THE

VIDEO GAME

GUIDE

VOLUME 1

1947-1989

Peter Cruickshank

First published in the UK in 2021 by Peter Cruickshank

ISBN 978-0-9927964-8-8

British Library Cataloguing in Publication Data.

A catalogue record for this book is available from the British Library.

Publisher's Note

Facebook.com/thevideogameguide

DEDICATION

To everyone who has ever found thrills, suspense, glory, wonder, escapism, love, loss and life in a video game.

Contents

ACKNOWLEDGMENTS

First of all, I would like to thank Iain Stirling who unwittingly helped sow the seeds for this book with our passionate talks about computer games of the 1980s during a holiday to Disney World with our families in 2019. Steff El Madawi for giving initial editing pointers and advice. My chief editor Steph Dagg for all her hard work. Paul Johnson, Ed Pulis and Alice Tennant for proofreading the book. To everyone who has advised and listened to me hark on about what would, one day, become the Video Game Guide. Finally for the support of my loving wife, Catherine.

INTRODUCTION

My first experiences with video games go back to the late 1970s playing arcades such as *Space Invaders* (1978), *Asteroids* (1979), and *Galaxian* (1979). My family's very first video game console here in the United Kingdom was a Binatone *TV Master System* (1976). Although this book is encyclopedic in nature, I would like to state that video games are as much about the passion and the emotions they evoke within us more than anything else. For it is our personal experiences that make them important to us and have a lasting effect on us for many years to come.

All these experiences are as real as anything that happens in our everyday lives. For every game mentioned in this book, there is someone out there on whom it has had a significant impact. From the most primitive, purely text-based adventure and roguelike games, where the player's imagination did the grunt work, to the vast immersive open-world games of today. All of these experiences should be cherished.

When we consider how far video games have come over the last seventy years we can only imagine where the future will take us and how they will evolve. We can predict that video games will look even more real and become even more immersive and that all of this is only the beginning.

I wanted to write a book about video games that focuses as much on their origins as it does on their more contemporary embodiments (covered in later volumes), that acknowledges games not only from Japan and the USA but from other parts of the world too. Giving the reader exposure to not only triple-AAA titled blockbuster games but also to indie and casual games. This book also covers many of the hardware innovations over the years and I hope this will give the reader an idea of the 'complete' history of video games while also acting as reference material and guide.

Peter Cruickshank

Note: A Glossary of terms can be found at the back of this book.

Video Game

Noun

A game played by electronically manipulating images produced by a computer program on a monitor or other display.

(Oxford Dictionary)

The 1940s

1940s Introduction

It wasn't until the middle of the twentieth century when what would later be considered the first video games were invented. The technicians who utilised this new emerging technology, known as computers, needed a way to illustrate the capabilities of these enormous and complex machines to the average layperson. What better way than an entertaining, fun game.

It is worth noting that many of these 'games' or simulations of this era were developed in universities, research labs, large corporations, or sections of government. Said examples were often never demonstrated to the media or the public at the time. Many never saw the light of day, or weren't documented in any reliable way, and are now lost to history.

The following examples are a glimpse of what we do know. Yet like so much of the past, they are only a small part of the story.

The cathode-ray tube amusement device and Gun Data Computers

Date: 1947

Region: USA

Inventors: Thomas T. Goldsmith and Estle Ray Mann.

Connecting a cathode-ray tube (CRT) to an oscilloscope, the user controls an artillery shell arcing towards specific targets using knobs and switches. Though the concept is like that of what would later become known as a video game, many people do not consider this device as such since the cathode-ray amusement device has no computing component. There is also contention as to whether it was ever built.

However, it is well-known that during the 1940s the military used similar technology to develop a series of what is known as the 'gun data computers' to calculate ballistic trajectories.

Turochamp

Date: 1948

Region: UK

Inventors: Alan Turing and David Champernowe

Platform: Automatic Computing Engine, and later for the Ferranti Mark 1.

Turochamp was a chess program. Written to calculate all possible moves at any point in the game and assign the best possible move for that state. Unfortunately, the program was too complex to be run on any computer of the time.

The 1950s

1950s Introduction

Even though it would be another twenty years before the term 'video game' would emerge, it was during the 1950s that what is defined as the first true video game was developed. However, as we will see, there is considerable contention as to whether this accolade goes to *Draughts* (1952), *OXO* (1952), *Pool/Billiards* (1954), or *Tennis for Two* (1958).

This decade also saw far-reaching fundamental hardware innovations, such as the first hard disk drive (1956) and the successful invention of the first integrated circuit (1958).

Bertie the Brain

Date: 1950

Region: Canada

Inventor: Dr Josef Kates

The Bertie the Brain computer was used to play tic-tac-toe, also known as noughts and crosses. The computer was four metres tall and used an array of light bulbs instead of a screen. There is contention as to whether this qualifies as a video game, as there were no moving graphics, only a primitive array of bulbs to display the shapes.

Nimrod

Date: 1951

Region: UK

Inventors: Raymond Stuart Williams and designed by John Makepeace Bennet

Platform: Nimrod

Tic-tac-toe and the game Nim were played on the vacuum tube computer, Nimrod at the Festival of Britain in May 1951. Built by Raymond Stuart Williams and designed by John Makepeace Bennet, Nimrod also uses bulbs rather than a monitor or other similar display and so may not qualify as a true video game, more a precursor.

UNISERVO Tape Drive

The UNISERVO tape drive was developed in 1951 for the UNIVAC 1 computer. It was the first available commercial tape drive. The storage capacity for a tape was 224 Kilobytes (224 KB or simply referred to as 224 K). This new way of storing data would later help those wishing to distribute software and, in turn, games.

Draughts

Date: 1952

Region: UK

Inventor: Christopher Strachey

Platform: Ferranti Mk1

Strachey had problems running his Draughts game in July 1951 on the Pilot ACE due to lack of memory. In 1952 he was able to program Draughts for the Ferranti Mk1. This time the game ran successfully.

Draughts is considered by some to be the first true video game as it was the first game to use a CRT display, rather than an array of bulbs.

OXO

Date: 1952

Region: UK (Cambridge)

Inventor: Mr A D Douglas

Platform: EDSAC computer

OXO was written for the EDSAC computer, the first computer to utilise a primitive from of RAM. It used vacuum tubes and three CRT Displays. The game is essentially noughts and crosses also known as tic-tac-toe. The player places a cross or a circle on a 3x3 grid, taking it in turns in an attempt to make a line of three in any direction.

This is another game that is considered by some to be the first true video game.

Pool/Billiards

Date: 1954

Region: USA (University of Michigan)

Inventors: William Brown and Ted Lewis

Platform: MIDSAC Computer.

Players can control the angle of the cue before taking their shots. The computer can calculate and display the movement of the graphics (balls, in this case) in real-time.

Pool/Billiards is another strong contender as the first true video game as it is the first game seen by the public to incorporate real-time moving graphics.

The Hard Disk Drive

The first hard disk drive (HDD) was released commercially in the USA in 1956 by an IBM team led by Rey Johnson.

Invented two years prior in December 1954, the HDD is an electro-mechanical storage device, a key component that would be used in many computers and games consoles well into the next century.

The Integrated Circuit

The first integrated circuit was successfully invented in the USA in September 1958 by Jack Kilby.

An integrated circuit is an electronic circuit usually formed from silicon, a key component in video game hardware. Despite many others working on the idea since 1949, Kilby's was the first functioning integrated circuit. Made from germanium, this primitive circuit would provide the groundwork for the evolution of the integrated circuit over the decades.

Tennis for Two

Date: October 1958

Region: USA (Brookhaven National Laboratory)

Inventor: William Higinbotham

The game simulates a game of tennis on an oscilloscope, as viewed from the side. With the use of a simple controller, two players could select the angle to return the ball and flick a switch when to return it.

Tennis for Two was very popular during the three-day Brookhaven National Laboratory's exhibition.

Mouse in the Maze

Date: 1959

Region: USA (MIT)

Inventors: Alan Kotok and Peter Samson

Platform: TR-0 computer

Mouse in the Maze is the first maze video game. A 'player' could place walls, cheese and, in certain incarnations of the game, glasses of martini by using a light pen. The mouse behaviour can then be observed.

Mouse in the Maze is sometimes seen as a precursor to modern-day simulation games such as *SimCity* (1989) and *The Sims* (2000).

PDP-1

The PDP-1 (Programmed Data Processor-1) computer was developed at MIT, USA in 1959 by Benjamin Gurley, the lead engineer of the team.

The PDP is the first 'minicomputer' to have a video game developed for it, that game being *Spacewar!* (1962). Other games developed for the PDP platform were *The Colossal Cave Adventure game/ADVENT/Colossal Cave/Adventure* (1976), *Zork: The Great Underground Empire* (1977), and *ESSEX MUD* (1980).

The 1960s

1960s Introduction

The 1960s saw the development of the prototype of the video game console with Ralph Baer's *Brown Box (1967)*. It also saw the first example of a head-mounted virtual reality (VR) system using computer graphics called *The Sword of Damocles (1968)*. However, it would be almost another half a century until VR would become commercially viable and make it into consumers' homes.

Spacewar!

Date: April 1962

Region: USA (MIT)

Inventor: Steve Russell

Platform: DEC PDP-1

Spacewar! is a two-player game. Set against a starfield backdrop, with a Star at the centre, a player must attempt to destroy the other player's ship with torpedoes while avoiding the other player's fire, as well as not being destroyed by colliding into the Star which exerts a strong gravity pull upon the ships. Each ship has limited fuel and torpedoes. There is also a hyperspace feature where a player's ship can jump to a completely random location on the screen.

Spacewar! became immensely popular within the programming community and there was a big demand for the game from institutions that had the PDP-1. Having experienced it on the PDP, other versions soon began to crop up for other systems. These versions are the first ports of a known game making Spacewar! The first multiplatform video game.

BASIC Programming Language

The Beginner's All-purpose Symbolic Instruction Code, or BASIC, programming language was developed at Dartmouth College, USA in May 1964 by John G. Kennedy and Thomas E. Kurtz design.

BASIC would be used to write many video games throughout the 1960s, 1970s, and 1980s.

Periscope/Torpedo Launcher

Date: 1965

Region: Japan

Developers: by Nakamura Manufacturing Co. and Sega Enterprises

Platform: Arcade

Periscope (originally named Torpedo Launcher) is not considered a video game; it is an electromechanical game. However, Periscope was one of many examples of a commercially released, coin-operated game. A precursor to the video game arcade; the shape of things to come.

The Brown Box

The Brown Box was developed in the USA in 1967 by Ralph Baer and his colleagues at Sanders Associates.

The Brown Box is the first multiplayer, multi-programmable video game system. Using a standard television as a display, games included ping-pong, checkers, golf, four different sports games, and a target shooting game, using a light-gun accessory. It is worth noting that in the ping-pong game, players could not only move up and down but also left and right, as well as manually controlling the direction of their returning ball.

The Brown Box is the first example of what would be later recognised as a video game console. Sanders licensed the Brown Box to Magnavox, who in 1972 released the system as the Magnavox Odyssey, the first commercially released video game console. Ralph Baer was the first person to successfully be granted a patent on the video game concept and would go on to sue and win against those infringing the patent, including Atari, Bally Midway, Mattel and Activision. Baer received the National Medal of Technology in 2004.

The Sword of Damocles

Date: 1968

Region: USA (MIT Lincoln Laboratory)

Developers: Ivan Sutherland and Bob Sproull.

The Sword of Damocles was the first head-mounted display, virtual reality system with computer graphics. The stereoscopic display puts the user in a virtual wireframe room. Not a game, in the strictest sense, but the first tentative step in this new technology.

Space Travel

Date: 1969

Region: USA

Developer: Ken Thompson

Platform: Multics operating system (later ported to the PDP-7)

Players must land their ship on planets and moons of our solar system as seen from a top-down view in this space simulation game. These heavenly bodies exhibit gravity according to their mass. The display is simple monochrome white lines on a black background.

Lunar Landing Game

Date: 1969

Region: USA

Developer: Jim Storer

Platform: PDP-8 minicomputer

Written in the FOCAL programming language, Lunar Landing Game, or simply Lunar, was a purely a text-based game involving typing in commands with the aim of successfully landing your lunar lander on the moon. The game would go on to influence and spawn a whole host of lander games establishing the Lunar Lander genre. The most famous of which is The arcade version *Lunar Lander* (1979).

The 1970s

1970s Introduction

This decade saw the emergence of the coin-operated video game arcade machine, as well as the first release of commercial home computers and consoles. The first two coin-operated machines were *Galaxy Game* (1971) and *Computer Space* (1971) made little impression on the American public. However, Atari's *Pong* (1972) was a huge commercial success, and by 1973 its cabinets had sold across the entire country and were even being shipped to other parts of the world. This heralded the first wave of arcade games which included *Breakout* (1976), *Asteroids* (1979), *Galaxian* (1979), and the worldwide phenomenon that was Taito's *Space Invaders* (1978). This latter inspired the entire shoot 'em up genre and became the longest-running widely-recognised video game franchise.

The very first home video game console was released with the *Magnavox Odyssey* (1972), which sold hundreds of thousands of units. Yet this paled in comparison to the success of the *Atari 2600 or VCS* (1977), which sold ten times this amount. Apple released its first computer with *the Apple Computer 1* (1976), closely followed by the more consumer-friendly *Apple II* (1977). Not to be outdone, Atari released the *Atari 8-bit computer* (1979), Commodore released the *Commodore PET* (1977) and Texas Instruments released the *T1-99/4 home computer* (1979), the first 16-bit home computer.

The 1970s saw the emergence of many new genres in video games. *Maze War* (1973) is seen as a precursor to the first-person shooter. It was also the earliest example of an avatar in a video game, as well as pioneering early 3D games featuring hidden wireframe graphics. *Empire 1* (1973) was the first turn-based strategy game, and perhaps the first-ever cooperative video game. *Gran Trak 10* (1974) was one of the earliest examples of a racing video game. *PEdit5,* also known as *The Dungeon* (1975), is often considered the first dungeon crawl RPG (role-playing game). *Gun Fight* (1975) would make use of the first music in a video game. Even though there had been text-based games in the previous decade, *The Colossal Cave Adventure* (1976) is generally viewed as the most influential text-based adventure game of all time. *Combat* (1977) was the first multi-directional shooter, and *Flight Simulator* (1979) is perhaps the first example of a commercially available flight simulator video game.

High Noon

Date of release: November 1970

Region: USA

Developer: Christopher Syosset

Platform: Call-A-Computer

High Noon was written in BASIC and is a purely textual, single-player, cowboy showdown game set in the wild west.

Galaxy Game

Date of release: November 1971

Region: USA

Developer: Bill Pitts and Hugh Tuck

Platform: Arcade

Galaxy Game is a variant of *Spacewar!* (1962) and is cited by some as the first commercial arcade video game in that a person had to pay to play it. However, only one machine was ever installed. This was at the coffee shop at Stanford University, California. Students Bill and Hugh charged 10 cents per game or a quarter (25 cents) for three games. As a bonus, if a player won a game, they would get to play a free game.

Computer Space

Date of release: November 1971

Region: USA

Developer: Syzygy Engineering

Publisher: Nutting Associates

Platform: Arcade

Created by Nolan Bushnell and Ted Dabney, Computer Space was a single-player or multiplayer, coin-operated variant of Spacewar! Released weeks after *Galaxy Game* (1971), Computer Space is often cited as the first commercially released arcade video game due to the fact that, unlike Galaxy Game, more than one was produced, although it only sold a little over a thousand cabinets. Its lack of success was believed to be due to its relatively complex controls.

Oregon Trail

Date of release: December 1971

Region: USA

Developers: Don Rawitsch and Bill Heinemann

Platform: HP 2000C Minicomputer

Oregon Trail, the first in a series of computer games, is an educational, text-based strategy game developed for computers that initially used teleprinters rather than a monitor. The fact that the game was installed in schools across the U.S.A. after 1975 meant that millions of children were exposed to a video game, possibly influencing some to explore this emerging industry.

Star Trek

Date of release: November 1971

Region: USA

Developer: Mike Mayfield:

Platform: SDS Sigma 7 and HP 2000C Minicomputer

Star Trek was a text-based strategy game where the player commands the *USS Enterprise* and must destroy Klingon warships. The game gained huge popularity throughout the latter half of the 1970s.

Atari

Nolan Bushnell and Ted Dabney founded Atari in the USA in June 1972.

Atari was the first company to frequently and consistently use the term 'video game' to describe their products and the business they were in. This term was soon picked up by the media of the time.

Atari are best known for establishing the video game industry in the arcades with *Pong* (1972) and the homes of America with their *Atari 2600 Home Console* (1977). Atari are known for other video games such as *Indy 800* (1975), *Breakout* (1976), *Star Raiders* (1979), *Asteroids* (1979), *Adventure* (1979), *Missile Command* (1980), *Battlezone* (1980), *Centipede* (1981), *Tempest* (1981), *Yar's Revenge* (1982) and *Star Wars* (1983).

C Programming Language

The C Programming language was released in 1972 by Dennis Ritchie. It is used in many video games.

Magnavox Odyssey

The Magnavox Odyssey was released in the USA in September 1972.

The Odyssey was the first home video game console. Developed by Ralph Baer at Sanders Associates, the console was only capable of displaying three monochrome square dots and a vertical line on a television screen and had no facility to produce sound. It also had only 64 Bytes of RAM, all for a retail price of $99.95.

The Odyssey was sold with dice, chips, paper money, and coloured plastic overlays to be placed on the screen to help with the integration of different games such as tennis, a skiing game, Simon says, ice hockey, cat and mouse, haunted House and more. Due to its limitations players often had to keep their own score or manage the rules of a game. Even though the Magnavox Odyssey is not the first official console to use 'cartridges' (that accolade goes to Fairchild Channel F (1976)) it did use game cards that inserted into the console in much the same way as a cartridge. The first commercial light gun was sold separately, which could be used with four other games.

Over the next three years, the Odyssey sold 350,000 units. In the next five years, several successive Odyssey models were released.

Pong

Date of release: November 1972

Region: USA

Developer: Atari

Publisher: Atari

Platform: Arcade

After realising their first game *Computer Space* (1971) was too complex for the average patron out for a drink, Nolan Bushnell was inspired by a demonstration of a tennis game on *the Magnavox Odyssey* (1972) and set computer engineer, Allan Alcorn the task of creating a similar game. Alcorn was able to introduce a scoring system, sound, a ball that got faster the longer you played, and changes to the angle on returning the ball dependent on where on the paddle you hit it. In stark contrast to *Computer Space*, Pong – a truncated word for Ping Pong – would be simplicity itself.

The instructions on the cabinet read: 'Deposit quarter. Ball will serve automatically. Avoid missing ball for high score.' The first Pong machine was placed in a local bar where Bushnell knew the owner. It wasn't long until a call was received reporting that there was a fault with the machine. It turned out that so many quarters had been put in the machine that it had backed up into the coin mechanism. It was then that Bushnell knew he had a hit, and he put all his remaining funds into creating another eleven machines.

People went crazy over Pong, and by 1973 the machine had made its way to the other parts of the United States and began shipping abroad. Pong was the first commercially successful video game in history. Atari released several sequels, each adding a new feature to the game: these included *Pong Doubles* (1973), *Quadro Pong* (1974), and *Super Pong* (1974). In 1975 Atari went on to release a home version. The Pong phenomenon spawned a whole host of Pong clones, hundreds of them. It seemed every electronic manufacturing company released their own version of it. Everyone wanted a piece of the pie. Pong is often cited as one of the greatest and most influential video games of all time.

Pong-Tron

Date of release: 1972

Region: Japan

Developer: Sega

Publisher: Sega

Platform: Arcade

Pong-Tron was Sega's first video arcade game cabinet and is a variant of Atari's Pong.

Empire 1

Date of release: 1972

Region: USA

Developer: John Daleske

Platform: PLATO System

Empire 1, also known as simply Empire, is a multiplayer, 2D, turn-based, space war game where the objective of the game is nothing short of conquering the galaxy. Your ship and nearby stellar objects are viewed from the top down. Empire is contested to be the first networked multiplayer arena shooter-style game.

Eight players could play together. Controls involved typing commands. Games could take hours or even days to complete. The PLATO terminals had a 512 x 512 monochrome vector CRT display, rather a large resolution for the time considering that contemporary arcade games ran on a 224 x 256 display.

Two more sequels would be released this same year: *Empire 2* and *Empire 3. Empire 4* was released in 1977.

Soccer

Date of release: 1972

Region: Japan

Developer: Taito

Publisher: Taito

Platform: Arcade

Soccer was the first arcade game to use a trackball controller, already used extensively in the military. It is also possibly the first soccer video game.

101 BASIC Computer Games

David H Ahl published *101 BASIC Computer Games* in 1973. The book contains descriptions and source code for games written by Ahl and others. It sold over 10,000 copies.

Maze War

Date of release: March 1973

Region: USA (NASA Ames Research Centre in California)

Developers: Steve Colley, Greg Thompson, and Howard Palmer

Platform: Imlac PDS-1

Maze War is considered one of the earliest known examples of a game as viewed from a first-person perspective. The player wanders through a 3D maze using a simple grid-based movement, and, dependent on the many variations, other players are displayed as merely dots, their names, figures, or, later, eyeballs. These are the earliest examples of an avatar (an image that represents other players) in a video game. Maze War also was the first video game to feature a mini-map. The aim is to shoot and eliminate the other players. This perhaps qualifies Maze War as the first multiplayer first-person shooter.

Laser Clay Shooting System

Nintendo releases its Laser Clay Shooting System in 1974 in Japan's amusement arcades.

Although this was not a video game, it is one of Nintendo's first arcade machines.

Spasim

Date of release: March 1974

Region: USA

Developer: Jim Bowery

Platform: PLATO computer network

Spasim is a multiplayer networked first-person space shooter and space flight simulator played on a 512 x 512 vector graphic display, a far higher resolution than other games of the time. Up to thirty-two players, four teams of eight players, could play Spasim.

Spasim would pave the way for other first-person space combat/simulation games, such as *Star Raiders* (1979) on the Atari platforms, and the revolutionary, *Elite* (1984).

Gran Trak 10

Date of release: May 1974

Region: USA

Developer: Atari

Publisher: Atari

Platform: Arcade

Gran Trak 10 is a single-player racing game viewed from the top-down perspective. It was the first arcade cabinet to feature a steering wheel, a gear shift, brake, and accelerator pedal.

Tank

Date of release: 1974

Region: USA

Developer: Kee Games (a subsidiary of Atari)

Publisher: Kee Games

Platform: Arcade

Developed by Steve Bistow and Lyle Rains, Tank is a two-player game where each player controls a tank inside a maze as seen from a top-down perspective. The objective of the game is to destroy your opponent's tank as many times as possible while avoiding being destroyed by them or any mines placed around the maze, all within the allotted time.

Tank sold over 10,000 cabinets and would spawn numerous sequels and clones.

Wild Gunman

Date of release: 1974

Region: Japan

Developer: Nintendo

Platform: Arcade

Wild Gunman is a light gun shooter electro-mechanical game using FMVs (Full Motion Video) of actors dressed as cowboys and bandits. It would later be translated into a video game in 1985 for the Nintendo Entertainment System.

Panther

Date of release: 1974

Region: USA

Developer: John Edo Haefeli

Platform: PLATO System

Panther is a multiplayer, first-person, vehicular combat, and simulation game. The aim of Panther is to destroy the other player's base.

Players are split into two teams. Each player controls a tank with different strengths and weaknesses. A map shows the game world comprising of mountains, each player's base location, and your allies. Fuel and ammunition are limited; however, players can give one another their fuel and ammo if they wish. All players can message each other during gameplay. Those who work together as an efficient team using good strategy have a better chance of destroying the enemy base first.

Panther is seen as a precursor to the popular arcade hit *Battlezone* (1980).

Speed Race/Wheels

Date of release: 1974

Region: Japan

Developer: Taito

Publisher: Taito

Platform: Arcade

Speed Race is a single-player racing game. The aim of the game is to race your car for as long as possible. The game is viewed from an above perspective, with the player having to avoid and pass other, slower cars on screen.

The arcade housed a monochrome screen and used a steering wheel and basic gear shift to control the player's car. Speed Race was released as Wheels in 1975 in North America by Midway games.

PEdit5/The Dungeon

Date of release: 1975

Region: USA

Developer: Rusty Rutherford

Platform: PLATO System

PEdit5 also known as The Dungeon is a single-player, dungeon crawl Role Playing Game (RPG), the first of its kind. Viewed from above, with the characters depicted in profile, only one room is seen at a time as the player, depicted as a figure with a sword and shield, moves through the dungeon finding treasure and fighting monsters, which can be avoided or dealt with using standard weapons or magic such as charm, blastbolt, invisibility, and sleep.

The Colossal Cave Adventure

Date of release: 1975 (with a full release in 1976).

Region: USA

Developer: William Crowther and Don Woods

Platform: PDP-10

The Colossal Cave Adventure, also known as ADVENT, Colossal Cave, or simply Adventure is a purely text-based video game. The player must explore a cave, find the treasures held within and then leave the cave alive. The narrative of The Colossal Cave Adventure is light and humorous and is considered to have heavily influenced many text-based games that came after it, as well as games such as *Adventure* (1979), *Mystery House* (1980) and *Zork* (1980).

Dnd

Date of release: 1975

Region: USA

Developers: Gary Whisenhunt and Ray Wood

Platform: PLATO system

Dnd is an RPG, heavily influenced by the table-top RPG Dungeons and Dragons. The game is viewed from a top-down perspective with the player viewed from the front holding shield and sword. Dnd is the first video game to feature bosses.

Moria

Date of release: 1975

Region: USA

Developer: Kevet Duncombe

Platform: PLATO system

Moria is a first-person RPG that was one of the first to allow players to travel in a party, in this case, up to ten people.

Indy 800

Date of release: 1975

Region: USA

Developer: Atari

Publisher: Atari

Platform: Arcade

Indy 800 is an eight-player driving game as viewed from above. The large arcade cabinet houses two steering wheels on each of its four sides. The players look down onto the horizontal display of the racetrack and cars. Each player has a different-coloured car. It is perhaps the first arcade game to have colour graphics using transistor-transistor logic.

Home Pong

Home Pong was released in the USA in 1975 by Atari.

This home console version of Pong was released for Christmas 1975 and sold exclusively through Sears retail stores. It sold around 150,000 units in a single season, which is an incredible amount when considering the Magnavox Odyssey sold a total of 350,000 in its entire lifetime.

Pong Clones

After Atari released Home Pong, it seemed every electronics manufacturer was developing what became known as their own 'home Pong clone console'. These were home machines that were built to play a version of the game Pong and often included several variants.

There were dozens of Pong clones, including the *Binatone TV Gaming Unit* (1976), *Coleco Telestar* (1976), and *The Color TV-Game 6* (1977).

Western Gun/Gun Fight

Date of release: November 1975

Region: Japan

Developer: Taito

Publisher: Taito

Platform: Arcade

Designed by Tomohiro Nishikado, Western Gun also known as Gun Fight, portrays two cowboys facing off in a gunfight from a side-on view. Players can move about and must shoot the other player before being shot themselves. It is easy to see how the mechanics of Pong were adapted for this game.

It is the first arcade game to use a microprocessor rather than transistor-transistor logic chips, meaning that the graphics could be faster and perceived as more fluid. Western Gun/Gun Fight was also the first video game to incorporate music, a short tune initiated when a player was killed.

EVR Race

Nintendo released their first game cabinet in 1975 with EVR Race.

'Players' simply bet on which horse (or in some cases, racing car) will win a race. It is debatable whether this is a video game at all as players aren't manipulating any displayed images. However, it is worth noting that this is along with its Laser Clay Shooting System (1974) was Nintendo's first move towards the video game industry.

Interceptor

Date of release: 1976

Region: Japan

Developer: Taito

Publisher: Taito

Platform: Arcade

Interceptor is a single-player, first-person shooter game. The player controls a jet fighter and must destroy as many enemy aircraft as possible. Players aim using crosshairs and shoot down enemy planes.

Interceptor was the first game to feature a form of sprite-scaling (enlarging or reducing the size of sprites to give the illusion that objects are closer or further away) and was the first arcade game to feature multi-directional scrolling.

Sea Wolf

Date of release: 1976

Region: USA

Developer: Dave Nutting Associates

Publisher: Bally Midway

Platform: Arcade

Sea Wolf is a single-player, military shooter, featuring a suspended periscope for the player to view the screen through. The aim of the game is to destroy enemy ships using your torpedoes.

It is the first video game to feature a high score. Sea Wolf was the most popular arcade game of 1976.

Apple Computer 1

The Apple Computer 1 was released in April 1976 by Steve Wozniak and Steve Jobs, the first of the Apple (Mac) platforms to be produced.

Death Race

Date of release: April 1976

Region: USA

Developer: Exidy

Publisher: Exidy

Platform: Arcade

Death Race was released in the USA in April 1976 by Exidy for the arcade. It is a one or two-player driving game viewed from a top-down perspective where you play as the Grim Reaper. The aim of the game is to kill as many people as possible in the allotted time. When you do a gravestone pops up signifying their death.

The cabinet featured two steering wheels, forward/reverse levers, and accelerator pedals. Death Race was one of the first games to create widespread controversy. There were many who weren't happy about an arcade game that seemed to promote running over innocent people. Exidy said that the sprites in question were actually Gremlins. However, those that were against the game were not convinced. The negative publicity created a significant rise in sales.

Breakout

Date of release: May 1976

Region: USA

Developer: Atari

Publisher: Atari

Platform: Arcade

Breakout was released in the USA in May 1976 by Atari for the arcade. Developed by Steve Wozniak and Steve Jobs, who would later found Apple Inc., Breakout involves similar gameplay to Pong. The player controls a paddle's horizontal position and must deflect a bouncing ball to destroy the bricks above. It is believed Breakout influenced the idea behind *Space Invaders* (1978).

Like Pong, Breakout was immensely successful and went on to spawn a long list of imitations. The Japanese demand for the game at the time was so great that Namco bought the rights to it. Yet this was still not enough, and the Japanese Yakuzza crime syndicate began manufacturing illegal Breakout cabinets.

Mattel Electronics Auto Race

The Mattel Electronics Auto Race was released in the USA in 1976 by Mattel. Auto Race is the worlds first handheld video game console. The device comprised of a Start/Reset switch, a four-gear switch and a red LED display. The aim of the game was to race your car as far as possible without hitting any other cars in the race. The cars were displayed as red dots as seen from above. The player could move into any one of three lanes to dodge the oncoming cars. The player's score was displayed at the top of the race track.

The game sold relatively well, and Mattel developed several other handheld games, including *Mattel Electronic Football* (1977) which would become immensely popular selling over a million. and Mattel Electronics *Missile Attack AKA Mattel Electronics Battlestar Galactica Space Alert* (1976/1978). These handheld devices proved so successful in the USA that in the holidays of 1977 they were even more popular than Atari 2600 (1976) console games.

These first Handheld devices were a shape of things to come, influencing such future handhelds as the *Nintendo Game & Watch series* (1980-1991), *Grandstand Tabletop electronic games* (1981), and the *Nintendo Game Boy* (1989).

Heavyweight Champ

Date of release: October 1976

Region: Japan

Developer: Sega

Publisher: Sega

Platform: Arcade

In Heavyweight Champ players utilised boxing gloves to control their character portrayed in monochrome from a side-view perspective. This is perhaps the first ever boxing video game.

Blockade

Date of release: October 1976

Region: USA

Developer: Gremlin

Publisher: Gremlin

Platform: Arcade

Blockade is the first of the Snake genre of video games, where the player moves their character around the screen using four directional buttons. The aim of the game is to survive longer than your opponent, without hitting the outside wall or colliding with the walls that each player leaves in their wake.

Blockade inspired several clones after its release; perhaps the most popular was the Light Cycle mini-game in the arcade game *Tron* (1982) and later *Snake* (1998) the much-played mobile version preloaded on Nokia phones.

Night Driver

Date of release: October 1976

Region: USA

Developer: Atari

Publisher: Atari

Platform: Arcade

Developed by Dave Sheppard, Night Driver is the first driving video game to be viewed from the driver's perspective.

Fairchild Channel F

The second generation of home video game consoles begins with the release of the Fairchild Channel F – the F stands for 'Fun'.

Released in the USA in November 1976 and designed by Jerry Lawson, it is the first Video game console to use a programmable ROM cartridge for its games. The Fairchild was capable of 128 x 64 screen resolution, an output of eight colours and came with 64 bytes of RAM. It sold 250,000 units.

Commodore PET

The Commodore PET was released in the USA in January 1977. It shipped with 4 KB of RAM and monochrome graphics for $795: equivalent to $3,510 in 2020. Along with the Apple II and the TRS-80, it was one of the best-selling personal computers of the decade.

The Color TV-Game 6

The Color TV-Game 6 was released in Japan only in June 1977 by Nintendo. It included six variants of Pong. Other more elaborate video game consoles in the series were released over the next couple of years.

The Color TV-Game is the highest-selling first-generation console with 1.5 million units. The first-generation includes the Magnavox Odyssey (1972) which sold 350, 000 units, Atari's Home Pong (1975) with 150,000 units and Coleco Telstar which sold a total of one million units.

Apple II

The Apple II was released in the USA in June 1977. It is Apple's first launch of a personal computer aimed at the consumer market. It was one of the first home computers able to display colour graphics and had 4KB of RAM.

The price of the computer wasn't cheap, starting at $1,298 for the 4KB version and $2,638 48KB version. It was an incredibly powerful computer, obviously very attractive for playing games, and the Apple II had some rather unique and defining games such as *Castle Wolfenstein* (1981), *Ultima 1: The First Age of Darkness* (1981), *Lode Runner* (1983), *Karateka* (1984), *The Bard's Tale* (1985), and *Prince of Persia* (1989).

The Apple II launched a whole line of computers finally ending in 1993 with the Apple IIe.

Space Wars

Date of release: 1977

Region: USA

Developer: Cinematronics

Publisher: Cinematronics

Platform: Arcade

Developed by Larry Rosenthal, Space Wars is the first vector graphics arcade game and is a variant on *Spacewar!* (1962).

This new arcade incarnation of the game introduced some new options and features. For example, ships took more than one hit to be destroyed, the star in the middle of the screen could exert negative or positive gravity. The star could be included or excluded completely.

Rather uniquely, every quarter deposited bought 90 seconds of gameplay. This was in stark contrast to every other game, where the player paid for a set number of lives and, theoretically, unlimited time.

TRS-80

The TRS-80 Micro Computer System was released in the USA in August 1977.

Created by the Tandy Corporation, the TRS-80 shipped with 4KB RAM, monochrome output, and impressive sound for the time. Some notable games such as *Zork* (1980), *Meteor Mission 2* (1980), *Asylum* (1981), *Penetrator* (1982), and *Sea Dragon* (1982) were developed for it.

Atari 2600

The Atari 2600 was released in the USA in September 1977.

Originally called the Atari VCS (Video Computer System), the Atari 2600 is a second-generation console with 128 bytes of RAM. Like the Fairchild Channel F, it used programmable ROM cartridges for its many games, thought to be around 470 by the end of its life. Nine games were available upon launch, including *Combat* (1977), a more evolved colour version of Kee Games' arcade game *Tank* (1974), which came bundled with the system. Also included were two joystick controllers.

Between 350,000 and 400,000 units were sold in 1977, and it would go on to sell a total of 30 million units. This was an unprecedented amount due to its ever-growing library of games and its many conversions of immensely popular arcade titles such as Space Invaders.

Atari's success was only matched by its dramatic decline. This was due to its lack of quality control on third-party titles as well as the infamously terrible *E.T. The Extra-Terrestrial* (1982) and conversion of *Pac-Man* (1982). This is thought to have contributed to the video game crash of 1983. But despite that, the Atari 2600 is thought to be the console that convinced the world that video games in the home had mass-market appeal.

Some of the most notable games for the Atari 2600 are *Super Breakout* (1978), *Adventure* (1979), *Space Invaders* (1980), *Pitfall* (1982), *Frogger* (1982), *Berzerk* (1982), *River Raid* (1982), *Pole Position* (1983), *Dig Dug* (1983) and *Ms. Pac-Man* (1983).

By the late 1970s, Atari accounted for 75% of the home video game market in the USA with the Atari 2600 making around $2 billion per year for the company.

Combat

Date of release: September 1977

Region: USA

Developer: Atari

Publisher: Atari

Platform: Atari 2600

Combat is a single-player or two-player multi-directional shooter and a variant of *Tank (1974).* It was one of the original launch titles for the Atari 2600, containing 27 different game modes. As seen from above, you control a tank, biplane, or jet fighter in a maze or, in the plane game's case, within clouds that hide you. It was a staple game for 2600 owners.

The concept of Tank/Combat has been copied in many other games including one of the mini-games in *Tron* (1982) arcade game.

Boot Hill

Date of release: 1977

Region: USA

Developer: Midway

Publisher: Midway Games

Platform: Arcade

Boot Hill is a sequel to *Western Gun/Gun Fight* (1975) and has the same basic, yet slightly more evolved game mechanics.

The Video Game Crash of 1977

A lot of companies had staked their entire business model on the success of their Pong clone machines. Unfortunately, there were far too many Pong clones out there and many of these manufacturers went under. This would perpetuate the point of view of many in the media that video games were a passing fad that would be no less than a footnote in history. The bankruptcy of so many electronics manufacturers and failing confidence in the video games industry at this point in time is now known as the Video Game Crash of 1977. However, Taito's Space Invaders (1978) would change everything.

BASIC Computer Games

David H Ahl publishes *BASIC Computer Games* in the USA in 1978. It is the first million-selling computer book.

Beneath Apple Manor

Date of release: 1978

Region: USA

Developer: Don Worth

Publisher: The Software Factory

Platform: Apple II

Developed by Don Worth, Beneath Apple Manor is a single-player, roguelike, dungeon crawler. The aim of the game is to obtain the golden apple located at the very bottom of the dungeon. Viewed from a top-down perspective, players must battle monsters and discover treasure.

Beneath Apple Manor was one of the first home video games to use procedurally generated environments, and even though it is often referred to (in retrospect) as a roguelike game, it was in fact released before *Rogue* (1980).

Essex MUD

Date of release: 1978

Region: UK

Developer: Roy Trubshaw and then Richard Bartle

Platform: DEC PDP-10

Also known as MUD, or MUD 1. Essex MUD (Multi-User Dungeon) is a text-based single-player or multiplayer adventure role-playing game where the aim is to gain as many points as possible by defeating enemies until one achieves the wizard rank, granting the character immortality and power over mortals.

Having enjoyed *Colossal Cave Adventure* (1975), Trubshaw was inspired to create MUD. He was able to make it possible for other players from different locations to play together and so MUD became the first online multiplayer game. It was also one of the first games to offer real social interaction between players. A couple of new terms would arise from such interaction. 'Griefers' were players who deliberately caused grief to other players. 'Noobs' or 'Newbies' were new players; these last two words are used frequently in modern-day gaming. In MUD players could create their own characters. Bartle created the first virtual female video game character called Polly when he noticed the other player, who were all male, always created male characters. MUD is one of the first games to be played on what was a precursor to the Internet. The game could be played on British Telecom's EPSS (Experimental Packet Switching System) by a handful of other Universities between 2 AM and 7 AM, in a sense, this could qualify Essex MUD as the first online video game.

FreeCell

Date of release: 1978

Region: USA

Developer: Paul Alfille

Platform: PLATO System

FreeCell is a solitaire card game that would eventually be included with every copy of the Windows Operating System from 1995 onwards, meaning to date that over a billion copies of the game have been shipped.

Space Invaders

Date of release: June 1978

Region: Japan

Developer: Taito

Publisher: Taito

Platform: Arcade

Space Invaders was released in July 1978 for the arcade. It was developed by Tomohiro Nishikado and published by Taito.

Just as Breakout is an evolved variant of Pong, so is Space Invaders an evolved variant of Breakout. The bricks are now alien invaders slowly descending whilst firing upon the player at the bottom. Instead of a paddle and a ball, the player can now shoot and destroy the invaders. Four bases provide the only protection from the invaders as they rain down their never-ending torpedo fire.

Nishikado drew inspiration from H.G. Wells' *War of the Worlds* for the design of the invaders. The game's sound was integral to increasing the player's excitement. The further the player progressed through a wave, the quicker the sound of the ominous invaders became. Space Invaders can be classed as the first real shoot 'em up, paving the way for many more to come.

It was an instant hit when it launched, filling up the Pachinko parlours and amusement arcades of Japan. Some establishments opened 24 hours a day 7 days a week, and the machines were in constant use. In Japan alone 100,000 cabinets were sold. Within three months Space Invaders had become so popular it is claimed that there was a national shortage of 100-yen coins. However, some say this is merely an urban myth. The Japanese PTA (Parent-Teacher Association) tried to ban the game for encouraging truancy. Politicians in the United Kingdom attempted unsuccessfully to restrict the playing of the game, as children there were also missing school. The Space Invaders phenomenon that pervaded the culture of the time cannot be understated. It often appeared on mainstream television, newspapers, magazines and music. By 1982 it had grossed $3.8 billion. Not only was it the best-selling video game, but it was also the highest-grossing entertainment product, and, adjusting for inflation, it still is the highest-grossing arcade game of all time at $14 billion. Space Invaders is also responsible for single-handedly ending the Video Game Crash of 1977 and starting what is often referred to as the Golden Age of arcade games (1978-86). It is often cited as one of the greatest and most influential video games of all time.

Space Invaders was ported to just about every platform there was, with the Atari 2600 version being exceedingly successful. The game spawned several sequels, including *Space Invaders Part II (AKA Space Invaders Deluxe)* (1979), *Return of the Invaders* (1985), *Super Space Invaders '91* (1990), *Space Invaders DX* (1993) and *Space Invaders Frenzy* (2017).

Gee Bee

Date of release: October 1978

Region: Japan

Developer: Namco

Publisher: Namco

Platform: Arcade

Designed by Toru Iwatani, Gee Bee is the natural evolution of the Breakout game. It is only fitting that video games would emulate and mix with the ever-so-popular pinball machines that inhabited bars and eateries years before the former emerged. In Gee Bee, you control two horizontal side-scrolling paddles. You must bounce the ball to break blocks, not only above but also to the sides. As with traditional pinball games, you gain points by hitting specific areas of the screen.

The game was not a commercial success, but it was a fun game to play and it is worth noting this was Namco's first arcade video game.

Adventureland

Date of release: 1978

Region: USA

Developer: Scott Adams

Publisher: Creative Computing Software

Platform: Various 8-bit home computers

The aim of Adventureland is to collect thirteen lost artefacts. Developed by Scott Adams, Adventureland is a single-player, fantasy, text adventure game. Scott Adams went on to publish several other games under his own publishing house Adventure International. His name became synonymous with the text adventure genre.

Adventureland was one of the first text adventure video game developed for home computers. It is a perfect example of the first wave of hobbyists writing their own video games in their own homes using microcomputers.

Atari Football

Date of release: October 1978

Region: USA

Developer: Atari

Publisher: Atari

Platform: Arcade

Programmed by Dave Theurer, Atari Football is the first non-racing game to feature vertical scrolling. It was very physically taxing to play and offered only 90 seconds of play for one quarter. More time was given if coins were put in the machine, in the same way as *Space Wars* (1977). Despite this, or perhaps because of this, it was extremely popular upon release.

Computer Othello

Computer Othello was released in Japan in 1978 for the arcade by Nintendo. A video game version of the board game Othello, it is Nintendo's first true arcade game.

Magnavox Odyssey^2

The Magnavox Odyssey^2 was released in the USA in December 1978.

The Magnavox Odyssey² is a second-generation console with 64 bytes of RAM. It was more of an all-purpose console, and because it included a full alphanumeric membrane keyboard it could also be used as a computer. It had an educational purpose as well as having a slot to put in a game cartridge.

The Magnavox Odyssey² also came with a cartridge of games. Many of the console's games were thought to be inferior to those of the Atari 2600. Even though the Magnavox Odyssey² would go on to sell over two million units over the next six years, this paled in comparison to Atari's sales figures.

Superman

Date of release: February 1979

Region: USA

Developer: Atari

Publisher: Atari

Platform: Atari 2600

Developed by John Dunn, Superman is a single-player action-adventure game based on DC's (Detective Comics) well-known superhero comic. The player controls Superman and must fly around the city in an effort to capture Lex Luthor and his men after they blow up a bridge. Upon completion, you must return to the *Daily Planet* in the fastest time possible.

Superman is the first superhero video game and one of the earliest licensed video games. It is also the first home video game to use multiple screens in its game world, and one of the first home console games to feature a pause button. More significantly it is possibly the first ever action-adventure game. Other well-known early action-adventure games are *Adventure* (1979), *Knight Lore* (1984) and *The Legend of Zelda* (1986).

The game was highly praised by critics and consumers alike. It probably helped that *Superman: The Movie* directed by Richard Donner had been released three months before. Superman won Best Game of the Year in the 1981 Arcade Awards.

Speed Freak

Date of release: March 1979

Region: USA

Developer: Vectorbeam

Publisher: Vectorbeam

Platform: Arcade

Designed and programmed by Larry Rosenthal, Speed Freak is one of the earliest first-person driving games and one of the first to use vector graphics.

Head On

Date of release: April 1979

Region: USA

Developer: Gremlin

Publisher: Sega

Platform: Arcade

Head On is a single-player racing game as viewed from the top down. The player must drive around a maze collecting dots while avoiding colliding with the other car. It easy to see how this would influence the game *Pac-Man* (1980).

Infocom

Infocom was founded in June 1979. Infocom was an American software developer best known for the *Zork* series (1980-97), *Planetfall* series (1983), *and Hitchhiker's Guide to the Galaxy* (1984) text adventure games, which are renowned for their flexibility and robustness in the genre. Infocom also included things like books, maps, cards, and other paraphernalia, more commonly referred to as 'feelies', with their games.

Lunar Lander

Date of release: August 1979

Region: USA

Developer: Atari

Publisher: Atari

Platform: Arcade

Lunar Lander used vector graphics to display the player's ship landing on a rough lunar surface. The player had to find a flat area to land on with a limited amount of fuel. As well as showing the player the amount of fuel left, the screen also displayed altitude, speed and your current score. Players could purchase more fuel by putting more coins in the machine. Very cunning.

Lunar Lander wasn't the first Lunar Lander game, yet it was successful enough in the arcades to popularise the Lunar Lander genre.

Temple of Apshai

Date of release: August 1979

Region: USA

Developer: Automated Simulations

Publisher: Automated Simulations

Platform: TRS-80

Temple of Apshai was released in the USA in August 1979 for the TRS-80 and Commodore PET. Developed by Automated Simulations, Temple of Apshai is one of the earliest dungeon crawl role-playing video games.

The display of your environment is viewed from a top-down perspective, in monochrome black and white. Despite the primitive graphics and slow gameplay, the game was a commercial success selling around 30,000 copies.

Galaxian

Date of release: October 1979

Region: Japan

Developer: Namco

Publisher: Namco

Platform: Arcade

Galaxian is a single-player shoot 'em up and a direct response to the Space Invader phenomenon. Galaxian is much faster paced than Space Invaders, and there is nothing between you and the enemy ships that swoop down upon the player in groups, rather than as a slowly descending unit.

Even though it was not the first arcade game to use colour graphics, it was utilised well in such animations as movement and explosions. Galaxian stood out from the crowd in a time when most arcades were either monochrome or used colour overlays on the screens to give a primitive illusion of colour.

Galaxian was incredibly successful and sold 40,000 cabinets in the USA alone.

Flight Simulator

Date of release: 1979

Region: USA

Developer: SubLogic

Publisher: SubLogic

Platform: Apple II

Written by Bruce Artwick, Flight Simulator is a single-player, first-person flight simulator of the Sopwith Camel aircraft. It featured a black and white 3D wireframe environment that ran at 3-6 frames per second and was able to consider 23 different aircraft characteristics. It is the first home 3D flight simulator.

Warrior

Date of release: October 1979

Region: USA

Developer: Tim Skelly

Publisher: Vectorbeam

Platform: Arcade

Designed by Tim Skelly, Warrior is a two-player fighting game with monochrome vector graphics viewed from the top down, where you play as one of two duelling knights. The aim is to defeat your opponent using your sword. Warrior is one of the first melee fighting games.

Microvision

The Microvision was released in the USA in November 1979 by the Milton Bradley Company.

Designed by Jay Smith (who would later design the Vetrex console released in 1982), the Microvision was the first handheld game console to use interchangeable cartridges. However, Microvision sales plummeted due to its small-screen resolution, a paltry 16 x 16 pixels, and lack of game support. It was discontinued two years later.

Atari 8-bit Computer

The Atari 8-bit Computer was released in November 1979. The Atari 8-bit family consisted of the Atari 400 and the Atari 800.

Due to having custom chips for graphics and sound, it was a very capable games machine, its arcade conversions being particularly impressive for the time. *Star Raiders* (1979) became known as the platforms 'killer app', a term used to describe a piece of software (in this case a video game) so desirable it is worth buying the hardware for. Other notable games were *Eastern Front 1941* (1981) *and Miner 2049er* (1982).

The Atari 8-bit family sold over two million units.

Akalabeth: World of Doom

Date of release: November 1979

Region: USA

Developer: Richard Garriot

Publisher: California Pacific Computer

Platform: Apple II

Akalabeth: World of Doom is a single-player first-person dungeon crawl RPG, heavily influenced by the tabletop game *Dungeons & Dragons*.

Garriot initially published the game himself. After catching the eye of California Pacific Computer Company, they went on to publish the game, crediting the author as 'Lord British'. (This was Garriot's dungeon master title when he played D&D.)

Akalabeth is seen as a precursor to the hugely successful RPG Ultima video game series (1981-1999). Sometimes Akalabeth is referred to as Ultima 0.

Asteroids

Date of release: November 1979

Region: USA

Developer: Atari

Publisher: Atari

Platform: Arcade

Created by Lyle Rains, Ed Logg, and Dominic Walsh, Asteroids is a single-player multidirectional space shooter viewed from above. The player controls a spaceship in an asteroid field. You must destroy the asteroids and any enemy ships in order to proceed to the next level. Asteroids break into smaller and smaller pieces until they are destroyed. The game is rendered on a vector display. The sound is akin to Space Invaders in that the rhythm increases the longer you play.

Asteroids was immensely successful when released and went on to spawn numerous clones. It quickly became the most popular video game in the arcades and was Atari's best-selling game of all time. Asteroids sold over 70,000 arcade cabinets. It was soon ported over to the Atari 2600 and Atari 8-Bit in 1981. The game has spawned many clones and has sequels of its own including *Asteroids Deluxe* (1981), *Space Duel* (1982) and *Blasteroids* (1987).

Tail Gunner

Date of release: November 1979

Region: USA

Developer: Vectorbeam

Publisher: Cinematronics

Platform: Arcade

Developed by Dan Sunday and Larry Rosenthal, Tail Gunner is a single-player, first-person space shooter where the player must shoot down waves of attacking enemies.

Tail Gunner is the first arcade game to have 3D wireframe animated objects. In this case, enemy planes can fly past the camera into the distance and then turn back towards the player.

Star Raiders

Date of release: 1979

Region: Worldwide

Developer: Atari

Publisher: Atari

Platform: Atari 400 and Atari 800 (Atari 8-bit computers)

Written by Doug Nebauer, Star Raiders is a single-player, first-person space simulator/shooter. It had impressive graphics, smooth gameplay, and engaging game mechanics such as a star chart, short- and long-range radar, and management of finite energy resources, to name but a few features. Ensuring the protection of the starbases is crucial as they are the only place to repair your ship, and this gives rise to further strategy on the players' part. When considering all its features, it is easy to see why Star Raiders is considered the killer app for the Atari 8-bit family and how it inspired games such as *Elite* (1984) and *Wing Commander* (1990).

Texas Instruments TI-99/4

The TI-99/4 home computer was released in the USA in 1979 by Texas Instruments. It is the first home computer to feature a 16-bit processor.

Monaco GP

Date of release: 1979

Region: USA

Developer: Gremlin Industries

Publisher: Sega

Platform: Arcade

Monaco GP is a single-player, racing game viewed from above on a colour Liquid-Crystal Display (LCD). The player must avoid the oncoming cars and finish the race before the timer runs out. The timer and score were displayed on various LEDs above the screen on the actual cabinet, like a pinball machine.

Monaco GP was ported to Sega's SG-1000 console in 1983.

Radar Scope

Date of release: December 1979

Region: Japan

Developer: Nintendo R&D2

Publisher: Nintendo

Platform: Arcade

Shigeru Miyamoto, who would later go on to create the *Donkey Kong, Mario* and the Legend of Zelda games, helped develop Radar Scope. The game is a single-player shoot 'em up similar in play style to Galaxian in that enemy ships swoop down and rain fire upon you. Radar Scope had two unique features. The first was its three-dimensional view. The second was that, unlike the usual shoot 'em ups that featured a one-hit kill on your ship, Radar Scope featured the ship's health, or perhaps a better analogy would be hull damage.

The game was incredibly popular in Japan but not in the USA. Nintendo ended up having to convert many of the leftover cabinets into *Donkey Kong* (1981) machines.

On-Line Systems

On-Line Systems, later Sierra On-Line, Inc. and after that Sierra Entertainment, Inc., was founded in 1979 by husband and wife Ken Williams and Roberta Williams.

Initially known for the successful graphical adventure game *Mystery House* (1980), the company would become famous for its graphic adventure games such as the *King's Quest* series (1980-2016), the *Quest for Glory* series (1989-1998), and the *Gabriel Knight* series (1993-2014).

Adventure

Date of release: 1979

Region: USA

Developer: Atari

Publisher: Atari

Platform: Atari 2600

Developed by Warren Robinett, Adventure is one of the first action-adventure home video games. The player is represented as a square, and you must search external and internal environments spanning across many screens that contain obstacles and mazes in search of a magical chalice. While roaming through the different screens, the player encounters hostile enemies including a bat that steals your items, dropping them at a randomised point in the game world and three dragons.

The exploration and puzzling aspects of this action-adventure game are a forerunner to *The Legend of Zelda* (1986), and its use of objects to gain access to new areas is a precursor to *Metroid* (1986).

Adventure held great appeal. As well as being recognised as a well-developed game, for the time, it is possibly best known for containing the first video game Easter egg. Programmers were not credited for their work, so Warren Robinett decided to leave his name hidden within a secret room. It took over a year until someone discovered the Easter egg, and by this time Atari had already sold many copies of the game. Adventure went on to sell over one million units.

Activision Inc.

Activision Inc. was founded in late 1979 by Atari developers who were unhappy about how they had been treated by their former employers. After the Video Game Crash of 1983, Activision diversified and went on to develop games not only for consoles but also for the computer market.

Activision is best known for its intellectual properties *Call of Duty* and *Guitar Hero*. In 2008 Activision merged with Vivendi Games and Blizzard Entertainment to form Activision Blizzard.

1970s Notable Omissions

1972

Star Trek (Arcade). Hunt the Wumpus. Cube.

1973

Pong Doubles. Space Race. Gotcha. Soccer.

1974

Quadrapong. Rebound. Shark Jaws. Super Pong.

1975

Maneater. Odyssey 100. PT-100.

1976

Blockade. Nürburgring 1. Road Race. Speed Race Twin. Moto-Cross. Tanktics

1977

Circus.

1978

APF MP 1000. Atari 2600 Football. Avalanche. Basketball. Block Game. Canyon Bomber. Frogs. Fire Truck. Outlaw. Tank 8.

1979

Bowling. Canyon Bomber. Space I. Space II. Space Invaders Part II (AKA Space Invaders Deluxe). Star Hawk.

1980

1980s Introduction

By the early 1980s, arcade machines were everywhere: not just in the amusement arcades themselves, but in restaurants, bars and cinemas. Their popularity grew to the point of oversaturation.

In homes across North America an abundance of bad console games and some very bad business decisions by those spearheading the industry, coupled with serious competition from the home computer market, caused many electronic manufacturers, video game publishers and developers to file for bankruptcy. The industry collapsed in the USA in what is now known as the Video Game Crash of 1983.

Yet in other parts of the world, the popularity of video games never wavered. With the immense popularity of the ZX Spectrum (1982) and Commodore 64 (1982) in Europe, and the Nintendo Famicom (1983) in Japan, the video game industry was as strong as ever.

In late 1985 the Nintendo Entertainment System (NES) managed to kick-start the games industry in the USA, although it didn't happen overnight. With titles like *Mario Bros.* (1983), *Tetris* (1984), *The Legend of Zelda* (1986), *Castlevania* (1986), *Metroid* (1986), *and Final Fantasy* (1987), the NES and the games industry eventually thrived once more in the States.

With the new wave of 16-bit machines, such as the Atari ST (1985), Amiga 1000 (1985), Amiga 500 (1987), and Sega Mega Drive/Genesis (1989), the difference in graphics between the arcade and the home experience was beginning to diminish. Arcade developers now had to come up with new and innovative ways to give consumers an experience they could not get in the home. They did this by developing techniques such as 'sprite scaling' (a technique where sprites could either grow or shrink to facilitate a three-dimensional environment) in games like *Hang-on* (1985), *Space Harrier* (1985), *Out Run* (1986) *and After Burner* (1987). *Some* of these also used cabinets that moved with the action. This was something that could not be emulated in the home.

Games like *Gauntlet* (1985) and *Teenage Mutant Ninja Turtles* (1989) would inspire an era of cooperative arcade games by offering huge cabinets with up to four sets of joysticks and buttons

This decade would also see the introduction of the handheld game devices, with

Nintendo's Game and Watch series (1980-1991) and Grandstand's series of electronic games (1980-1984). This would culminate in the immensely successful cartridge-based handheld Nintendo Game Boy *(1989)* and its killer app *Tetris* (1989).

Significant developments were made in 3D gaming from the established, real-time (seen or hidden line) wireframe graphics of *Battlezone* (1983), *Star Wars* (1983) *and Elite* (1984), to flat-shaded polygons, the first being *I Robot* (1984). Some other significant 3D games of the latter part of the decade were *The Sentinel* (1986), *Zarch/Virus* (1987), *Hard Drivin'* (1989), *and S.T.U.N. Runner* (1989), to name but a few.

The 1980s also saw the birth of several new genres, including the side-scrolling shoot 'em up, with *Defender* (1981) and *Scramble* (1981). *Space Panic* (1980) *and Donkey Kong* (1981) introduced and then popularised the platform genre. *Mystery House* (1980) would introduce graphics to the text adventure. *Haunted House* (1981) is arguably the first example of a survival horror game, albeit a tame one. *Castle Wolfenstein* (1981) would be the first game that would rely heavily on stealth, quietly introducing the stealth or sneak 'em up genre later popularised by *Metal Gear* (1987). *Sokoban* (1982) is one of the earliest examples of a puzzle video game. The *Arcade Machine* (1982) is the first example of a game creation game. *Utopia* (1981) was the first example of a (commercial) real-time strategy game. *Front Line* (1982) was the first in the scrolling run and gun genre. *Little Computer People* (1985) was possibly the first example of a life simulation game before it was firmly established with *SimCity* (1989). *Operation Wolf* (1987) was the first first-person rail shooter.

Traditional RPGs of the West such as *Ultima 1* (1980) and *Wizardry* (1981) would develop over the years in the East with games such as *The Black Onyx* (1984), *Dragon Quest* (1986), *Phantasy Star* (1987) and *Final Fantasy* (1987), heralding a new genre of Japanese role-playing games (JRPGs). That is not to say that RPGs in the West did not evolve: *Ultima IV: Quest of the Avatar* (1985) and *Wasteland* (1988) certainly marked a departure from their own inspiration of the 1970s and early 1980s games. This decade also saw the advent of the video game character with *Pac-Man* (1980), followed by other popular characters such as Mario, Donkey Kong, Q*Bert, Link, and Mega Man.

Sinclair ZX80

The Sinclair ZX80 was released in the UK in January 1980 by Science of Cambridge, later to be known as Sinclair Research. Developed by Clive Sinclair and Jim Westwood, the Sinclair ZX80 would become renowned as the first mass-market home computer for under one hundred British pounds - £99.95 or £79.95 in kit form. This was far cheaper than its contemporaries and, for many, made home computing an actual reality in the days when the majority of people couldn't afford a personal computer. The ZX80 could only output black and white with no sound to a standard television. It came with 1 kilobyte of RAM, making it extremely limited. As with many computers of the time, games were stored on standard audio cassettes, which were loaded onto the computer using a standard tape player plugged into the ZX80. The keyboard was a simple membrane that had shortcut BASIC commands on specific keys to make it easier for coding.

The ZX80 certainly had many shortcomings. However, there is no doubt that for many people it was their only way of accessing the world of computing in the comfort of their own home, and some of these people would go on to develop video games themselves.

Armor Attack

Date of release: March 1980

Region: USA

Developer and Publisher: Cinematronics

Platform: Arcade.

Designed by Tim Skelly (*Warrior* (1979)), Armor Attack is similar in gameplay to *Tank* (1974) or *Combat* (1977). From an overhead view, the player controls a jeep and must destroy enemy tanks and helicopters.

Armor Attack uses vector graphics and a screen overlay for its maze. The game was extremely fast-paced. It was later released for the Vetrex in 1982.

Game and Watch – Ball/Toss-Up

Ball, known as Toss-Up in the USA, the first Game and Watch game, was released in Japan in April 1980 by Nintendo. Ball was developed by Gunpei Yokoi. The player had to simply press the right or left button to have the character throw and keep the balls juggling in the air. It is believed that Yokoi came up with the idea for the small portable gaming device whilst observing a bored businessman playing with a calculator on the train.

Game and Watch devices usually comprised a small monochrome LCD screen, featuring a single-player game, which could also be used as a clock, and with some having an alarm. Well over fifty different models were produced, which included widescreen models, multi-screen models, some of which opened up in the same fashion as the Nintendo DS (2004), tabletop models, panorama models, super colour models, micro vs. models, crystal screen models, and the special model.

The Game and Watch series of products was very successful, with some titles selling up to a million units and accumulating for Nintendo sales of more than forty-three million worldwide over the next decade. Some of Game and Watch's most notable titles included *Popeye* (1981), *Mickey Mouse* (1981), *Snoopy Tennis* (1982), *Donkey Kong* (1982), *Donkey Kong II* (1983), *Mario Bros.* (1983) and *Donkey Kong Jr.* (1983).

Stratovox/Speak & Rescue

Date of release: May 1980

Region: Japan

Developer: Sun Electronics

Publisher: Sun Electronics

Platform: Arcade

Stratovox also known as Speak & Rescue, was a standard single-player, fixed space shooter. In this instance, the swooping aliens flew down from left to right. On the right was a moon with ten figures. The enemy ships picked up the figures to take them away, which the player tried to prevent.

Stratovox was the first video game to feature voice synthesis: a computer simulation of human speech. Stratovox says "Help me, help me!", "Lucky", "Very good!" and "We'll be back." It was hoped that the voice synthesis feature would be another way to attract customers to the arcade cabinets.

King & Balloon

Date of release: June 1980

Region: Japan

Developer: Namco

Publisher: Namco

Platform: Arcade

King & Balloon is a standard fixed shooter and actually runs on modified *Galaxian* (1979) hardware. In fact, some elements, such as the multi-coloured starfield backdrop, are still there. In King & Balloon, the player controls two little green figures standing upon a parapet and holding a cannon. The player must shoot down a multitude of balloons. The aim is to protect the king standing beneath the balloons that swoop down to pick him up. The player can destroy a balloon that is holding the king, and this will free him. (A similar game mechanic is found in *Defender* (1981), where the player's role is to protect and attack, rather than just attack.) The cannon can be destroyed by collision with the balloons or their shots. The player has an infinite number of cannons. Lives are lost when the king is taken off-screen.

King & Balloon was another game to feature speech to entice potential customers. It was also released in 1984 for the MSX home computer.

Pac-Man

Date of release: July 1980

Region: Japan

Developer: Namco

Publisher: Namco

Platform: Arcade

Pac-Man, known as Puck-Man in Japan, was designed by Toru Iwatani, who wanted to create a game that would appeal to women as well as men, thus broadening its audience. It is said that Iwatani came up with the idea for Pac-Man when taking a slice of pizza, leaving a simple head shape with a mouth. Pac-Man is a maze game. The aim of which is to score as many points as possible and clear each screen by manoeuvring the titular character through each maze, enabling him to 'eat up' all the pellets that he encounters. Four different-coloured ghosts – Inky, Pinky, Blinky and Clyde – move throughout the maze, each demonstrating a unique behaviour to make the gameplay as varied as possible. If Pac-Man encounters a ghost the player loses a life. The number of lives the player has is indicated by the number of Pac-Man icons displayed beneath the bottom-left corner of the maze. There are four larger 'power pellets' in each of the four corners of the maze, and when Pac-Man eats one of these, the ghosts flash blue and Pac-Man can 'chomp' the ghosts for a short time, which forces the ghosts to return to the centre of the maze after which they are a threat once again. Fruit items appear in the middle section of the maze, twice during each level, awarding extra points when eaten. The controls are simplicity itself: a single joystick. The pitch of the games sound increases throughout play to heighten the tension. The introduction of music and game-play sound is a perfect match for the game's frenetic theme. After several cleared screens, a cinematic will play, usually involving Pac-Man being chased across the screen by a ghost in a humorous vignette. These autonomous scenes are the first examples of video game cut scenes.

Pac-Man, like many arcade games, was supposed to have no end, yet there is a bug in the game that prevents the player from finishing and therefore progressing beyond level 256. Sometimes known as the 'split-screen bug. The player reaches level 256, and the right half of the screen is filled with seemingly random symbols. Since half the pellets are missing, the game does not allow a player to clear the screen and move on, making it possible to achieve a perfect score of 3,333,360 points. To do so a player must achieve a maximum score on the first 255 levels without losing a single life and score as many points as possible using all extra lives.

Despite receiving a lukewarm response from manufacturers and critics, Pac-Man was incredibly popular with the consumer, and what became known as 'Pac-Mania' or 'Pac-Man Fever' swept across the world. Due to the game's popularity and its iconic character, merchandise flew off the shelves, including toys, consumables, and clothing. A Pac-Man single went to number nine in the U.S. charts, selling 2.5 million copies. A Pac-Man animated TV series was produced by Hanna-Barbera, airing on ABC and attracting 20 million viewers. All of this made Pac-Man the first video-game franchise. Atari sold twelve million units for the Atari 2600. The arcade alone made over $1 billion during its first year, making more money than anything in the music or movie industry at the time. Due to this success, Pac-Man went on to have many sequels and clones, most notably *Ms. Pac-Man* (1982), *Pac-Mania* (1987), *Pac-Man World* (1999) and *Pac-Man Championship Edition* (2007).

Star Castle

Date of release: 1980

Region: USA

Developer: Cinematronics

Publisher: Cinematronics

Platform: Arcade

Designed by Tim Skelly and programmed by Scott Boden. In Star Castle, the player controls a spaceship that must destroy the enemy cannon at the centre of the screen. The cannon is protected by three layers of shielding, each made up of twelve sections. The player must destroy the rotating shield in order to fire upon the cannon, while the cannon releases homing mines through the shield to destroy the player's ship. Star Castle was a vector-based game with colour overlays in the middle to give the illusion of different coloured shields.

Missile Command

Date of release: July 1980

Region: USA

Developer: Atari

Publisher: Atari

Platform: Arcade

Designed by David Theurer, Missile Command stood apart from many other video games of the time. Despite being, in essence, a shoot 'em up, the main theme throughout the game is the defence of the six cities at the bottom of the screen from numerous missile strikes, depicted by dots and their trailing vectors. The player controls crosshairs on-screen and can use any of their own three missile batteries by pressing one of three buttons to launch ground-to-air missiles that explode at the designated point in the sky, destroying any oncoming enemy missiles in that immediate area. Like most games in this genre, there are a never-ending number of levels to clear and the gameplay, speed and therefore the difficulty of the game increase the longer it is played.

Missile Command was very successful upon release and went on to sell over 2.5 million copies when it was ported over to the Atari 2600 in 1981. It has spawned many clones and sequels over the years. It is perhaps the first video game to reflect the socio-political issues of the time, namely the nuclear tension between the USA and the Soviet Union. In fact, Theurer suffered from nightmares of a nuclear attack whilst coding the game.

Carnival

Date of release: 1980

Region: North America

Developer: Gremlin

Publisher: Sega

Platform: Arcade

Carnival is a single-player, standard fixed shooter. The player must shoot three rows of targets, which move across the screen. The targets consist of ducks, rabbits, owls and extra ammunition. Above the targets is a wheel that turns with flags on spokes; these flags must also be shot to clear the screen. The player's limited ammunition is shown at the bottom of the screen. If the player runs out of ammunition, then the game is over. This feature where the player must be as accurate as possible to clear the screen creates some serious tension and can also very rewarding.

Carnival is made distinct by two notable features: the music that plays throughout – *Sobre las Olas* by Juventino Rosas – is the quintessential sound of funfairs and carnivals, and this is the first video game to feature a bonus round, accessed after a level is cleared by shooting a bear target that moves across the screen.

Carnival was later released for the Atari 2600 and Atari 8-bit, ColecoVision and Intellivision.

Dragster

Date of release: 1980

Region: USA

Developer: Activision

Publisher: Activision

Platform: Atari 2600

Designed by David Crane, in Dragster the player views both their own and their opponent's car from a side view. The player must carefully race against their opponent while being careful not to blow the engine.

The gameplay is very simplistic, even for the time. However, it is worth noting that Dragster was Activision's first game. Activision would go on to develop much better games programmed by David Crane, most notably the popular hit *Pitfall* (1982).

Eamon

Date of release: 1980

Region: USA

Developer: Donald Brown

Publisher: None

Platform: Apple II

Developed by Donald Brown, Eamon, also known as The Wonderful World of Eamon, is a fantasy-themed, text-based RPG where the player takes part in quests set in a magical world filled with monsters.

What set Eamon apart from its predecessors was that Brown released his game free and in the public domain; he openly encouraged and invited others to add to his game.

A master disk, which Brown called 'the main Hall', was utilised to save and upload an already-established character's state. This could then be used to transfer a player's character to a completely new adventure written by a third party.

HAL Laboratory, Inc.

HAL Laboratory, Inc. was founded in 1980. The Japanese Video game developer's first games included *Taxman* (1981), a Pac-Man clone for the Apple II, and *Radar Rat Race* (1981) for the Commodore 8-bit computers.

Even though HAL began by making games for Commodore and the MSX, they went on to develop almost exclusively for every Nintendo console ever produced, becoming synonymous with the Nintendo brand. From its extensive library of games, HAL Laboratory, Inc. is best known for *Earthbound* (1994) (known as Mother 2 in Japan), the *Super Smash Bros. series*, and their many *Kirby games*.

Intellivision

Intellivision was launched in 1980 by Mattel Electronics. A second-generation home console, the Intellivision pitted itself openly in the media against its main competitor, the Atari 2600, informing the consumer of its superior graphics and sound. Which few could argue.

The Intellivision also boasted a host of exclusive games, particularly its sports games supported by major sports associations leading to titles such as *NFL Football* (1980), *NBA Basketball* (1980), *NHL Hockey* (1980), *Major League Baseball* (1980) and *PGA Golf* (1980).

By 1983 over three million consoles had been sold, a very respectable amount, but not enough to topple the market leader, the Atari 2600.

Mystery House

Date of release: 1980

Region: USA

Developer: On-Line Systems

Publisher: On-Line Systems

Platform: Apple II

Designed and Illustrated by Roberta Williams and programmed by Ken Williams, Mystery House was one of the first graphical adventure games. The husband and wife team were inspired to make their own game after playing *Colossal Cave Adventure* (1975).

In Mystery House, the player and seven other people find themselves locked in an old, abandoned mansion. As the player progresses through the game, exploring the mansion's many rooms, they discover the recently murdered individuals with whom they entered the house at the start of the game. The player must seek a way to discover the identity of the murderer and escape from the house.

Roberta Williams realised that almost all games in this genre were purely text-based, and so she came up with the idea to include illustrations: she drew seventy scenes for Mystery House. The idea for the story was inspired by Agatha Christie's novel *And Then There Were None* (1939). Initially, Mystery House sold over 10,000 units through mail order alone. Later, through the Sierra Venture line, it sold a further 80,000 units worldwide.

Olympic Decathlon

Date of release: 1980

Region: USA

Developer: Timothy W.Smith

Publisher: Microsoft

Platform: TRS-80

Programmed by Timothy W. Smith, Olympic Decathlon included accurate simulations of all ten decathlon events (the first of this genre) and would pave the way for other sports games, such as *Track & Field* (1983) and *Hyper Sports* (1984).

Rogue

Date of release: 1980

Region: USA

Programmed by Michael Toy and Glenn Wichman

Platform: a freely distributed game for Unix-based mainframe systems.

Rogue is a dungeon crawling game where the aim of the game is to survive the dungeons and locate the Amulet of Yendor, which is to be found in the lowest level of the dungeons. The player will encounter monsters and different items along the way that may help them on their quest. The game world is revealed as the player explores and is made entirely from text-based characters, also known as ASCII (American Standard Code for Information Interchange) characters. For example, dots and lines make up the structure of the rooms, the player's character is displayed as an @ symbol, a snake is represented by an S, and so on and so forth. Despite being a rather primitive-looking game, Rogue has some very appealing features. The essence of Rogue is that the whole game world is procedurally generated, meaning that it has infinite re-playability: no two games will ever be the same. Also, there are very limited opportunities to save the game. Rogue would define roguelikes as a genre: a game that is exciting and intense since permanent death (permadeath) is a very real possibility. No saves, no checkpoints – the player must start all over again. This type of game is even more popular than ever for some in recent years due to many games having checkpoints or the opportunity to save at any time.

Rogue went on to produce many ports and clones. The most notable ports are the colour Rogue DOS version in (1983) and the Rogue Atari ST version in (1986): both versions substitute the original ASCII for 2D Graphics. The most prominent Rogue clones are *Hack* (1982) and *NetHack* (1987). Rogue has also influenced many games such as the *Diablo series* (1997-current date).

Phoenix

Date of release: 1980

Region: USA

Publisher: Centuri and Taito

Platform: Arcade

Phoenix is a typical single-player, space shoot 'em up, also known as a shmup, and is similar to games such as *Galaxian* (1979) and *Galaga* (1981). You must shoot down a set number of enemies who, from time to time, dive-bomb in an attempt to destroy the player's craft.

Phoenix had a couple of unique elements, one of which was that the player could use a shield to protect their craft from the alien bird-like creatures that would crash into it. Once used, the shield needed five seconds to recharge. Secondly, Phoenix was possibly the first arcade game to feature a boss, in the form of a giant mothership, at every fifth level. It was later released on the Atari 2600.

Red Baron

Date of release: 1980

Region: USA

Developer: Atari

Publisher: Atari

Platform: Arcade

Red Baron is a single-player, first-person 3D flight simulator and shooter. The player controls a World War I biplane and must destroy all enemy targets, including planes, pillboxes, turrets and Zeppelins. The game was developed along with *Battlezone* (1980). The game used three-dimensional wireframe vector graphics with a colour overlay. Red Baron had an interesting feature where it adjusted its current difficulty level, up or down, based on the performance of the last thirty-two players, including the top three scores.

Even though Battlezone was the more popular of the two games, Red Baron is an adequate precursor for dog-fighting games to come, such as *Air Raiders* (1982), *F-15 Strike Eagle* (1984) and *Ace of Aces* (1986).

Space Invaders on the Atari 2600

Space Invaders was released in the USA in 1980 for the Atari 2600. It was the first home video game to sell a million units. It quadrupled sales of the Atari 2600 console, making Space Invaders the Atari 2600's first killer app.

Space Invaders Tournament

Such was the success of the Atari 2600 port of Space Invaders that Atari organised the Space Invaders Tournament in 1980 in Los Angeles. Over 10,000 people participated in the event Won by William Heineman, now Rebecca Ann Heineman. The Space Invaders Tournament was the first electronic sports (esports) event.

Fishing Derby

Date of release: 1980

Region: USA

Developer: Activision

Publisher: Activision

Platform: Atari 2600

Created by David Crane, Fishing Derby is a one- or two-player game and depicts two fishermen sitting on opposing docks, as seen from a side-on view. The bottom two-thirds of the screen is taken up by water where the fish are found. The player uses their joystick to aim their hook onto a fish and reel it in. However, there is a shark swimming amongst the fish, ready to intercept the player's catch. The aim of the game is to be the first player to catch 99lbs of fish. The deeper the fish, the heavier they are, but the greater the risk of being eaten by the shark.

Fishing Derby is surprisingly fun, and unique in a market of maze games and shooters. It was a refreshing change and appealed to both children and adults.

Wizard of Wor

Date of release: 1980

Region: USA

Developer: Dave Nutting Associates

Publisher: Midway

Platform: Arcade

Wizard of Wor is a one- or two-player maze game, where the players control space knight characters called worriors. Within the maze are also several monsters that the player must shoot to clear the screen and progress to the next level. There are a set number of enemies to kill, though only a maximum of six appear on the screen at any one time. The other more difficult enemies spawn when a monster has been dispatched; these other monsters can become momentarily invisible yet are always visible on the radar at the bottom centre of the screen. Players can shoot at one another or decide to play cooperatively. Most two-player games involved taking turns or being pitted against one another, and so the cooperative aspect was rather unique and rewarding.

Wizard of Wor is a somewhat challenging game to play, so much so that when it was released under the name The Incredible Wizard for the Bally Astrocade game console, a cash prize was offered to the first person who could complete the game.

TRS-80 Color Computer

The TRS-80 Color Computer was released in the USA in September 1980. Created by the Tandy Corporation, the TRS-80 Color Computer shipped either with 4 KB, 16 KB or 32 KB of RAM, colour output, eight colours in total and supported many notable well-made games, such as *Pac-Man* (1980), *Canyon Climber* (1981), *Downland* (1981) and *Zaxxon*

(1982).

Warlords

Date of release: 1980

Region: USA

Developer: Atari

Publisher: Atari

Platform: Arcade

Warlords can be played by up to four players. Each player controls a castle placed in one of the four corners of the screen. The players must protect their wall from a fireball by deflecting it using a shield. The fireball bounces around the screen, destroying sections of the castle walls if not protected. The aim of the game is to use this game mechanic to break down your opponents' walls and break through their defences. A castle is destroyed if the fireball gets past the wall and makes contact with the castle icon inside. Whoever is left alive wins the game. Whenever a player is defeated, or a certain amount of time has passed, more fireballs are introduced, increasing the difficulty. The player uses a spinner controller to move their shield. It is interesting to see how Pong (1972) evolved into Breakout (1976) and Breakout evolved into Warlords. The four-player aspect was quite rare in its day.

For the upright cabinet version, the game is reflected onto a mirror on which a perspective drawing of the castles as seen from above is drawn. This gives the scene a unique, three-dimensional look. What also made Warlords a popular game in the arcade was that it was one of the few games where four friends could battle it out together. Warlords was later released for the Atari 2600.

Crazy Climber

Date of release: October 1980

Region: Japan

Developer: Nichibutsu

Publisher: Nichibutsu

Platform: Arcade

In Crazy Climber the player is portrayed as a green-jumpsuited figure scaling the side of a building, which disappears off the top of the screen. A graphic of the player's progress up the entirety of the skyscraper can be seen on the left. The opening and closing of windows cause the climber to fall, as well as several other obstacles, including a giant ape.

Crazy Climber was the first platforming climbing game. It was later released for the Atari 2600, Famicom and Playstation.

Rally-X

Date of release: November 1980

Region: Japan

Developer: Namco

Publisher: Namco

Platform: Arcade

Rally-X is a top-down maze game. The player controls a blue car and must collect all the yellow flags to earn points and move on to the next level. Three red cars pursue the player's car and attempt to collide with it, in which event the player loses a life. The player's car can deploy a smokescreen that slows down the pursuing cars. The game area is larger than the screen, and so a mini-map of where the flags and cars are located is displayed on the right-hand side. The player also has a limited amount of fuel to collect all the flags.

Rally-X was presented at a trade show along with Battlezone, Defender, and Pac-Man. The consensus was that Rally-X would be the most profitable game. Even though it enjoyed relative success, both Defender and Pac-Man proved to be the far more popular games, with the initially overlooked Pac-Man becoming the most successful arcade game of all time. Rally-X was later released for the MSX.

Space Panic

Date of release: November 1980

Region: USA

Developer: Universal

Publisher: Universal

Platform: Arcade

Developed by Chris Crawford, Space Panic is believed by some to be the first true platformer. The player controls a figure who can run across platforms and climb ladders. Several aliens traverse the gaming area, seeking to destroy the player's character. The player must dispose of the aliens by digging holes into the platforms, waiting until the alien gets stuck in the hole and then knocking them out of the hole: the alien will expire from falling to the lower level. More difficult enemies can only be killed by aligning a series of holes vertically, allowing the player to lure an alien to the top hole and then knock it down. There is a limited supply of oxygen to complete each level.

Space Panic was not very successful, perhaps due to the many new elements it introduced, or to the fact that it runs too fast, making it difficult for the player to successfully play the game. It is said that the average game lasted only thirty seconds. Space Panic would influence games such as *Lode Runner* (1983), and one of my personal favourite arcades, *Mr. Do's Castle* (1983).

Battlezone

Date of release: November 1980

Region: USA

Developer: Atari

Publisher: Atari

Platform: Arcade

Designed by Edward Rotberg, Owen Rubin and Roger Hector, Battlezone is a single-player, first-person 3D shooter, where the player takes control of a tank. The aim of the game is to destroy as many enemy tanks as possible, and the occasional UFO, which all explode into satisfying three-dimensional chucks when destroyed. The environment comprises several large rocks dispersed throughout the landscape, which the player uses for cover and a mountainous landscape on the horizon.

Battlezone had some features that set it apart. The cabinet housed a suspended periscope similar to *Sea Wolf* (1976), through which the player would view the game. It featured green-on-black wireframe 3D graphics using its vector display. Also, it is worth noting that since the outside world was blocked off from the player's sight, they would be immersed in a new 3D environment, albeit a somewhat primitive one. Edward Rotberg and Atari were commissioned by the US Military to develop a similar game for training purposes, so impressed were they by Battlezone.

Some consider Battlezone to be the first virtual reality video game. It was later ported to several platforms, most recently as a true virtual reality game *Battlezone PSVR (PlayStation Virtual Reality)* (2016).

Berserk

Date of release: November 1980

Region: USA

Developer: Stern Electronics

Publisher: Stern Electronics

Platform: Arcade

Designed by Alan McNeil, Berserk is a multi-directional, run and gun shooter game played in a series of mazes. The player is displayed as a humanoid figure who, upon entering a maze, is set upon by killer robots. The player must shoot and/or dodge the robots and their returning fire, as well as avoid the electrified fences, and make it out through an exit where the next maze loads up. The game world comprises 65,536 mazes or rooms. If the player lingers within a room for too long a character called Evil Otto will appear, depicted as a large yellow face. The player will be killed if touched by Evil Otto, and since there is no way to kill Evil Otto the player must exit the room as soon as possible.

The game was notably different from some of its contemporaries due to its speech synthesis. The robots on-screen would utter "Intruder alert! Intruder alert!" or "The intruder must not escape," and would entice the player with the phrase "Coin detected in pocket". Berserk was later released for the Atari 2600, the Vetrex and the Atari 5200.

Broderbund

Games developer, Broderbund, was founded in the USA by brothers Doug Carlston and Gary Carlston in November 1980. Their first game was *Galactic Empire* (1980). They then went on to develop many games for 8-bit home computers, such as *Choplifter* (1982), *Lode Runner* (1983) and *Prince of Persia* (1989). Broderbund also developed *Myst* (1993) and are known for the *Carmen Sandiego series* (1985-91) of educational mystery video games.

DECO Cassette System

The DECO Cassette System was released in December 1980 by Data East. It worked in a similar manner to the way in which a computer could use a tape system to run its games, but for the arcade. Amusement arcade owners could buy a base cabinet and, over time, order a new game stored on a large cassette. Games were copied from the tape onto the cabinet's RAM chips. Once this process was complete, taking only two to three minutes, the new game could be played. On the upside, it was a flexible system, but on the downside, the tapes were less reliable than solid-state chips. Data East made many of their own games for the DECO Cassette System as well as intellectual properties from other publishers.

Zork 1

Date of release: December 1980

Region: USA

Developer: Infocom

Publisher: Personal Software

Platform: TRS-80 and PDP-10

Developed by Tim Anderson, Marc Blank, Dave Lebling and Bruce Daniels between 1977 and 1979, Zork 1 also known as Zork: The Great Underground Empire – Part 1, is a text-based fantasy adventure game that begins at the exterior of a white house with the well-known opening:

West of House

You are standing in an open field west of a white house, with a boarded front door.

There is a mailbox here.

Soon after entering the house and collecting several objects, the player enters a vast subterranean world populated with a variety of monsters. The aim of the game is to collect all twenty treasures of Zork. The game is notable for its flexible replies to player input and its rich narrative. Zork 1 is considered one of the most important games of the RPG genre. It was a best-seller for years after its release, selling hundreds of thousands of copies, and has been ported to many platforms.

1980 Notable Omissions

Computer Bismarck. Galactic Empire. Heiankyo Alien. Major League Baseball. Moon Cresta. NBA Basketball. NFL Football. NHL Hockey. PGA Golf. Prisoner. Quasar. Sasuke vs commander. Scram. Space Firebird. Spectar. Tank Battalion. Targ. The Prisoner. Wizard and the Princess.

1981

ANALOG Computing

The magazine *ANALOG Computing* was first published in January 1981. Founded by Lee H. Pappas and Michael DesChesnes, *ANALOG* (Atari Newsletter And Lots Of Games) *Computing* was published for Atari 8-bit owners. It ran until 1989. *ANALOG Computing* was one of the first publications to feature regular articles exclusively about video games.

Scramble

Date of release: February 1981

Region: Japan

Developer: Konami

Publisher: Konami

Platform: Arcade

Scramble is a single-player, side-scrolling shooter. The aim of Scramble is to progress through the levels shown at the top of the screen and destroy the enemy vessels that launch from the ground and later attack from the air. The player's ship can shoot horizontally and is also equipped with bombs to destroy enemy ships and facilities on the ground. Fuel is shown at the bottom of the screen and the player must bomb fuel sites to replenish their fuel. The constant horizontal-scrolling forces the player along the game world, making careful maneuvering crucial especially when spaces through caverns become tight. The game is won on the sixth level where the player must destroy the base.

Scramble is the first forced horizontal-scrolling shooter, meaning that the set pace of the screen's movement, often from left to right or upwards, limits the player's movement within the game world, setting the stage for many more similar side-scrolling shooters to come. Scramble was released outside of Japan in March of the same year.

Gorf

Date of release: February 1981

Region: North America

Developer: Midway

Publisher: Midway

Platform: Arcade

Developed chiefly by Dave Nutting, Gorf (Galactic Orbiting Robot Force) is a standard fixed shoot em' up, except that each of the five levels is distinctly different. The first level is very similar to *Space Invaders* (1978), but the major difference is that you are protected by a giant domed shield that is gradually shot to pieces by the descending enemy ships. The second level has ships that shoot continuous laser beams, making manoeuvrability tight and limited. The third level is almost exactly like *Galaxian* (1979). The fourth level has the player shooting ships while going through a space warp. In the fifth and final level, you must shoot through the flag ship's domed shield, breakthrough its hull until you can destroy its main reactor. One of Gorf's most notable features was its emphasis on synthesized speech.

Gorf is one of the first games to let players buy extra lives before starting to play. However, only a maximum of seven starting lives can be attained.

Sinclair ZX81

The Sinclair ZX81 was released in the UK in March 1981 by Sinclair Research. Developed by Clive Sinclair and Jim Westwood, the ZX81 was to be manufactured as cheaply as possible to push the selling price down, making it accessible to as many customers as possible. It was an upgraded variant of the ZX80: Westwood was able to combine eighteen of the ZX80's chips into one single chip. The ZX81, like its predecessor, could only output black and white and no sound to a standard television. It came with 1 kilobyte of RAM (about enough to type 24 lines of code), though a 16K RAM pack/module upgrade (about enough to type 400 lines of code) was available and necessary to play many games. Games were stored on cassette, which was loaded onto the computer, using a standard tape player plugged into the ZX81. The keyboard was a simple membrane that had shortcut BASIC commands on specific keys to make it easier for coding. The ZX81 sold for the incredibly low price of £69.95 or £49.95 in kit form. It was released by Timex in the USA for $99.95. The ZX81 was very successful selling over 1.5 million units.

Defender

Date of release: March 1981

Region: USA

Developer: Williams Electronics

Publisher: Atari

Platform: Arcade

Developed by Eugene Jarvis, Defender is a single-player, horizontal shoot 'em up where the game world is several times the screen size and wraps around upon itself horizontally, meaning if you fly in either the left or right direction from point A then soon enough you will arrive back at that same point. The player must destroy waves of enemies who attempt to abduct astronauts from the planet's surface. Astronauts carried to the top of the screen turn into lethal enemy mutants. Astronauts can be saved by accurately shooting the enemy ship, at which event the Astronaut will fall gently back to the surface. Radar displays the locations of enemy ships and astronauts. As well as a lightning-fast laser, the player has a limited number of smart bombs that destroy every enemy on the screen. There is also a hyperspace button to be used in desperate situations. However, since the screen is often littered with enemies, enemy fire and mines, this can often lead to instant death.

Defender is considered one of the most difficult video games ever created. The controls comprised a joystick and five buttons, which was a few too many for some players. It certainly attracted players who liked a challenge. Defender was immensely popular selling over 50,000 units. It was soon ported to over a dozen platforms and had numerous copies and clones.

Amidar

Date of release: 1981

Region: Japan

Developer: Konami

Publisher: Stern

Platform: Arcade

Amidar is a standard maze game set on interlinked quadrilaterals laced with dots. The player's character is an ape that must eat up all the dots to clear the level. When a quadrilateral's dots are all eaten, it is filled with a colour. As with most maze games, enemies attempt to seek and destroy you. The player has a 'jump' button that can be used three times per level and makes all enemies on the screen jump for a moment, thus enabling the player to pass them unharmed if timed right. The bonus level involves the same basic game mechanics. However, in this case, each quadrilateral has a three figure-number contained within, representing bonus points awarded.

Super Cobra

Date of release: March 1981

Region: Japan

Developer: Konami

Publisher: Konami

Platform: Arcade

Super Cobra is the sequel to *Scramble* (1981) and is basically the same game (a single-player, side-scrolling shooter) with a few differences. For example, the player now flies a helicopter instead of piloting a ship, there are ten levels instead of six, and the player, upon losing all lives, can continue precisely where they left off if they put another coin in before the time expires.

Despite being almost the exact same game as its predecessor and released within the same year, it was a commercial success and was ported to most computers and consoles of the time.

Astrosmash

Date of release: 1981

Region: USA

Developer: Mattel

Publisher: Mattel, Sears

Platform: Intellivision

Designed by John Sohl, Astrosmash is a single-player, fixed space shooter. The player controls a laser gun that must destroy oncoming meteors, spinning bombs, UFOs and guided missiles. Unlike most games in this genre, enemies simply pass by the bottom of the screen and enemy ships like the UFO do not fire upon your laser. The player can only lose a life through contact with an enemy. The game is very fast-paced, yet skilled players can last for some time. This led to a high score contest, where the best players from around the United States and Canada were flown to Houston, Texas, to attend the finals.

Astrosmash was ported to the Atari 2600 and Aquarius home computer. It sold over one million units, making it one of the top five selling games for the Intellivision.

Centipede

Date of release: 1981

Region: USA

Developer: Atari

Publisher: Atari

Platform: Arcade

Designed by Dona Bailey and Ed Logg, Centipede is a single-player, fixed shooter where the aim of the game is to destroy the segmented centipede that works its way down the screen left to right, or vice versa. The screen is littered with mushrooms. The centipede reverses direction and drops down to the next level of the screen when hitting the edge of the screen or one of the many mushrooms. Other creatures appear in the game, laying down more mushrooms, for instance. This makes the game more challenging as the more often the centipede intercepts a mushroom, the quicker it descends to the bottom of the screen. However, the player can shoot not only the centipede to destroy its segments but also the mushrooms, and the other creatures too, essentially gaining more time and giving themselves a better chance to destroy all segments of the centipede. When a segment of the centipede is shot, it turns into a mushroom and the two sections left will split apart and move independently – creating two smaller centipedes where previously there was one. This will happen again and again, eventually breaking the centipede into single pieces which must all be dispatched.

Centipede was aimed at both genders. After launch, it was estimated that roughly half of its players were women, and indeed Centipede was the first arcade game to be chiefly designed by a woman (Dona Bailey). Centipede was incredibly successful and was ported to many platforms.

Frogger

Date of release: June 1981

Region: Japan

Developer: Konami

Publisher: Sega/Gremlin

Platform: Arcade

Designed by Robert Papas, in Frogger the player takes the role of a frog attempting to cross a busy road and then a river, as seen from a top-down perspective. The player starts at the bottom of the screen and uses a joystick only to move in any one of four directions to avoid the traffic. There is a safe zone in the middle of the screen to give the player a moment's respite. However, there is a timer, so the player must continue jumping onto the backs of turtles and logs (for some reason water kills the frog) to reach the top of the screen and into one of the safe slots provided. Each time the player successfully puts a frog home in its slot, the timer resets and the player must run the gauntlet again in an attempt to put the next frog in an available slot. Once all five slots are filled the player progresses to the next level. Each level increases in difficulty.

Frogger was yet another successful arcade game in the Golden Age of Video Games (1978-86) and has spawned many copies and clones.

Raster Blaster

Date of release: June 1981

Region: USA

Developer: Bill Budge

Publisher: BudgeCo

Platform: Apple II

Developed by Bill Budge, Raster Blaster is a home computer pinball simulation and is a precursor to a spite of other Pinball video games such as *Pinball Construction Set* (1983). The game featured realistic physics and was very popular for the Apple II, selling over 25,000 units.

Ultima 1: The First Age of Darkness

Date of release: June 1981

Region: USA

Developer: Origin Systems

Publisher: California Pacific Origin System

Platform: Apple II

Developed by Richard Garriot, whose previous game *Akalabeth: World of Doom* (1979) is sometimes referred to as *Ultima 0*, Ultima 1 is officially the first in the long series of Ultima RPGs. The player plays the part of 'The Stranger' who must find and destroy the gem of immortality in the possession of the evil wizard, Mondain. Long before *Dragon Quest* (1986) and *Final Fantasy* (1987), Ultima introduced a multitude of features that would become the established way to design an RPG video game, recognized by many as the new gold standard. Ultima 1 was the first to introduce an all-colour world view as seen from the top-down, where the player could roam and explore. Enemies on the world map would simply appear and combat would automatically initiate (This was a game mechanic emulated later in *Final Fantasy (1987)*). The dungeon-crawling aspect is played in a first-person 3D mode, where players would encounter monsters and discover treasures. Ultima 1 was the first game where a player could die of starvation and so consumables management played a key part in survival. It was also the first time players could steal items from towns. Ultima 1 was the first game to cross genres and break the boundaries of its traditions. It went from a world of magic and monsters into time travel, even sporting a space-shooter element at one point in the game.

Ultima 1 was well received and soon had a cult following spawning an entire series. This series is split into three parts as follows: The Age of Darkness, comprising of Ultima I-III, The Age of Enlightenment, comprising of Ultima IV-VI and The Age of Armageddon, comprising of Ultima VII-IX. The last game in the Ultima series was *Ultima IX: Ascension* (1999).

Kaboom!

Date of release: July 1981

Region: USA

Developer: Activision

Publisher: Activision

Platform: Atari 2600

Designed by Larry Kaplan, Kaboom! is an unauthorised clone of *Avalanche* (1978). In Kaboom! the player must use a three-tier bucket to catch multiple bombs being thrown from the top by a character known as the 'Mad Bomber.' If the player fails to catch a bomb, they lose a life. The gameplay is very fast-paced and rather simplistic yet solid.

Kaboom! was a very successful Atari 2600 game, selling over one million units.

Donkey Kong

Date of release: July 1981

Region: Japan

Developer: Nintendo R&D1

Publisher: Nintendo

Platform: Arcade

Designed by Shigeru Miyamoto, Donkey Kong is a single-player, platform game where the player controls the character, Mario, who was initially called Jumpman. He must ascend to the top of a construction site, jumping over barrels and climbing ladders to save his girlfriend, Pauline, from a giant ape called Donkey Kong. The game offers a power-up item to collect; thereafter Mario can use a hammer to smash the oncoming barrels. Donkey Kong offers four distinctly different stages. At each stage, Mario must climb higher and the difficulty increases. In stage 4, Mario must remove eight rivets from a platform that supports Donkey Kong. When done, Donkey Kong will fall, and Mario is reunited with Pauline. Upon completion of stage four, the player progresses to the next level. The stages are repeated but the speed of the game increases. In the first stage on level 6, Mario will die within a few seconds due to an error in the game. Technically this means the player has completed the game.

Donkey Kong introduced the characters of Mario and Donkey Kong. Shigeru Miyamoto portrayed Mario as a carpenter initially before he became the well-known plumber he is today. His trademark look came about since the resolution of the sprites was so limited. Mario wore a hat because there weren't enough pixels to display hair and he was given a moustache because, again, there were too few pixels to draw an accurate mouth. The name Donkey Kong as the name of the ape came about because Miyamoto spoke little English. He searched through a Japanese-English dictionary because he wanted to name the ape 'Stubborn Gorilla' He found the word 'donkey' as a synonym for 'stubborn' and 'Kong' relating to 'ape'.

At a time when the arcades were full of space shooters, mazes, driving and sports games, Donkey Kong, with its strong emphasis on characters and narrative, really stood out from the crowd and became immensely popular. Donkey Kong's success can be seen in the numerous sequels for each of these two debut characters. There are too many to mention them all here. However, to focus on Donkey Kong himself, the most notable sequels would include *Donkey Kong jr* (1982), *Donkey Kong Country* (1994), *Donkey Kong 64* (1999), *Donkey Kong Jungle Beat* (2005), *Donkey Kong Country Returns* (2010) and *Donkey Kong Country Tropical Freeze* 2013). Donkey Kong was Nintendo's first real success in the arcades.

IBM Personal Computer

The IBM Personal Computer (what would later become IBM PC Compatible) was released in August 1981. In the late 1970s and early 1980s, the personal computer market was dominated by the Apple II (1977), the Commodore PET (1977) and the TRS-80 (1977). IBM, previously known for their mainframe computers, entered the personal computer market with an open architecture standard, benefiting and encouraging third-party developers. The IBM PC cost $1,565 and was shipped with 16 KB RAM and featured colour graphics. IBM pushed a huge marketing campaign making the IBM PC very attractive for home users.

Microsoft Adventure originally released in 1979, itself a port of *Colossal Cave Adventure* (1976), was one of its launch titles. Hundreds of independents produced software for the IBM PC platform. By 1983 the IBM PC would come to dominate the high-end home computer market in the USA. Other companies, such as Compaq and American Megatrends, developed computers that were IBM Compatible meaning that any of these computers would be able to use the same hardware and software. This was the first step towards the modern-day Personal Computer or PC platform on which many video games are played.

Eastern Front (1941)

Date of release: August 1981

Region: USA

Developer: Chris Crawford

Publisher: Atari

Platform: Atari 8-bit.

Eastern Front (1941) is a single-player turn-based strategy game where you play the part of the Germans fighting the Russians on the Eastern Front during World War II. The game features different map topology as well as rivers, mountains, forests and swamps. The screen only shows a very small part of the map. According to Chris Crawford, Eastern Front (1941) is the first wargame with a smooth-scrolling map. Differences in seasons also affect gameplay. The player controls many different unit types and can give them all a variety of orders.

Eastern Front (1941) was highly praised for its technical gameplay mechanics and artificial intelligence, making it a very challenging game. Eastern Front (1941) is considered one of the Atari 8-Bit's most successful games, selling over 60,000 units.

Grandstand Electronic Games

Grandstand Leisure Products released the first in its series of table-top and handheld electronic games in the UK and Japan in 1981. Hoping to cash in on the popularity of Nintendo's Game & Watch handheld series of games, Grandstand Leisure Products manufactured several of their own portable devices. The Grandstand Electronic Devices were much loved by many children of the 1980s

Some of the most notable games were *Astro Wars* (1981), *The Big Game* (1981), *Firefox F-7* (1981), *Caveman* (1982) and *Scramble* (1982).

The Dungeons & Dragons Computer Fantasy Handheld Electronic Game

The Dungeons & Dragons Computer Fantasy Handheld Electronic Game was released in the USA in 1981 by Mattel. The player moves through a dungeon made up of 100 junctions, or rooms as they are called. The aim of the game is to find the arrow, then find the dragon and kill it. Players must beware of bats and pits. If you have a grappling hook you can climb out of the pit, but if not, the game is over. The left part of the LCD screen displays the player in the room. On the right is displayed the proximity of a pit or the dragon. However, the player never knows in which direction these perils lie.

Dungeons & Dragons Computer Fantasy Handheld Electronic Game is the first Dungeons & Dragons video game.

Lady Bug

Date of release: 1981

Region: USA

Developer: Universal

Publisher: Universal

Platform: Arcade

Designed by Kazutoshi Ueda, Lady Bug is a single-player, maze game where the player plays as the Lady Bug who must eat up all the flowers, hearts and letters throughout the screen to continue to the next level. A graphical border counts down the time until an enemy bug will be released from the centre of the maze. Skull sprites will also kill the player. Three randomly selected and placed letters appear on each level. These make up the word SPECIAL and EXTRA. Collect all the letters for SPECIAL and the player is given a free game. Collect all the letters for EXTRA and the player receives an extra life. This kind of 'bonus' mechanic would be used extensively in future arcade games. Lady Bug's most unique feature is the introduction of gates. There are twenty gates that pivot in the middle. The player can turn these gates, changing the layout of the maze. Players can use this game mechanic to access different areas of the maze and escape enemy bugs.

Lady Bug wasn't that successful in the arcades but did rather well when ported to the ColecoVision (1982) console.

Quest for the Rings

Date of release: 1981

Region: USA

Developer: Magnavox

Publisher: Magnavox

Platform: Odyssey²

Quest for the Rings is a fantasy adventure game for between 2-5 players, where the aim of the game is to find ten magical keys. It is a rather unique video game in that you play it in conjunction with a board game. It was not the first to include what are known as 'feelies' (books and models etc.), however, it is one of the few games where such things are integral to gameplay. A full-colour gloss-finished guidebook was included, together with a colour fold-out hard-back map, a colour keyboard overlay and an assortment of game pieces, including metal coins. One player plays the part of the ringmaster and hides the keys within castles of their choice. Once the game is started on the Magnavox console, players can choose their class of hero. They then choose a location on the map. They are transported to that location on the screen where they must avoid monsters while attempting to collect a key if one is there.

Quest for the Rings was awarded 'Most Innovative Game' in the 1982 Arcade Awards (Arkies).

Space Dungeon

Date of release: 1981

Region: Japan

Developer: Taito

Publisher: Taito

Platform: Arcade

Designed by Rex Battenberg, Space Dungeon is a multi-directional shooter where the aim of the game is to collect as many treasures as possible, then find and exit the level through the 'collect bonus' room all the while avoiding a multitude of different enemies seeking to destroy you. Each screen represents a room, and a level is made up of 36 rooms. The player can make use of radar at the top of the screen to obtain information on the adjacent rooms and their own place within the level. There are 100 levels in Space Dungeon: levels 1 to 99, then a level 0, and if completed the game starts again at level 1.

One quaint quirk of the game is an opening rhyme at the beginning of levels 2-9: e.g. 'The thief's in view on level 2.' 'More to see on level 3.'

Zork II: The Wizard of Frozbozz

Date of release: 1981

Region: USA

Developer: Infocom

Publisher: Infocom

Platform: Atari 8-bit and TRS-80

Zork II is the direct sequel to the text-based fantasy adventure game *Zork 1* (1980) and continues where the story left off.

Zork II was highly praised by critics and well received by players.

It was soon ported to many of the popular home computer platforms of the time.

Utopia

Date of release: 1981

Region: USA

Developer: Mattel Electronics

Publisher: Mattel Electronics

Platform: Intellivision

Developed by Don Daglow, Utopia is a two-player, turn-based strategy game. Each player controls an island and must attempt to create the most prosperous society. This is indicated by points at the bottom. Each player can gather resources and build an infrastructure as well as interfering with their opponent's progress.

Utopia is perhaps worth considering as a precursor to the modern-day Real-Time Strategy (RTS) game. Even though the gameplay is turn-based it does have some real-time elements such as weather.

Vanguard

Date of release: 1981

Region: Japan

Developer: TOSE

Publisher: SNK

Platform: Arcade

Programmed by Dave Payne, in Vanguard the player must fly their ship through the interior of an asteroid, avoiding obstacles and shooting down enemy ships. The game is broken down into zones: at the end of each zone, there is a boss to destroy. At the end of the final level, the player must defeat an alien called the Gond. The player's ship can fire in any one of four directions. Fuel is limited but can be replenished by destroying enemy ships. Energy pods are scattered throughout the zones; these will render your ship invulnerable for a limited time. Sound plays a large part in the game. As well as announcing each level's name, a sample from the movies *Star Trek: The Motion Picture* and *Flash Gordon* play when starting the game and collecting energy pods respectively.

Vanguard is one of the first shoot 'em ups with multi-directional scrolling.

Wizardry: Proving Grounds of the Mad Overlord

Date of release: 1981

Region: USA

Developer: Sir-Tech

Publisher: Sir-Tech

Platform: Apple II

Developed by Andrew C. Greenberg and Robert Woodhead, Wizardry is a first-person RPG dungeon crawling video game. Known as Wizardry I for short, it is the first of nine in the Wizardry series, the last being Wizardry 8 (2001); one of the games was a spin-off game though and is not numbered. It was one of the first video games to use a party-based system. The player controls six different characters, choosing their race, class and stats. The aim of Wizardry is to descend through the ten levels of the dungeon below Trebor's Castle and ultimately defeat the arch-wizard Werdna (Andrew spelt backwards) and retrieve a powerful amulet. The dungeon is full of monsters, puzzles and warp zones that make it easy to get lost. However, some players loved the challenge of trying to map the game with pencil and paper.

Games such as Wizardry and *Ultima* (1981) heavily influenced the JRPG genre inspiring games such as *Dragon Quest* (1986), *Final Fantasy* (1987) and *Chrono Trigger* (1995).

Castle Wolfenstein

Date of release: September 1981

Region: USA

Developer: Muse Software

Publisher: Muse Software

Platform: Apple II

Castle Wolfenstein was designed by Silas S. Warner. Set in World War II, you play as a captured ally soldier. A fellow prisoner gives you a gun he's acquired (how he hid it from the guards is anyone's guess) and tells you that the battle plans for Operation Rheingold are hidden somewhere in the castle. The aim of the game is to find the plans and escape the castle alive. There are supply boxes spread throughout the game world, which comprises sixty screens. Enemy guards can be shot or held hostage, searched, then shot. The player can acquire an enemy uniform and sneak past the guards, thus saving scarce ammunition. This makes it an essential game mechanic. The SS guards are harder to kill and can identify you when wearing the enemy uniform. The player views the game from a top-down perspective. However, as with many games depicted in this way, the characters are seen from a side-on perspective.

Castle Wolfenstein sold over 20,000 units in less than a year and was ported over to other popular formats of the day. Castle Wolfenstein is considered one of the first stealth games or sneak em' ups. Some of the most notable games in the Wolfenstein series are, *Wolfenstein 3D* (1992), (often considered the Grandfather of the modern-day first-person shooters), *Return to Castle Wolfenstein* (2001), *Wolfenstein* (2009), *Wolfenstein: The New Order* (2014) and *Wolfenstein II: The New Colossus* (2017).

Galaga

Date of release: September 1981

Region: Japan

Developer: Namco

Publisher: Namco

Platform: Arcade

Designed by Namco, Galaga is the sequel to *Galaxian (1979)* and plays much the same in that it is a fixed space shoot em' up. Galaga has some improvements and new features over its predecessor. The enemy ships appear on screen in groups, rather than an entire fleet. At the end of level 3, the player is awarded an extra ship that bolts onto the side of the existing ship, giving the player twice the firepower until one of the ships is destroyed. A boss ship within the fleet is equipped with a tractor beam and can capture your ship. If you manage to destroy this enemy ship without destroying your captured ship, it will return to you.

Of all the shooters of this kind, Galaga is often regarded as the best in this era of video games.

Electronic Games Magazine

Electronic Games Magazine was launched in the USA in October 1981. It was the first video games magazine to be published in the United States which covered games across different platforms. Space Invaders won 'Game of the Year' award, in this first set of arcade awards known as the 'Arkies'.

Tempest

Date of release: October 1981

Region: USA

Developer: Atari

Publisher: Atari

Platform: Arcade

Designed by Dave Theurer, Tempest in effect is a three-dimensional vector-displayed Space Invaders, that would later be known as a Tube Shooter. The player views the inside of a tube made up of (usually) sixteen sections. At the near side is the player and, in the distance, coming towards you, are the enemy. The player controls the ship across the near edges by rotating a knob. Originally this rotated the tube instead, but testers complained it made them feel sick and so Theurer changed the control method to movement of the ship instead. As well as being able to shoot the enemies, the player has limited use of a 'Superzapper' that destroys all enemies on the screen. When a level is cleared the player warps forward to a different tube layout.

Tempest was one of the first games to allow players to choose at what stage to begin the game. Some players found a bug in the game where, if you attained a specific amount of points, the game would give them 40 extra credits. Tempest was fast-paced and stood out from the crowd becoming an instant hit, perhaps because it looked and played so differently from most other arcades of the time.

Stargate

Date of release: October 1981

Region: USA

Developer: Vid Kidz

Publisher: Williams Electronics

Platform: Arcade

Created by Eugene Jarvis and Larry DeMar of developer Vid Kidz, Stargate is the sequel to *Defender* (1981) and is fundamentally the same game: you must destroy the aliens attempting to carry off the astronauts on the ground. There are a few differences from the aforementioned *Defender*, such as new enemy ships, a limited cloaking device for your ship making it invulnerable for a short time, and a stargate that can be flown into and takes you instantly to an astronaut in trouble. However, this last feature, like the hyperspace feature, can drop you into the middle of a bunch of enemies.

Stargate was the first arcade to feature buttons that would show the player previous players high scores if pressed. Some versions of Stargate are referred to as Defender II.

Turbo

Date of release: October 1981

Region: Japan

Developer: Sega

Publisher: Sega

Platform: Arcade

Designed by Steve Hanawa, Turbo is a single-player, racing game, where the player's car is seen from an elevated position from directly behind. The aim of the game is to pass thirty cars before the timer runs out.

Turbo was highly praised for its smooth animation and its varied locales which included driving through cityscapes, the countryside, by the ocean, through tunnels and over bridges. Many considered it to be the best racing game of its day.

It was soon ported to the Intellivision and later for the ColecoVision.

Qix

Date of release: October 1981

Region: USA

Developer: Taito America

Publisher: Taito

Platform: Arcade

Designed by Randy and Sandy Pfeiffer, in Qix the player controls a small diamond and must use the four-directional joystick with the quick draw or slow draw buttons to draw closed shapes on the screen. Upon completion, the shape is filled in: blue for quick draw and red for a slow draw. Once 75% of the screen is filled, the player moves onto the next level. The player must avoid touching the sparks that follow them along any lines they've drawn, and the Qix, which is a series of lines that moves anywhere on the screen.

It is difficult to define what genre Qix is. It is part puzzler, part action, and it also becomes a maze game once the player begins drawing on the screen.

Qix wasn't a great success, but it certainly had a cult following.

Fantasy

Date of release: October 1981

Region: Japan

Developer: SNK (Shin Nihon Kikaku)

Publisher: SNK

Platform: Arcade

Fantasy is classed as a single-player, action/adventure game, though it is unique amongst its contemporaries as it only has a single joystick and no button for jumping or shooting. There were other arcade game like this, but most of these were maze games or basically stayed the same as the player progressed through the levels.

Fantasy is quite different. The first level has the player attempting to land a hot air balloon or a sailing ship while avoiding enemy fire. The second level has you on deck, as seen from the top-down, trying to save your girlfriend: in fact, this is the whole premise of the game. The player can only defeat the enemies by having them killed by friendly cannon fire. The third level has the player in the balloon avoiding enemies. The fourth is a standard platformer like *Donkey Kong*. The next few levels are all variations of the other game mechanics, touching on many genres and accomplishing them well.

Bosconian

Date of release: November 1981

Region: Japan

Developer: Namco

Publisher: Namco

Platform: Arcade

Bosconian is a single-player, multi-directional scrolling space shooter set on a large, open map. The aim of the game is to destroy all the enemy ships and space stations on the map, then progress to the next level. Space stations continue to release squadrons of ships until they are destroyed. The space stations can be destroyed by destroying all six sections, or even more efficiently by a well-aimed shot into the central exhaust port: very satisfying. The game can be beaten, in a way. Once level 255 is complete, the player is taken to level 0 where the game behaves abnormally. If level 0 is passed, then the game starts all over again at level 1. This could be interpreted as completion since the game restarts as before.

Bosconian features radar on the right of the screen and is one of the first Video games to feature continuation upon death if the player inserts another coin.

Computer and Video Games (CVG)

Computer and Video Games (*CVG*) magazine was first published in November 1981. It featured news, reviews, tips and tricks for video games. It stopped publishing in 2004, making it one of the longest-running video game magazines.

BBC Micro

The BBC Micro was released in the UK in December 1981 by Acorn Computers Ltd. The BBC Computer Literacy project aimed at schools throughout the UK would include a bespoke computer, an accompanying television series and literature. Acorn, Dragon and Sinclair all made bids for this major contract, which required meeting a list of stringent specifications. Acorn won the bid and soon after their prototype became the British Broadcasting Corporation's Microcomputer System or BBC Micro for short.

Several models were created. Initially the Model A with 16 KB of memory, and the Model B with 32 KB of memory. Later came the 128 KB and 500 KB versions. However, in the early 1980s, it was the Model B that found its way into 80% of UK schools. It also sold well to the public despite its price. The model A cost £235 and the model B £335, far more expensive than the ZX81 (1981) or what would become the even more popular Sinclair Spectrum (1982).

The BBC Micro fulfilled its role and is considered a well-made and robust machine and

Even though it was quite late onto the UK computer gaming scene, probably due to its initial focus on education, it has some excellent games. Most notable games for the BBC Micro were *Chuckie Egg* (1984), *Elite* (1984), *Repton* (1985), *Bug Eyes* (1985), *Thrust* (1986), *Imogen* (1986) and *Exile* (1988).

1981 Notable Omissions

Asteroids Deluxe. Astro Wars. Canyon Climber. Crush, Crumble and Chomp! Crossfire. Coleco Tabletop Games. Battle of Atlantis. Downland. Dribbling. Entex Selector Game. Firefox F-7. Jump Bug. KawanaKajima no Kassem/Attakai. Lock 'N Chase. Pleiades. Polybius (fictitious video game). President Elect. Softporn Adventure. Space Dungeon. The Big Game. Treasure Island. Venture. Video Hustler.

1982

3D Monster Maze

Date of release: 1982

Region: UK

Developer: Malcolm Evans

Publisher: J.K. Greye Software

Platform: Sinclair ZX81

3D Monster Maze is a single-player, first-person adventure, and, some might say, survival horror game. The aim of the game is to find the exit and escape from the maze without being eaten by the Tyrannosaurus Rex. Lines of text will inform the player of the status and proximity of the dinosaur, such as REX LIES IN WAIT (meaning he has not sensed you), HE IS HUNTING YOU (he can hear you but has not seen you), REX HAS SEEN YOU, and RUN HE IS BEHIND YOU.

The game was highly praised for its technical achievement on such a limited machine and the fear it induced in its players. 3D Monster Maze was one of the first 3D home computer games and is cited by some as the first survival horror video game.

Zaxxon

Date of release: January 1982

Region: worldwide

Developer: Sega/Gremlin

Publisher: Sega/Gremlin

Platform: Arcade

Zaxxon is a single-player, isometric shooter where the aim of the game is to fly over the enemy fortress avoiding obstacles and destroying as many enemies as possible to gain the maximum amount of points. Fuel must be shot at to ensure that the player does not run out. The player must also consider their altitude in the game, flying over walls and other obstacles or they will crash. An altimeter and the shadow of the ship on the ground, aid with this part of the gameplay. There are also outer space sections, and an end of level boss called a Zaxxon Robot.

Zaxxon was the first video game to use Axonometric Projection – an efficient way for the hardware of the time to display 3D isometric-looking graphics. The name Zaxxon was inspired by the word Axonometric. Zaxxon was the first arcade video game to be advertised on television. Zaxxon was praised by critics and consumers. Not surprisingly it was ported to most platforms of the time. It won Best Science Fiction/Fantasy Coin-Op Game of the year at the 1984 Arcade Awards and Best Stand-Alone Game of the year at the 1985 Arcade Awards.

Ms. Pac-Man

Date of release: February 1982

Region: USA

Developer: General Computer Corporation

Publisher: Midway

Platform: Arcade

It was a forgone conclusion that Pac-Man (which was, and still is, the best-selling arcade game of all time) would have a sequel. Originally Pac-Man would be the protagonist for that sequel and the game was to be called Super Pac-Man. Yet it was thought that perhaps a female Pac-Man would be better: after all, many women played Pac-Man.

However, the origin of Ms. Pac-man did not come from the original developers/publishers, but from three American students – Doug Macrae, John Tylko and Kevin Curran. Their start-up company General Computer Corporation was all about installing a connecting circuit board, which they built, into an established arcade cabinet. This would modify the game enough to give it new look. Fresh interest, and more money. Pac-Man game cabinets were now changed into a game called 'Crazy Otto', possibly influenced by the character Evil Otto in *Berzerk* (1980). Luckily for the General Computer Corporation, Midway saw the value of their work and the game would finally be recognised as the now-familiar Ms. Pac-Man

Ms. Pac-Man is essentially the same as Pac-Man, but there are some notable differences as well as the protagonist being female. There are four different maze layouts which appear in different colours, interspersed throughout the levels. The spaces between the walls are filled in. The fruit enters through one warp hole and floats around the screen for a limited time until exiting through another, rather than just sitting in the middle of the screen. There are two sets of warp holes on some of the levels instead of just the one. The ghost enemy behavioural patterns have been changed. Ms. Pac-Man also introduces new music and sound effects. It also has its own original cut-scenes. Even though it was the original Pac-Man that broke all the records, Ms Pac-Man is considered by many to be the superior game.

Haunted House

Date of release: February 1982

Region: USA

Developer: Atari

Publisher: Atari

Platform: Atari 2600

Developed by James Andreasen, Haunted House is a single-player, survival horror game. The aim of the game is to move through the three floors and basement of the pitch-black haunted house in search of three pieces of an urn while avoiding bats, spiders and Mr Graves, whose ghost haunts the house. The player's character is displayed as a pair of white eyes with black pupils. Footsteps sound as you walk about the house. You must use your infinite number of matches to locate the pieces or urn in the dark.

Haunted House is one of the first examples of a survival horror video game.

Moon Patrol

Date of release: February 1982

Region: Japan

Developer: Irem

Publisher: Irem

Platform: Arcade

Developed by Takashi Nishiyama, Moon Patrol is a single-player, side-scrolling shooter where the player controls a moon buggy and must destroy UFOs, tanks and mines while jumping over craters. There are five levels in the game, during which the environment and enemies will change. At the top of the screen, a progress bar depicts how far through each level you are. Also shown is a warning system to give you some idea of where the next attack will come from.

Moon Patrol was the first game to utilise parallax scrolling. This technique involved moving the background graphics more slowly than the foreground when scrolling, to give the illusion of depth and realism. Moon Patrol was ported to most platforms of the day and there were many clones.

Dig Dug

Date of release: April 1982

Region: Japan

Developer: Namco

Publisher: Namco

Platform: Arcade

Dig Dug is a single-player maze game where the aim of the game is to clear each screen of enemies, either by getting in close and pumping them full of air until they explode, or alternatively digging away soil and have rocks drop on them. There are two types of enemies: Pookas, who have a large redhead with goggle eyes, and the more dangerous Fygars, who are green dragons that breathe fire at you. The screen is seen as a cutaway of the player digging through the soil, making paths in their wake.

Dig Dug was a commercial success and spawned several sequels and clones. It is rated as the sixth most popular arcade game of all time on The Killer List of Video Games (KLOV) website, which is considered by many to be the definitive online encyclopaedia for arcade games.

Star Wars: The Empire Strikes Back

Date of release: 1982

Region: USA

Developer: Parker Brothers

Publisher: Parker Brothers

Platform: Atari 2600

Designed by Rex Bradford, Star wars: The Empire Strikes Back is a single-player, scrolling shooter where the aim of the game is to destroy as many AT-ATs (which any Star Wars fan will know stands for 'All Terrain Armoured Transport') as possible, preventing them from destroying the rebel base. You control Luke Skywalker's Snowspeeder. To destroy an AT-AT you must shoot at the head or body multiple times. The AT-AT will change colour as you land more and more shots, eventually destroying it. You then move onto the next incoming AT-AT. The enemy shoots back and the player's Snowspeeder changes colour dependent on the amount of damage received. The player can land on the ground and the Snowspeeder will quickly be repaired. From time to time the Snowspeeder flashes which means Luke is shielded by the force and is invulnerable for a short time. When all enemies are destroyed the player moves onto the next level where AT-ATs walk quicker and must be destroyed more efficiently, lest they reach the rebel base, meaning game over.

Even though *The Empire Strikes Back* was the second movie from the original Star Wars trilogy, it is the first ever Star Wars video game.

1982 Arcade Awards

In March, *Electronic Games Magazine* hosts the 1982 Arcade Awards.

Pac-Man wins Best Commercial Arcade Game.

Asteroids on the Atari 2600 wins Best Video Game of the Year.

Star Raiders on the Atari 400/800 wins Best Computer Game of the Year.

ZX Spectrum

The ZX Spectrum was released in the UK in April 1982. The ZX Spectrum was an 8-bit personal computer that shipped with 16 KB RAM or 48 KB RAM and seven colours, that could be brightened to double the amount of colour output. Including black, this made a total of fifteen colours. The cost was £125 for the 16 KB version or £148 for the 48 KB version. Love it or loathe it, the rubber key keyboard wasn't as precise as a mechanical keyboard but was a vast improvement on the membrane keyboards of the previous models.

Games were stored and loaded using a standard tape recorder. As the successor to the ZX80 (1980) and ZX81 (1981), the ZX Spectrum, often referred at the time as 'The Speccy' or 'Speccy 48K', continued to be the entry-level PC in the UK. Its low price point coupled with its growing library of games ensured that it was a massive hit, bringing video games to the masses in the home. In the early 1980s in the UK most computer owners either had a Spectrum or the Commodore 64 (1982). It was a simple matter to copy games onto blank cassettes and the playground was rife with children swapping and copying games.

Contrary to popular belief, this perhaps helped boost the games industry as children's interest in video games at this time reached fever pitch and inspired a host of bedroom coders.

It is thought that there may be somewhere between ten to twenty thousand video games released for the ZX Spectrum platform. Some of the most notable were *The Hobbit* (1982), *Chuckie Egg* (1983), *Manic Miner* (1983), *Skool Daze* (1984), *Knight Lore* (1984), *Elite* (1984), *Jet Set Willy* (1984), *The Way of the Exploding Fist* (1985), *Head over Heels* (1987) and *Dizzy* (1987).

Pitfall

Date of release: April 1982

Region: USA

Developer: Activision

Publisher: Activision

Platform: Atari 2600

Designed by David Crane, the aim of this single-player, side-scrolling platformer is to control Pitfall Harry across various obstacles such as deadly pits, rolling logs, snapping crocodiles, and poisonous scorpions in an effort to collect 32 treasures within a 20-minute time limit. Harry can jump, swing on vines and climb ladders to achieve this goal.

Pitfall has inspired several sequels and clones from *Hunchback* (1983) for the arcade and various 8-bit platforms, to *Temple Run* (2011) on mobile. All have their roots in this original game. Pitfall was one of the Atari 2600's best-selling games with around four million units sold. It is thought that part of this popularity may be due to the contemporary release of the film *Raiders of the Ark* directed by Steven Spielberg. However, it cannot be emphasised enough that Pitfall was a well-developed game in its day. Positive word of mouth is the real reason why any game has sustainable high sales, as was the case with Pitfall.

Night Life

Date of release: April 1982

Region: Japan

Developer: Kōei

Publisher: Kōei

Platform: NEC PC-8801 Personal Computer

Night Life was the first erotic computer game. Meant to be an aid to sexually active couples, the 'game' featured simple monochrome line art and text. It was a precursor to the erotic game genre, also known as Eroge.

Electronic Arts (EA)

Electronic Arts (EA) was founded in the USA in May 1982 by ex-Apple employee Trip Hawkins. EA is the second-largest publisher of video games in the world at the time of writing.

EA publishes titles such as *Battlefield* (2002-2022), the *Crysis* series (2007-2020), *Command & Conquer* series *(1995-2020), Dead Space* series (2008-2011), *Dragon Age* series (2009-current date), *EA Sports, Mass Effect* series (2007-2017), *Medal of Honor* series (1999-2020), *Need for Speed* (1994-2019), *Titanfall* series (2014-2017) and *The Sims* series (2000-2018).

Atari 5200

The Atari 5200, also known as the Atari 5200 SuperSystem, was released in the USA in May 1982. An 8-bit, second-generation console, the Atari 5200 was supposed to compete with the Intellivision and be the successor to the immensely popular yet ageing Atari 2600. However, due to its incompatibility with the 2600's vast and successful library, graphics that were only marginally better than its predecessor, the console's ugly bulkiness and (at times) impractical controller, the console never achieved the success that the 2600 had paved the way for.

Despite that, the 5200 sold over a million units, although the successor of the Atari 2600 could and should have sold so much more. Most notable games for the 5200 are *Pitfall II: The Lost Caverns* (1984), *Pole Position* (1983), *Star Wars: The Arcade Game* (1983) and *Jungle Hunt* (1983).

Lucasfilm Games

The video game publisher Lucasfilm Games (what would later become LucasArts in 1990), was formed in May 1982 by George Lucas. Because Atari held the video game rights to Star Wars, Lucasfilm Games looked to creating original IPs in house. Many in the company thought this gave them more creative freedom and a chance to try something new.

Lucasfilm/ LucasArts would go on to create such renowned games as *Maniac Mansion* (1987), *The Secret of Monkey Island* (1990), *Sam & Max Hit the Road* (1993) *and Grim Fandango* (1998). *They did eventually go onto develop many Star Wars games including Star Wars: Dark Forces* (1995) and *Star Wars Jedi Knight II: Jedi Outcast* (2002).

Choplifter

Date of release: May 1982

Region: USA

Developer: Dan Gorlin

Publisher: Broderbund

Platform: Apple II

Choplifter is a single-player, multi-scrolling shooter that has the player control a helicopter, destroying buildings and freeing the hostages within. Landing nearby, the hostages will board the helicopter. A maximum of sixteen hostages can be carried at any one time, where the player must then return them to the home base. The player must avoid or destroy enemy tanks and aircraft that can shoot down the helicopter. Hostages can be killed by the enemy and friendly fire.

Choplifter has been praised for its movie-like narrative and the animations of the hostages. The game was ported to several platforms of the time. An arcade remake of Choplifter was released in 1985. This was rather unusual at the time, as most video games were ported from the arcade to home platforms, not the other way around. It is a testament to the appeal of Choplifter.

Yar's Revenge

Date of release: May 1982

Region: USA

Developer: Atari

Publisher: Atari

Platform: Atari 2600

Developed by Howard Scott Warshaw, Yar's Revenge is a single-player fixed shooter where you play as the creature called the Yar. The aim is to breach a barrier and destroy the evil Qotile on the other side of the screen.

The name Yar came from spelling Ray Kassar's (Atari's boss) first name backwards. The game shipped with a comic book which acted as a prologue, explaining that the Yar was avenging the destruction of one of its worlds, Razak IV. Yar's Revenge received a rather unenthusiastic reception from critics, yet it must have been appealing to the consumer as Yar's Revenge was Atari's best-selling original title for the Atari 2600.

Donkey Kong Game and Watch Handheld

The Donkey Kong Game and Watch Handheld was released in Japan in June 1982 by Nintendo. Having had incredible success in the last two years with their single screen series of Game and Watch Handheld Electronic Games, Nintendo introduced their vertical multi-screen models. Donkey Kong is based on the arcade game of the same name. The player controls Mr. Game and Watch (a standard character who appears in many Game and Watch games), in place of the traditional Mario and must make his way up to the top of a building by jumping over and avoiding obstacles. Each time the player reaches the top, they take away a small section that helps support Donkey Kong at the top. Once all four supports have been taken off, Donkey Kong falls, and Mr. Game and Watch can save his girlfriend. The whole level then starts again. Each time the level starts the pace of the game becomes that much quicker.

Donkey Kong, as with many Game and Watch games, was incredibly popular and sold hundreds of thousands of units. The Donkey Kong Game and Watch Handheld is the first piece of hardware to ever feature a traditional D-pad controller.

Joust

Date of release: July 1982

Region: USA

Developer: Williams Electronics

Publisher: Williams Electronics

Platform: Arcade

Designed by John Newcomer and programmed by Bill Pfutzenreuter, Joust is a single or two-player game where the aim is to knock your opponents from their mounts, while at the same time preventing them from doing the same to you. The player controls a knight sitting on a flying ostrich: by tapping the flap button you can control the speed of your ascent or descent. The joystick controls the direction. If you hit an opponent from above, then they turn into an egg that you must pick up before they hatch into a new knight. If they hit you from above you lose a life. You must defeat all the other knights to proceed to the next level. Each level contains platforms and deadly perils that must be avoided. In the two-player mode, players can either play together to defeat the enemies or treat one another as just another enemy on screen. The screen wraps around on the sides so that if you fly off one side of the screen, you will appear on the other side.

Joust was a respectable success and was praised by critics and consumers alike. Its popularity influenced similar copycat games. Joust itself was later ported to many other home platforms.

Atlantis

Date of release: 1982

Region: USA

Developer: Imagic

Publisher: Imagic

Platform: Atari 2600

Designed by Dennis Koble, Atlantis is like *Missile Command (1980)* in that you must protect the City of Atlantis by shooting down invading ships. When all the settlements of Atlantis are destroyed (which inevitably happens as the game is unwinnable), a small saucer-shaped ship is seen escaping. This leads to another game by Imagic called *Cosmic Ark (1982).*

Imagic ran a competition where players could send photographs of their highest scores for Atlantis. Winners would receive a copy of Atlantis II, a modified version of the original game.

Donkey Kong Jr.

Date of release: August 1982

Region: Japan

Developer: Nintendo R&D1

Publisher: Nintendo

Platform: Arcade

The sequel to the successful *Donkey Kong* (1981), Donkey Kong Jr. is the only video game that features Mario as the villain. The game begins with two Marios in fact, trapping Donkey Kong and taking him to the top left of the screen. The player controls Donkey Kong Jr. and must avoid the enemies that Mario releases, making your way to the top to get the key and free your father. However, at the end of each of the first three levels, Mario pushes the cage away before you can do this. Each level is different, and level four involves the player pushing six keys up to their locks, while avoiding enemies to finally free Donkey Kong, whereupon he falls and is caught by his son. Donkey Kong Jr. carries him off-screen with Mario in pursuit, who is kicked into the air by Donkey Kong's foot.

As with the original, Shigeru Miyamoto integrated a lot of character and narrative into the game. Donkey Kong Jr. was very successful and was ported to a multitude of platforms.

Hamburger/BurgerTime

Date of release: 1982

Region: Japan & North America

Developer: Data East

Publisher: Data East/Bally Midway

Platform: Arcade

BurgerTime known as Hamburger in Japan is a single-player, platform game where you play as Chef Peter Pepper who must run over different burger ingredients, effectively dropping them to the plates waiting below, while avoiding enemies. The player has a limited amount of five pepper shots with which to stun said enemies. There are six different levels to complete. Upon completion, the player starts again at the first level.

BurgerTime was well received and had two sequels with *Peter Pepper's Ice Cream Factory* (1984) and later a two-player sequel in *Super BurgerTime* (1990).

ColecoVision

The ColecoVision was released in the USA in August 1982. ColecoVision is an 8-bit second-generation console and was graphically superior to the current market leader, the Atari 2600, as well as the Atari 5200 and Intellivision, closing that distance between the arcade versions and the home versions of video games.

ColecoVision initially launched with twelve games including the incredibly popular *Donkey Kong* (1982) and *Zaxxon* (1982). The controllers were like the Atari 5200, with a joystick and number pad. Plastic overlays could be slotted over the number pad for certain games.

There were some inspired expansion modules and peripherals for the ColecoVision. With these, you could play Atari 2600 games, purchase a driving controller, trackball or advanced joystick set. Another integrated a keyboard into the console called the Coleco Adam computer (1983).

Graphically the games were superior to anything available in the home. Some of the ColecoVision's most notable games were *Super Action Baseball* (1983), *Pepper II* (1983), *Mario Bros.* (1983), *Mr Do!* (1983), *BurgerTime* (1984) and *Tapper* (1984).

Commodore 64

The Commodore 64, also known as the C64, was released in August 1982. The Commodore 64 is an 8-bit computer with 64 KB of RAM and 16-colour output. It sold for $595 and was the successor to the Commodore VIC-20 (1980). One of the main selling points of the C64 was its 64 KB of RAM, which was good value for money at the time. Also, its software library numbered in the thousands: it had an incredible choice of games. Graphically it was superior to most systems of the day, partially due to the way it handled colour and because of its hardware-driven sprites, which meant that sprites (independent moving graphics) looked a lot better than on other computers of the time. The C64 also had a very impressive sound chip for its time and price point.

Homebrew games and the demo scene exploded on the C64 platform. Hobbyists would write their own games (homebrew) or create audio-visual demos (demo scene) emphasising and pushing the boundaries of what the hardware could do.

In time the Commodore 64 became the best-selling home computer in history. It is estimated that it may have sold up to 17 million units worldwide. With such incredible sales and a large user base, it is not surprising that the C64 is home to some of the best 8-bit video games of all time. Most notable were *Impossible Mission* (1984), *International Karate +* (1984), *Ultima IV: The Quest for the Avatar* (1985), *Paradroid* (1985), *The Bard's Tale* (1985), *Bubble Bobble* (1986), *Defender of the Crown* (1987), *Maniac Mansion* (1987), *Skate or Die* (1987), *Wizball* (1987) and *Wasteland* (1988).

David's Midnight Magic

Date of release: 1982

Region: USA

Developer: David Snider

Publisher: Broderbund

Platform: Apple II

David's Midnight Magic is a pinball simulation game based on the pinball machine *Black Knight* (1980). The game was well-received by critics and the public alike and won Computer Game of the Year at the 1983 Arcade Awards.

Demon Attack

Date of release: 1982

Region: USA

Developer: Imagic

Publisher: Imagic

Platform: Atari 2600

Designed by Rob Furlop, Demon Attack is a single-player, fixed shoot 'em up where the player must destroy wave after wave of space demons. Enemies will swoop down, and others will split into smaller enemies when shot. The original game had 84 waves of enemies. Shortly after release, though, some players had reportedly completed the game. Furlop then changed the game so that the next batch of Demon Attack couldn't be finished.

Demon Attack won Best Video game of the year at the 1983 Arcade Awards.

Starpath Supercharger

Released in the USA in August 1982 for the Atari 2600, the Starpath Supercharger was an expansion device that slotted into the 2600 like a game cartridge. You then plugged the Supercharger into a standard audio cassette player. After that, it was just a case of loading the game by pressing the play button on the cassette player. This meant long load times, lasting minutes, but on the plus side it and added about 6000 bytes (6KB) to Atari's 128 bytes of RAM. Games running with this device looked a lot smoother than standard Atari 2600 games.

Some of the most impressive games using the Starpath Supercharger were *Frogger* (1982), *Dragonstomper* (1982) and *Survival Island* (1982).

Football Manager

Date of release: 1982

Region: UK

Developer: Kevin Toms

Publisher: Addictive Games

Platform: Sinclair ZX80, ZX81 and ZX Spectrum.

Football Manager is based on the English league football, otherwise known as soccer. The player must manage real-world players and their statistics, as well as finances and transfers. The aim of the game is to make it from the fourth division to the top of the first division (as it was known in those days). The player can also compete in the FA Cup. The game is predominantly text-based. Only the highlights are played out in an isometric graphical format, and this only happened on certain platforms.

Beginning as a mail-order game and then finding its way into computer retail outlets, Football Manager was ported to many platforms and was a commercial success, selling half a million units. Football Manager is the first football management simulation game and spawned three sequels with: *Football Manager 2* (1988), *Football Manager World Cup Edition* (1990) and *Football Manager 3* (1992).

Gravitar

Date of release: 1982

Region: USA

Developer: Atari

Publisher: Atari

Platform: Arcade

Developed by Mike Hally and Rich Adam, Gravitar is a single-player, multi-directional shooter and is a mix of *Asteroids* (1979) and *Lunar Lander* (1979). The player controls a wedge-shaped ship that moves towards a planet (and hence a level) of their choice. Once within a certain distance, the real gameplay begins as the player is presented with a landscape, enemy ships and bunkers that fire on you. However, the real difficulty in Gravitar is dealing with said enemies while ensuring the gravity of the planet doesn't cause you to crash onto its surface. Fuel must also be collected using the tractor beam button. Each planet is completely different. Some offer 360 degrees of surface that you must work around, destroying bunkers and collecting fuel. Others are claustrophobic caverns with barely any room to manoeuvre. In later levels, the difficulty ramps up to ridiculous levels as players must cope with reverse gravity or invisible planets.

Despite its difficulty, Gravitar is a fine game and certainly underappreciated in its day. It was not ported to any other machines apart from the Atari platform. However, it did inspire the popular game *Thrust (1986)* which was ported to many 8-bit computers. Gravitar was one of the few video games to feature a level-select option.

Hack

Date of release: 1982

Region: USA

Developer: Jay Fenlason.

Platform: Usenet

Hack was developed and released in 1982 by Jay Fenlason.

Hack is a roguelike game, very similar to *Rogue* (1980), in that the player must traverse dungeons, encounter monsters and use items to stay alive. It too displays the world using text-based characters, also known as ASCII characters. Later versions of Hack would substitute ASCII characters for graphics instead. Hack later evolved into the game *Nethack* (1987).

Pole Position

Date of release: September 1982

Region: Japan

Developer: Namco

Publisher: Namco

Platform: Arcade

Designed by Toru Iwatani (designer of *Pac-Man (1980)*), Pole Position is a Formula One racing game where you view the car from a third-person perspective. Using a steering wheel, gear shift and pedals the player must first complete the qualifying lap to earn a place in the race against seven other cars. You must avoid water and other cars, as well as the billboards on the side of the road. The quicker you finish the laps the more points you earn.

Pole Position used scaling sprites to depict the illusion of driving along a three-dimensional track and passing the other cars. It is the first game to base its racetrack on a real-life one, that being the Fuji Speedway in Japan.

Pole Position was the most successful arcade game of 1983 and inspired a whole host of racing games for the arcade and in the home. It is considered by some to be the most influential racing game of all time. Pole Position is also the first 16-bit arcade game and won Best Coin-Op Game of the Year at the 1984 Arcade Awards. It didn't take long for the game to be ported to most 8-bit platforms of the day. Its success ensured several sequels. These were *Pole Position II* (1983), *Final Lap* (1987), *Final Lap 2* (1990), *Final Lap 3* (1992) and *Final Lap R* (1993).

Pengo

Date of release: September 1982

Region: Japan

Developer: Coreland

Publisher: Sega

Platform: Arcade

Pengo is a single-player maze game where you control Pengo, the penguin, who must successfully eliminate the Sno-bees to move onto the next level. The maze is made up of blocks that can be pushed towards the Sno-bees, crushing them. Another way to dispatch a Sno-Bee is if both you and the Sno-bee are standing at the outer wall. Pengo can vibrate the wall, stunning the Sno-bee, and then run over them. Other Sno-Bees hatch from eggs and can be eliminated before they do. These last two methods are riskier than the first as the window of opportunity is rather small. Three diamond-like blocks cannot be destroyed. If these are pushed and lined up together, the player receives bonus points. After two minutes the Sno-bees will change and move quicker around the maze.

Pengo has spawned many clones over the years, but my personal favourite, by far, is the little-known *Bubble Trouble* (1996) by Ambrosia Software. In May 2010 an eight-player multiplayer arcade version of Pengo was created in Japan.

Mr. Do!

Date of release: September 1982

Region: Japan

Developer: Universal

Publisher: Universal

Platform: Arcade

Mr. Do! is a single-player maze game, very similar to and released soon after *Dig Dug* (1982). The aim of the game is for Mr. Do! (who for some reason is a clown) to dig his way through the ground and collect all the cherries to move onto the next level. Enemies called Creeps can be killed either by throwing his bouncing ball at them or by digging away at the ground supporting a giant apple, which, if timed right, will drop onto the enemies. Occasionally, one of the letters spelling EXTRA will appear, and if this can be destroyed in the same manner, then this letter will light up at the top of the screen. You need to get all five letters for an extra life.

Mr. Do! was a successful game. It and its sequels were ported to many systems throughout the 1980s and 1990s. Mr. Do! was the first in the Mr. Do! series. The other games in the series are *Mr. Do's Castle* (1983), *Mr. Do's Wild Ride* (1984), and *Do! Run Run* (1984).

Time Zone

Date of release: 1982

Region: USA

Developer: On-Line Systems

Publisher: On-Line Systems

Platform: Apple II

Written and directed by Roberta Williams (*Mystery House* (1980)), Time Zone is a single-player text and graphical adventure game. As the player, you travel through time meeting well-known historical figures and solving puzzles.

Time Zone was an incredibly ambitious project: it contained around 1,500 locations, most of these accompanied with full-colour artwork, and 39 puzzles to solve. An unprecedented six double-sided floppy disks were needed to store the entire game. Due to its ambitious scope, Time Zone may mark the first occasion where the current model of game development was utilised, with production being broken down into different disciplines due to its scale, rather than a few people being able to create an entire game, Roberta Williams needed a team of programmers and artists to work on the project.

The original price of $99 in 1982 (which would be $273 adjusting for inflation in 2021) may make it one of the most expensive video games ever sold relative to other games of the time. The game received mixed reviews: some thought it wasn't worth the high price point, while others praised its ambition.

Tron

Date of release: 1982

Region: USA

Developer: Bill Adams

Publisher: Bally Midway

Platform: Arcade

Tron is a single-player mixed-genre action game, based on Disney's movie of the same name which was also released in 1982. Tron is made up of four mini-games. Perhaps the most well-known is the Light Cycles game where the aim is for the player to move around the screen in their light cycle and survive longer than the opposing Non-Player Characters (NPCs) on the screen by not crashing into either the outer wall or the walls of light the cycles leave in their wake. The trigger button on the joystick acts as an accelerator when needed. In the Battle Tanks game, the player controls a tank in a maze as seen from a top-down perspective and must destroy the other tanks on screen. The joystick moves the tank, and the trigger fires the gun, while the dial controls the direction of the gun turret which can turn a full 360 degrees. The I/O Tower has the player guide Tron into the I/O Tower. Grids bugs must be shot and cleared out of the way to achieve this goal. The MCP Cone mini-game involves Tron shooting a rotating shield and getting past without it touching him. When all four of these games have been completed the player must play them again. However, the difficulty increases.

Tron's distinctive music and sound from the movie, as well as its overall look, gave it a unique appeal to players. It was a very successful game making $30 million by 1983. Tron won Coin-Op Game of the Year at the 1983 Arcade Awards.

The Hobbit

Date of release: 1982

Region: worldwide

Developer: Beam Software

Publisher: Melbourne House

Platform: ZX Spectrum

The Hobbit is a text-based adventure game based on J. R. R. Tolkien's book *The Hobbit*. Many of the screens have basic illustrations and take several seconds to draw on-screen on the original cassette version. The text-based interaction was very complex and intuitive for its time. The game was very flexible when controlling and being influenced by objects. Game world objects and characters have a quantitative weight and size and can be damaged or broken. Characters would act of their own accord rather than waiting around for instructions. Such NPCs (non-player characters) could wander off or get themselves killed, sometimes making finishing the game difficult or impossible. This gave each play-through an element of randomness, making each game different from the last. Unlike many text-based games where the next event wouldn't happen without user input, in The Hobbit things would happen in the game world all the time unless the player pressed the pause button.

The game was very successful, and even though there are no concrete sales figures it is thought that The Hobbit sold hundreds of thousands of units and may be the best-selling text-based adventure game of all time. It was ported to many 8-bit computers. The Hobbit also won Best Strategy Game in the 1983 Golden Joystick Awards.

Jungle Hunt

Date of release: 1982

Region: Japan

Developer: Taito

Publisher: Taito

Platform: Arcade

Jungle Hunt is a single-player, side-scrolling action-adventure game where you play as a jungle explorer and must save a woman from being eaten by cannibals. There are four distinctly different levels. In the first level, the player must correctly time jumps between swinging ropes or fall and lose a life. On the second level, you swim through a river infested with crocodiles. The third level has the player running up the side of a volcano, jumping over flaming boulders. In the fourth level, the player must jump over the cannibals and rescue the girl suspended over a boiling cauldron. After this, the game shows the girl kissing the jungle explorer. Upon completing all four levels the game begins at level one again only the difficulty increases.

Jungle Hunt was one of the first video games to use parallax scrolling to give the illusion of depth and realism. Earlier versions of the game featured a Tarzan-like hero until Taito was sued by the Edgar RIce Burroughs estate for using the character's likeness. It was then that the protagonist was changed to an early twentieth-century English jungle explorer. Jungle Hunt was ported to many of the 8-bit consoles and computers of the time.

Invasion of the Space Invaders

Martin Amis published his semi-autobiographical book *Invasion of the Space Invaders: An Addict's Guide to Battle Tactics, Big Scores and the Best Machines* in 1982, exploring the effects of the arcade phenomenon in the 1980s.

Microprose

The game publisher Microprose was founded by Bill Stealey and Sid Meier in 1982. Microprose are known for their strategy and military vehicle simulation games. Most notable are *F-15 Strike Eagle* (1984), *Sid Meier's Pirates* (1987), *F-19 Stealth Fighter* (1988), the *Civilisation series* (first released 1991) and the *X-COM series* (first released 1994).

Miner 2049er

Date of release: 1982

Region: USA

Developer: Big Five Software

Publisher: Big Five Software

Platform: Atari 8-bit

Designed by Bill Hogue, Miner 2049er is a single-player platform game. Set in the year 2049, you play as Bounty Bob and must explore all ten levels of Nuclear Ned's uranium mine in search of the evil Yukon Yohan. Bounty Bob himself can run and jump and climb ladders. The real appeal of the game is in its fantastic level design and its many inspired gaming mechanics, taking the platforming genre to another level. Similar to Pac-Man, the player must move over every part of the level to complete it. In this case, filling it in rather than taking something away. Enemies can kill Bounty Bob on contact unless he collects a key item, in which case the enemies are vulnerable and can be collected. They do not respawn on the screen. Bounty Bob must also watch out for radioactive waste and giant moving pistons that can crush him. Other game mechanics to help move around the screen include ladders, slides, moving platforms, and a matter transporter. On the final screen, Bob must make use of a cannon by collecting TNT on the left of the screen and using it to reach the higher levels. The more TNT you use the higher the level the player can reach. All these excellent ideas, and the fact that all ten levels (when most games similar to this had only four or five) were very different from one another, made Miner 2049er a very popular and successful game.

Miner 2049er inspired the game *Manic Miner* (1983), *Blagger* (1983) and *Dynamite Dan* (1985). Miner 2049er won Best Electronic Game of the Year (Players' Pick) at the 1984 Arcade Awards.

Star Strike

Date of release: 1982

Region: USA

Developer: Mattel

Publisher: Mattel

Platform: Intellivision

Designed by Hal Finney and Brett Stutz, Star Strike is a single-player shoot 'em up. The aim of the game is to destroy an alien superweapon set to destroy Earth. The player controls a spaceship flying down a trench, shooting down alien fighters and bombing five red weapon silos to destroy the alien weapon. The player has only one life; however, the ship can take several hits before being ultimately destroyed. Hits on the player's ship affect manoeuvrability or result in other faults to simulate damage. A counter at the top of the screen counts down from 8000 to 0. When it reaches zero the alien weapon fires, the Earth is destroyed, and the game is over.

The similarity between Star Strike and the attack on the Death Star at the end of the movie *Star Wars: A New Hope* (1977) wasn't lost on anyone. Star Strike was ported to the Atari 2600.

Robotron: 2084

Date of release: 1982

Region: USA

Developer: Vid Kidz

Publisher: Williams Electronics

Platform: Arcade

Designed by Eugene Jarvis and Larry DeMar, Robotron: 2084 is a single-player, twin-stick shooter as seen from a top-down perspective, where killer robots have rebelled against their human masters. The player must save the humans on the screen from the robots and earn as many points as possible. There are different enemy robots to contend with in Robotron: 2084. Some robots simply try and kill you upon contact, while others will shoot at you. The Hulk Robotron is indestructible and can only be slowed but not destroyed, and the Brain Robotron can possess humans turning them into Progs. The controls are simple. The left joystick controls the movement of your character. The right joystick controls the direction the player fires. The player can fire in one of any eight directions while moving.

Robotron: 2084 is well-known for being one of the most difficult arcade games of all time. The screen is teeming with enemies and the player must fight to stay alive every second. The only forgiving elements are its reactive controls and the fact that the humans in all the chaos cannot be harmed by friendly fire. Robotron: 2084 set the standard and popularised the twin-stick shooter. Inevitably it was ported to many 8-bit and 16-bit platforms.

Swordquest: Earthworld

Date of release: October 1982

Region: USA

Developer: Atari

Publisher: Atari

Platform: Atari 2600

Designed by Dan Hitchens and Tod Frye, Swordquest: Earthworld is a single-player action-adventure game, the first of four planned in the Swordquest series of games. The idea behind Swordquest was very ambitious for its time. Swordquest: Earthworld shipped with a DC (Detective Comics) comic book and a poster. If you joined a club, you also received a t-shirt. The aim of the game was to find all the clues in the game and send them to Atari. The players who found the most were invited to the Atari headquarters to play a 90-minute custom-made Swordquest game. The player who finished first won a prize: a talisman made of 18-carat solid gold, studded with twelve diamonds.

The other games in the Swordquest series had similarly lavish prizes, apparently worth around $25,000 each. The prize for the second game, *Swordquest: Fireworld*, was a gold chalice, and for the winner of *Swordquest: Waterworld* a gold crown. The winner of *Swordquest: Airworld* would receive the 'Philosopher's stone,' an ornate gold box. The four winners would compete for the ultimate prize of a sword, its gold handle encrusted with precious stones, worth around $50,000.

The games themselves were rather plain action-adventure games, moving from one room to the next collecting objects or manoeuvring past obstacles. The prizes themselves and the possibility of winning were the allure of these games. The clues were numbers. The player had to figure out that these numbers referred to page numbers and panel numbers in the comic book. In the comic book were hidden words. Players had to work out which one of these words was significant.

Due to the Video Game Crash of 1983, Atari's financial difficulties forced it to sell the company and so the competition for *Swordquest: Waterworld* was never held. The entire competition ended there. The whereabouts of these expensive prizes are currently unknown and have become the stuff of Video game legend.

NEC PC-98

The NEC PC-98 was released in Japan in October 1982. The PC-98 was a high-end Japanese personal computer, meant primarily for home office use. It shipped with a 16 Bit CPU, 128 KB RAM, although this could be expanded, and had a 256-colour palette. With hardware years ahead of the average PC or console, it was inevitable that Japanese creatives would come up with some graphically stunning games.

The NEC PC-98 was initially designed to clearly display Japanese writing, so many of the games were visual novel games, with beautiful art and animation. The developers for this machine were also known to release a lot of erotic games and demoware, a departure from the mainstream in the West.

The PC-98 built up a strong following of enthusiasts who continued to support it, creating content throughout the 1980s and 1990s. Most notable games for the PC-98 were *Rusty* (1993), *Policenauts* (1994) which was written and directed by Hideo Kojima (Best known for designing the Metal Gear series of games), *Yu-No: A Girl Who Chants Love at the Bound of this World* (1996) and *Dead of the Brain* (1999).

Q*bert

Date of release: November 1982

Region: USA

Developer: Gottlieb

Publisher: Gottlieb

Platform: Arcade

Designed by Warren Davis and Jeff Lee, Q*bert was completely different to anything else around at the time and is difficult to classify. It is a mix between platformer, action and the puzzle genre. The game area is made of cubes built into a pyramid configuration as viewed from an isometric perspective. The aim of the game is for the player to control Q*bert and jump on top of every cube on the screen. When Q*bert lands on a cube, it changes colour. Once all the cubes have changed colour the player moves onto the next screen. There are four screens to every level. In later levels, Q*bert must jump on cubes twice to attain the desired colour. There is a key at the top of the screen to indicate the colour you are aiming for, so you don't lose track. The player must avoid enemies that also move around the gaming area. Q*bert can lure them near the edge and escape using either one of two moving platforms that take him back to the top cube. These can only be used once, though. Q*bert himself is a quirky blob with cartoon eyes, little legs and a stumpy tube-like nose. One of his most unique features is the way he speaks. The arcade uses speech synthesis and Q*bert speaks in a garbled nonsensical voice with a word bubble that depicts the character's speech '@!#?@!' when he's killed by an enemy. In fact, this was going to be the original name of the game, but it was changed to Q*bert at the last minute.

Q*bert released to commercial and critical acclaim. It sold over 25,000 arcade cabinets. The Q*bert character, like Pac-Man before him although to a lesser extent, became a recognisable character in popular culture, spawning merchandise with his likeness. Q*bert won Most Innovative Coin-Op Game at the 1984 Arcade Awards.

Front Line

Date of release: November 1982

Region: Worldwide

Developer: Taito

Publisher: Taito

Platform: Arcade

Designed by Tetsuya Sasaki, Front Line is a single-player, vertical scrolling, run and gun game where you play as a soldier. The aim is to reach the enemy fort and destroy it. Enemy soldiers and tanks must be dealt with to achieve your goal. The player views the battlefield from a top-down perspective and the screen scrolls as you move up through the game area. The player has a gun and grenades. You can also drive a tank to defeat the enemy. A standard joystick moves the player and a button is pressed for throwing grenades. However, to fire at targets the player must make use of a rotary button that can point the character's gun in one of eight positions and the whole mechanism must be pushed down. This rotary button control was very rare and made Front Line rather unique. Front Line is cited by some as the first run and gun game.

Microsoft Flight Simulator 1.0

Date of release: November 1982

Region: USA

Developer: Microsoft

Publisher: Microsoft

Platform: IBM PC

Obtaining the licence from SubLogic's *Flight Simulator* (1979), Microsoft released Microsoft Flight Simulator 1.0 in November for the IBM PC. This new version had a new coordinate system, weather and time of day. MS FS was one of the first home video games with 3D flat-shaded graphics.

MSFS 1.0 was later used to test if PCs were IBM compatible (see IBM Personal Computer 1981).

Vectrex

The Vectrex was released in the USA in November 1982 by General Consumer Electronics. Conceptualised by John Ross, the Vectrex is an 8-bit second-generation video game console that shipped with 1 KB of RAM and has a unique in-built display. It sold for $199. The Vectrex is the only vector display home console. It is also the only home console to have a screen set in a portrait orientation (excluding some handheld systems) rather than landscape. This was because consoles plugged into the television. The screen only displayed a black and white image, so games were shipped with colour overlays to make them appear in colour.

Displaying vector images meant that it lent itself very well to games like *Asteroids* (1979) and other vector-based arcade games. Initially, the system sold well due to its amazingly crisp graphics, ultra-smooth movement and the fact that it lent itself well to newly emergent 3D looking games. However, it launched not long before the Video Game Crash of 1983 and sales soon began to drop.

The Vectrex shipped with one built-in game *Mine Storm* (1982), which was like *Asteroids* (1979). Other notable games were *Scramble* (1982), *Berzerk* (1982), *Polar Rescue* (1983), and *Spike* (1983).

Dragonstomper

Date of release: 1982

Region: USA

Developer: Starpath

Publisher: Starpath

Platform: Atari 2600

Designed by Stephen Landrum, Dragonstomper is a graphical RPG where the aim of the game is to defeat the dragon and retrieve a magical amulet. The player is displayed as a dot and must explore the wilderness and dungeons and fight monsters to complete your quest.

Dragonstomper required the Starpath Supercharger, an expansion device, which ran games on cassette. Some believe that Dragonstomper was the first true RPG for the Atari 2600 console.

The Arcade Machine

Date of release: 1982

Region: USA

Developers: Doug Carlston and Chris Jochumson

Publisher: Broderbund

Platform: Apple II

The Arcade Machine was a game creation system enabling the users to create and edit shoot 'em up type games that had become so popular over the last few years. Games could be saved to a self-bootable disk to be played on other computers, allowing creators to share their games.

The Arcade Machine was quite successful and was soon ported to the Atari 8-bit platform.

River Raid

Date of release: December 1982

Region: USA

Developer: Activision

Publisher: Activision

Platform: Atari 2600

Designed by Carol Shaw, River Raid is a single-player, scrolling shooter as seen from a top-down perspective. The player controls a jet fighter and must fly above the river shooting down enemy jets, helicopters and warships. Fuel must be collected lest the jet run out and crash. The land acts as a barrier so the players must navigate down the river making sure not to crash into the ground.

River Raid was very successful, selling over a million units. It was ported to most 8-bit platforms of the day. It also won Best Action Video game in the 1984 Arcade Awards.

E.T. The Extra-Terrestrial

Date of release: December 1982

Region: USA

Developer: Atari

Publisher: Atari

Platform: Atari 2600

Designed by Howard Scott Warshaw, E.T. The Extra-Terrestrial is a single-player, adventure game based on the immensely successful movie directed by Steven Spielberg. The aim of the game is to find three pieces of a device to allow E.T. to 'phone home'.

Due to late negotiations, Warshaw had only five and a half weeks to finish the game for the Christmas season of 1982. This is often cited as the reason why the game was so bad, and partly why some say it is the worst video game of all time. E.T. is also said to be one of the biggest commercial failures in video game history and contributed to the video game crash of 1983. Atari would never fully recover from this. Due to over-production, it was believed that millions of cartridges were buried in Alamogordo, New Mexico. In 2014 this was discovered to be partly true when hundreds of thousands of E.T. cartridges, as well as other Atari titles, were uncovered at the site.

Not surprisingly E.T. The Extra-Terrestrial was never ported to any other platform.

Sokoban

Date of release: December 1982

Region: Japan

Developer: Thinking Rabbit

Publisher: Thinking Rabbit

Platform: NEC PC-8801 Personal Computer

Designed by Hiroyuki Imabayashi, Sokoban is a puzzle game where the aim is to move crates around the warehouse into pre-assigned spaces to progress to the next level. Each warehouse has a different size and configuration. Crates can only be pushed, so the player must be careful not to push crates into corners unless it is a finishing move to put the crate into one of the spaces.

Like most well-designed puzzle games, Sokoban's premise is simple, yet depending on the layout of specific screens/boards can take some time to complete. The game has been praised for its (at times) difficulty and addictiveness.

Sokoban was very successful and sold over 400,000 units. It was ported to several 8-bit platforms of the time and spawned many iterations over the years, including *Sokoban Perfect* (1989) for the NEC-PC-9801 and *Sokoban Touch* (2016) for Android and Apple iOS.

1982 Notable Omissions

Air Raiders. Armour Ambush. Aztec. Bagman. Black Widow. Blue Print. Bubbles. Caveman. Cosmic Ark. Deadline. Dragon 32. Frenzy. Gridrunner. Hungry Horace & Horace Goes Skiing. Imagine Software. Millipede. Necromancer. Nibbler. Pimania. Popeye. Shamus. Space Duel. Spider-Man. Spy Daisakusen. Starcade (video game TV show). Star Trek Arcade. Star Voyager. Survival Island. Time Pilot. Tunnels of Doom. The Dragon and the Princess. Tron: Deadly Discs. Tron: Maze-a-Tron. Tutankhamun. Ultimate Play the Game. Ultima II: The Revenge of the Enchantress. Wayout. Wizardry II: The Knight of Diamonds.

1983

1983 Arcade Awards

In January the *Electronic Games Magazine* hosts the 1983 Arcade Awards.

Tron wins Coin-op Game of the Year.

Demon Attack for the Atari 2600 wins Best Video Game of the Year.

David's Midnight Magic for the Apple II wins Computer Game of the Year.

Xevious

Date of release: January 1983

Region: Japan

Developer: Namco

Publisher: Namco

Platform: Arcade

Designed by Masanobu Endo, Xevious is a single-player, vertical-scrolling shooter where the aim of the game is to destroy the Xevious forces and prevent them from taking over the Earth. The player controls a ship called the *Solvalou* that can shoot air targets and bomb enemies on the ground. An on-screen target aids the player with their aim. There are many different enemy types and end of level bosses. An interesting mechanic is that the game will provide more difficult enemies if the player is having an easy time of it. If you can destroy the enemy radars you encounter, this system is disabled, and the game will revert to less difficult enemies. The ground far below is made up of desert, sea, rivers and forest. Other features include roads and even Nazca lines can be seen. Another nice attention to detail was the way the player's bombs leave craters in their wake.

Xevious was the first video game to use pre-rendered graphics and even though they may look primitive today, in 1983 they certainly stood out as head and shoulders above other similar games. This game would become the precursor and inspiration for many vertical-scrolling shooters, paving the way for the sub-genre known as 'bullet hell' which still has a huge following in Japan. Xevious was very popular and was ported to many platforms. Even if some of these platforms did struggle to replicate the originals graphics, they were still quite playable and the Famicom version released in 1984 became that console's first third-party killer app, selling 1.2 million units. Xevious led to several sequels most notably *Super Xevious* (1984) and *Xevious 3D/G* (1997).

Sinistar

Date of release: February 1983

Region: USA

Developer: Williams Electronics

Publisher: Williams Electronics

Platform: Arcade

Sinistar is a single-player, multi-directional shooter where the player controls a small, fast-moving spaceship against a starfield background, as seen from a top-down perspective. The aim of the game is to blast crystals off the planetoids scattered around the game world, which is several times larger than the screen size, to arm yourself with sinibombs needed to defeat the game boss, Sinistar, a giant metallic demon face. Grey ships fly around the screen trying to shoot you down, while red ships attempt to mine the crystals before you do in an attempt to build Sinistar somewhere off-screen. A radar at the top of the screen displays the locations of all the planetoids and enemies, including the deadly Sinistar. When Sinistar has been built the player can hear his deep booming voice announce, "Beware I live." Sinistar also exclaims "Beware, Coward," "Run Coward," "Run run run!" These sound bites have been used in multiple games over the years. Sinistar lets out a grisly roar, his eyes glow red and his mouth moves, as he hunts down and destroys you.

The sound is fantastic, especially in the sit-down cabinet version since this was the first arcade video game to use stereo sound. Sinistar is without a doubt a fantastically menacing protagonist, one of the best at this point in video game history. To destroy Sinistar, sinibombs must be used: each one destroys a small part of him. It takes thirteen sinibombs to destroy Sinistar. Once he is destroyed, you move onto the next level where the number of different enemies and planetoids change.

Unfortunately, Sinistar was never ported to any platforms, but there were several clones. Sinistar was the first game to use a 49-way optical joystick, designed by Williams Electronics.

Archon: The Light and the Dark

Date of release: 1983

Region: USA

Developer: Free Fall Associates

Publisher: Electronic Arts

Platform: Atari 8-bit

Archon: The Light and the Dark is a single-player, strategy game similar to chess where the aim of the game is to either take control of five power points or remove all your opponent's pieces. The player controls fantasy pieces such as wizards, goblins and golems on a chess board, each with unique abilities. When these pieces intercept one another, the screen transitions to a field of combat where the player controls a character and must use its unique abilities to defeat the enemy, which itself has its own specific attack and defences. Once the outcome is determined, the game transitions back to the board. This interesting mechanic made Archon: The Light and the Dark a very strategic and unique game.

Over the years the game was ported to many 8-bit and 16-bit platforms. A respectable sequel was released for MS-DOS: *Archon Ultra* (1994). Archon: The Light and the Dark won Most Innovative Video Game/Computer Game at the 1984 Arcade Awards.

Ant Attack

Date of release: 1983

Region: UK

Developer: Sandy White

Publisher: Quicksilva

Platform: ZX Spectrum

Ant Attack is a single-player isometric, action game. The aim is to rescue the boy, if you play as the girl, or rescue the girl if you play as the boy, located somewhere in the ancient city of Antescher (a reference to the graphic artist M C Escher, whose work inspired the games look). The city's only inhabitants are giant ants who attempt to hunt down the player. The player can avoid the ants or use a limited number of grenades against them. The player can move in any of four directions, as well as up and down to navigate over, under and around the 3D structures of the city.

The game was praised for its technical achievement on the Spectrum platform and the feeling of trepidation it induced its players. Ant Attack was one of the first isometric home computer games and also one of the few video games where the player can choose their gender. It is also another precursor to the survival horror game.

Journey

Date of release: March 1983

Region: USA

Developer: Bally Midway

Publisher: Bally Midway

Platform: Arcade

Journey is a single-player action game. The aim of the game is to control and reunite the members of the American rock band, Journey, with their instruments through a series of different mini-games.

The most interesting aspect about Journey is the history behind the digitised faces of the band members on the characters the player controls. Ralph Baer, sometimes referred to as the father of the home video game console with his Brown Box (1967) and Magnavox (1972), conceptualised the idea of installing a cheap black and white camera into an arcade machine. The idea was that a player's face could be captured and displayed on the player's game character. Another idea was to capture a player's face and have them displayed on the high score board. The idea was tested in Chicago but was unfortunately dropped after someone exposed themselves on camera. This technology was used specifically for the digitised band members of Journey and is the first example of digitised graphics in a video game.

A cassette player was installed in the arcade cabinet with the play button on, but the power off. When the final stage is reached, the power is switched on and the cassette player plays Journey's *Separate Ways (Worlds Apart)*. Bally Midway hoped that the popularity of the band would make the arcade game a hit. However, partly due to the Video Game Crash of 1983, the reception was lukewarm, and it is believed only about a thousand cabinets in total were ever made.

Mappy

Date of release: March 1983

Region: Japan

Developer: Namco

Publisher: Namco

Platform: Arcade

Mappy is a single-player, side-scrolling platform game. The aim is for Mappy, the police mouse, to retrieve all the stolen items in the cat mansion and proceed to the next screen. Enemy cats are known as Meowkies and the boss cat called Goro attempt to stop Mappy. Trampolines can be used to jump up to higher platforms but will break if Mappy jumps on them four times. The cats can't hurt Mappy while in the air, only on the platforms. There are several doors that when open emits a microwave that can be used to dispatch nearby enemies when timed right. During bonus rounds, Mappy must bounce across a series of trampolines collecting as many balloons as possible. The game contains 256 levels.

Apart from the Famicom, Mappy was not ported to any other platforms at the time. However, it was later ported to a multitude of consoles, handheld and mobile devices. A few Mappy sequels were developed, including *Mappy-Land* (1986) arcade, *Hopping Mappy* (1986) and *Mappy Kids* (1989). A thirteen-part cartoon Mappy web series was released between 2013 and 2014.

JetPac

Date of release: May 1983

Region: UK

Developer: Tim Stamper and Chris Stamper

Publisher: Ultimate Play the Game

Platform: ZX Spectrum

JetPac is a single-player, platform shooter where the aim of the game is to assemble your rocket and collect fuel, enabling you to take off. The player controls a spaceman with a jetpack who flies around, picking up falling pieces of the rocket and dropping each one on top of the preceding piece. Once complete they must pick up fuel and put that into the rocket. Aliens infest the screen and must be avoided or dispatched. Once a rocket is complete, the spaceman can board it and leave the surface. After this has been done, the game begins again on a different planet.

JetPac received high praise for its simple yet compelling gameplay. The game sold 300,000 units and made over £1 million. JetPac is the first game in the Jetman series that include JetPac (1983), *Lunar Jetman* (1983), *Solar Jetman: Hunt for the Golden Warship* (1990) and *JetPac Refuelled* (2007). JetPac won Best Original Game of the Year at the 1983 Golden Joystick Awards.

Jumpman

Date of release: 1983

Region: USA

Developer: Epyx

Publisher: Epyx

Platform: Atari 8-bit

Designed by Randy Glover, Jumpman is a single-player, puzzle platformer. The base on Jupiter has been sabotaged by terrorists. The aim of Jumpman is to disarm all the bombs on the screen. This is done by merely touching them, at which point they disappear from the screen. Upon touching the last bomb, the player progresses to the next level. Each level has a name, giving the player some idea of what they are about to face. The player must avoid things such as killer robots, vampire bats, bombs and other lethal projectiles. Jumpman can run, jump (obviously), climb ladders and descend ropes.

Jumpman was ported to several home computers of the time. It has also seen several unofficial ports and remakes by fans of the game.

Astron Belt

Date of release: May 1983

Region: Japan

Developer: Sega

Publisher: Sega

Platform: Arcade

Astron Belt is a single-player, rail-shooter, laserdisc video game. The player controls a spaceship as viewed from a third-person perspective. The aim of the game is to destroy the enemy ships. The background space scenes and explosions incorporate digitised footage from sci-fi movies. This mix of media can be jarring or intriguing, depending on your tastes.

Astron Belt is the first laserdisc video game. It was released only a month earlier than the better-known and very popular *Dragon's Lair* (1983), a game that Astron Belt inspired when shown at the AMOA (the Amusement & Music Operators Association) show earlier in 1982. However, it is worth noting that *Dragon's Lair* was the first laserdisc video game released in the USA and many people's first exposure to this new technology. Astron Belt was only ported to the MSX Home Computer.

Capcom

Capcom was founded in Japan in May 1983 by Kenzo Tsujimoto.

Capcom is an incredibly successful publisher and developer of video games. Their best-known games are the *Mega Man series* (1987 onwards), *Street Fighter series* (1987 onwards), *Resident Evil series* (1996 onwards), *Devil May Cry series* (2001 onwards) and *Monster Hunter series* (2004 onwards). Some other noteworthy games are *Phoenix Wright: Ace Attorney* (2001), *Okami* (2006) and *Asura's Wrath* (2012).

Star Wars

Date of release: May 1983

Region: USA

Developer: Atari

Publisher: Atari

Platform: Arcade

Designed by Mike Hally, Star Wars is a single-player, 3D vector-displayed, first-person rail space shooter based on the popular movie *Star Wars: A New Hope*. You play the part of Luke Skywalker flying his X-Wing on an assault against the Death Star. The aim of the game is to make your way through each stage, destroying TIE fighters, gun turrets and towers, and eventually shooting the exhaust port at the end of the trench stage to destroy the Death Star. Except for the first Death Star, each Death Star is split into three stages: the space stage, the Death Star surface stage and the trench stage. Players must shoot at and intercept enemy fire, or dodge obstacles to prevent the loss of shields and being destroyed. Once the first Death Star is obliterated, the assault on the second Death Star begins: this introduces more TIE fighters, artillery bunkers during the surface stage, and obstacles in the trench stage. The third Death Star introduces even more TIE fighters and towers during the surface stage. Once the third Death Star is destroyed the game begins again but with increased difficulty.

Another big draw of the game was its sound. Digitised samples of the movie's main characters, as well as the popular *Star Wars* theme music, played throughout gameplay, immersing the player in the cinematic experience. This was particularly enhanced in the sit-down cockpit version of the cabinet. The controls are like those of an aircraft to some degree. Players can control pitch and move left and right, but at some points during the game control is taken away from the player to take you to the next part of the game. The controls are very smooth and responsive.

Star Wars was ported to most platforms of the day, yet it was difficult for home consoles and computers to recreate the excitement of the sound and visuals of the arcade. Star Wars was well received and sold nearly 13,000 units. Star Wars had two direct sequels: *Star Wars: Return of the Jedi* (1984) and *Star Wars: The Empire Strikes Back* (1985). Star Wars won Best Coin-Op of the Year at the 1985 Arcade Awards.

MSX

The MSX Personal Computer was released in Japan in June 1983 by Microsoft Japan. Conceived by Kazuhiko Nishi, the MSX introduced the idea of a standardised computing format, in the same way, that VHS (Video Home System, 1976) had standardised Video Recorders. Any product with the MSX logo would be compatible with the platform. The first machine shipped with an 8-bit CPU and 16 KB of RAM. Later models had a 16-bit CPU and up to 512 KB of RAM.

The MSX line of computers would sell over five million units. Unfortunately, due to the well-established Commodore 64, it never took root in the all-important US market. It would be years until Microsoft would standardise the majority of computer gaming under one platform.

Hundreds of games were released for the MSX system. Some of the most notable are *Eggerland Mystery* (1985), *King's Valley* (1985), *Bomberman* (1986), *Metal Gear* (1987), *Parodius* (1988) and *Puyo Puyo* (1991).

Dragon's Lair

Date of release: June 1983

Region: USA

Developer: Advanced Microcomputer Systems

Publisher: Cinematronics

Platform: Arcade

Designed by Rick Dyer and Don Bluth, Dragon's Lair is a laserdisc fantasy animation game. The player controls the knight, Dirk the Daring, and must save Princess Daphne from Singe, the dragon. Dirk must avoid obstacles and defeat various enemies to achieve his goal. A simple joystick to move Dirk in one of four directions and a button to make Dirk attack with his sword are the only controls. As this was a laserdisc game, the player did not move the character in real-time. Instead, on-screen prompts told the player in which direction to move the joystick, or whether to press the attack button. This would then result in either a success animation being played, where Dirk would avoid a deadly obstacle, dispatch an enemy, or a fail animation would play showing one of many amusing death scenes that Dragon's Lair would become renowned for. The player only had a very short amount of time to initiate the correct response meaning that they must focus and hold their nerve lest they make a mistake. However, seeing as the game is linear within its branching paths, an experienced player would know what action to take and could be ready.

The art style for Dragon's Lair is straight out of a 1980s' Disney animation. Don Bluth worked at Disney for many years before setting up his own animation studio in 1979. Both Bluth and Dyer were intrigued by the emerging laserdisc technology. Bluth set out to create an arcade game with stunning graphics that would replicate the Disney look. Its only main drawback was that the game would be playing a series of short animations based on user input. With graphics that looked decades ahead of its time, Dragon's Lair was an instant success. Despite its limitations, consumers were bowled over by not just its graphics but also the high production value of animation and sound. Even when idle the game introduces potential players to the characters and story, illustrating the gameplay and amusing death animations. Here was a cartoon that you could play. It was a breath of fresh air and an interesting take on the video arcade game, although it would never replace the traditional arcade game. People could never deny a sense of amazement the first time they heard and saw Dragon's Lair.

The game was ported to many home platforms, but it was difficult to emulate the graphics of a laserdisc game on such limited machines. There were a few Dragon's Lair sequels released for many different platforms over the years, though the only official arcade release was *Dragon's Lair II: Time Warp* (1991). Dragon's Lair won Best Coin-Op Game Audio/Visual Effects in the 1984 Arcade Awards.

Planetfall

Date of release: July 1983

Region: USA

Developer: Infocom

Publisher: Infocom

Platform: multiple 8-bit home computers

Designed by Steve Meretzky, Planetfall is a single-player, comedy science-fiction text adventure. After crash landing on a doomed starship, you must solve the mystery of an alien structure on a desolate planet, with the help of a child-like robot called Floyd.

Planetfall shipped with several 'feelies' including a manual, ID card and postcards.

Planetfall was well-received by critics and consumers alike who praised the writing and especially the character of Floyd. His unfortunate demise in the game brought some players to tears. For this reason, Planetfall was a quiet milestone in video game history. Rarely if ever had the medium elicited such an emotional response from the player, staying with some for many years after.

Bomberman

Date of release: July 1983

Region: Japan

Developer: Hudson Soft

Publisher: Hudson Soft

Platform: NEC PC-8801 and other Japanese-manufactured PCs

Bomberman is a mix of the maze and strategy genres. The aim is to destroy all the enemies on-screen with your bombs and progress to the next level. Each level is laid out in a grid of rock and empty spaces. Bomberman, a cute-looking robot, must use his bombs to destroy rocks and open other areas to eliminate the enemy and find the door to the next level. Bombs explode along the four grid lines and have a limited area of effect so Bomberman must get close to enemies or predict their movements to some degree. The bomb's effect and the number of bombs that can be laid at a time can change if specific power-ups are discovered. There are fifty levels in the original Bomberman.

The game was so successful that it was ported to almost every major platform of the time and spawned several clones. Bomberman was the first in a series of many games over the years, not all of which were maze games like the original. Bomberman is well known for its multiplayer aspect in what is called battle mode, whether it be one-on-one, or four players, or even ten-person local multiplayer on the Sega Saturn. A ten-player version called Hi-Ten Bomberman was developed and played on a custom made hi-definition TV in Japan in 1993 at the Ninth Hudson Soft Caravan, a gaming event that was shown at 44 venues across Japan. The *Hi-Ten Bomberman* (1993) is the first video game to be played on a hi-definition screen.

Some of the most noteworthy Bomberman games are *Bomberman '93* (1992), *Super Bomberman 2* (1994), *Mega Bomberman* (1994), *Bomberman 64* (1997), *Bomberman 64: The Second Attack* (1999), *Bomberman Tournament* (2001), *Bomberman Jetters* (2002) and *Bomberman Land* (2007).

Mario Bros.

Date of release: July 1983

Region: Japan

Developer: Nintendo R&D1

Publisher: Nintendo

Platform: Arcade

Designed by Shigeru Miyamoto and Gunpei Yokoi (both of whom developed the Donkey Kong games), Mario Bros. is a single-player or multiplayer platform game. The aim of the game is to dispatch all the pests infesting the sewers. Mario or his brother Luigi do this by jumping up and knocking the platform the pests are standing on from underneath, then kicking them off-screen before they flip themselves back on their feet. Jumping up and hitting the 'POW' icons from below causes all the enemies on the screen to flip over onto their backs. This can be used three times before disappearing. As well as pests, coins emerge from the sewer pipes. These can be collected for more points.

Mario Bros. is the first game where Mario is portrayed as a plumber rather than a carpenter. It is also Luigi's first appearance in a video game. Although later Mario games would be some of the most lucrative in video game history, the first outing of the Mario brothers was only moderately successful. Despite this Mario Bros. was ported to most systems at the time. Mario Bros. would go on to become one of the most successful video game series of all time, generating well over $30 billion at the time of writing. Mario himself is one of the most if not *the* most famous video game character of all time.

Some of the most notable games in the Mario series are *Super Mario Bros.* (1985), *Super Mario Bros. 3* (1990), *Super Mario World* (1990), *Super Mario 64* (1996), *Super Mario Galaxy* (2007), *New Super Mario Bros. U* (2012), *Super Mario 3D World* (2013) and *Super Mario Odyssey* (2017).

Nintendo Famicom

The Nintendo Famicom was released in Japan in July 1983 by Nintendo. Designed by Masayuki Uemura, the Famicom, also known as the Family Computer, is an 8-bit cartridge-based third-generation video game console. It shipped with two controllers and could display a total of 25 colours on-screen. The Famicom originally had three of Nintendo's most popular games released alongside it. These were Arcade ports of *Donkey Kong* (1981), *Donkey Kong Jr.* (1982) and *Popeye* (1982).

The Famicom is perhaps most famous for being the original Japanese version of what would later become the Nintendo Entertainment System, or NES, released two years later in 1985 and was pivotal in kick-starting the video game industry in America after the crash of 1983. The two systems are essentially the same. The major differences are that the Famicom had different plastic moulding of red and white. It had storage slots for the controllers. One of these controllers had a microphone. They also had different kinds of expansion ports.

The Famicom and NES were the most successful consoles of the third generation and the best-selling of all time until the mid-1990s, selling a total of around 62 million units worldwide. Some of the most notable games for the Famicom were *Mario Bros.* (1983), *Castlevania* (1983), *The Legend of Zelda* (1986), *Final Fantasy* (1987), *Mother* (1989) and *Super Mario Bros. 3* (1990).

SG-1000

The SG-1000 was released in Japan in July 1983 by Sega. The SG-1000 is a third-generation, cartridge-loading, 8-bit console with 1 KB of RAM and an output of 16 colours. The joystick controller was hardwired into the console. Peripherals included a joypad, racing wheel and keyboard.

The SG-1000 was followed by a few iterations that in total sold 160,000 units, a mere fraction compared with the Nintendo Famicom which was released on the same date. It is, however, Sega's first home video game console and a precursor to the more successful Sega Master System (1985).

Some of the SG-1000's most notable games were *Sega-Galaga* (1983), *Gulkave* (1983), *Girl Garden* (1984), *H.E.R.O.* (1985) and *Wonder Boy* (1985).

Chuckie Egg

Date of release: 1983

Region: UK

Developer: A&F Software

Publisher: A&F Software

Platform: BBC Micro, Dragon 32 and ZX Spectrum

Designed by Nigel Alderton, a 'bedroom coder' who taught himself how to program on the Sinclair ZX81, Chuckie Egg is a platformer, where the aim of the game is to collect all the eggs on-screen before the timer runs out. The player controls Hen-House Harry who can run, jump, climb ladders and travel on moving platforms. Collecting bird seed pauses the timer momentarily. However, the hens eat the bird seed. Harry can be killed by the hens or, in later levels, by a giant yellow duck, which is in a cage in the top left part of the screen for the first eight levels.

The control and movements of Harry are very smooth and, refreshingly, he isn't killed by small drops as was the case with many other platform games of the time. The gameplay is quick and strategic, and it is obvious why Chuckie Egg was so incredibly popular at the time, selling over a million units.

The game was soon ported over to the other popular computer platforms of the time. Chuckie Egg spawned a sequel in *Chuckie Egg 2* (1985), which, although not a bad game, never achieved the popularity of the original.

Crystal Castles

Date of release: 1983

Region: USA

Developer: Atari

Publisher: Atari

Platform: Arcade

Designed by Scott Fuller, Franz X. Lanzinger and Sam Lee, Crystal Castles is a single-player, isometric maze game, where the aim is to collect as many gems as possible before the multitude of enemies does. You control Bentley Bear (a bear dressed in a wizard's outfit) and must run around each castle collecting all the gems. The player controls Bentley's movement with a trackball and makes him jump with a button. Bentley starts with three lives. If he loses a life a speech balloon says "BYE!" When losing his second life he says "OUCH!", and on losing his final life, he says "#?!", insinuating a curse word. There are nine levels with four castles each and the final, tenth level has just one, making a total of thirty-seven. Upon completing a castle several key notes from the *Nutcracker Suite* play. When the tenth and final Castle has been completed the text "I GIVE UP: YOU WIN / YOU MUST BE A VIDEO WHIZ" displays on the screen with your score. The *1812 Overture* plays celebrating the player's victory.

Crystal Castles is one of the few video games to have an actual ending, as opposed to the usual unending levels, kill screen or disruptive bugs, making completion impossible. Crystal Castles was ported to most 8-bit platforms of the day.

Lode Runner

Date of release: July 1983

Region: USA

Developer: Douglas E. Smith

Publisher: Broderbund

Platform: multiple 8-bit home computers

Lode Runner is a single-player, puzzle platform game. The aim of the game is to collect all the gold on the screen while avoiding being captured by the guards. Each screen is made up of platforms and ladders. The player can quickly chip a hole in the floor which a guard will fall into. The guard takes several seconds getting out and filling the hole back in, during which time you can walk over the top of them. Once all the gold is collected, the player moves onto the next level. The original 1983 release of Lode Runner has 150 levels. Players must attempt to foresee how the guards may trap them into a corner and so a certain amount of strategy is involved. Also, in later levels coins can be difficult to acquire without a bit of forethought.

The original incarnation of Lode Runner was called *Kong* and the graphics were purely ASCII characters. The second version, called *Miner*, used more representative graphics but was initially turned down by Broderbund for being too simplistic. After improving the graphics and adding a level editor, Lode Runner was accepted by Broderbund. Lode Runner is one of the first platform games to include a level editor. Some of the levels which were created by children in Smith's neighbourhood, as a way of testing the level editor, found their way into the final game.

The game was very successful and was ported to most platforms of the time, many of which have variations and additions to the original. It was even ported to the arcade (a computer game being ported to the arcade is extremely rare), and versions of Lode Runner have been ported consistently over the decades to this current day. Few games have been developed for so many platforms, a testament to its timeless gameplay. Lode Runner was awarded Computer Game of the Year at the 1984 Arcade Awards.

Dandy

Date of release: 1983

Region: USA

Developer: Atari Program Exchange

Publisher: Atari

Platform: Atari 8-bit

Designed by John Howard Palevich, Dandy (a play on the abbreviation for Dungeons and Dragons – D&D) is a single- or multiplayer, top-down, dungeon crawl game, where the aim is to find the key and escape each level, with the ultimate goal of escaping the dungeon itself. The player controls a small figure who moves around huge, maze-like dungeons confronting a multitude of enemies, who can be killed with your bow and arrow. Some enemies are easy to kill with one shot while others take several shots. These enemy sprites change form when hit to inform the player of their current state of health. Some enemies are produced in monster generators. These must be destroyed or else the player risks being overwhelmed. Enemies drain a player's health upon contact. Health can be replenished by eating food that can be found in the dungeon. Potions can also be collected and will instantly obliterate all enemies on the screen if used. The 'Heart of gold' is a collectable item that can revive a fallen companion.

Dandy was the first four-player cooperative home video game. It was ported only to the Amstrad, Commodore 64 and Spectrum computers. Dandy directly inspired the hugely successful arcade game *Gauntlet* (1985), which shares many of the same game mechanics.

Gyruss

Date of release: 1983

Region: Worldwide

Developer: Konami

Publisher: Konami

Platform: Arcade

Designed by Yoshiki Okamoto, Gyruss is a single-player, tube shooter. The aim is to destroy as many enemies as possible and reach Earth. The player begins by working through waves of enemy ships to first reach Neptune, then Uranus, Saturn, Jupiter, Mars and finally Earth. Upon reaching each planet, the player enters the chance round, where they can destroy as many ships as possible to get bonus points. After the Earth chance round, the entire game begins again, yet the difficulty increases. Gyruss has a similar game mechanics to *Tempest* (1981) in what is termed the tube shooter, where moving left or right will not only take you along the bottom of the screen but along the sides and the top. The player's ship always points towards the centre of the screen where stars emanate as you fly through space.

Gyruss has been ported to many platforms over the years, most recently to mobile devices.

M.U.L.E.

Date of release: 1983

Region: USA

Developer: Ozark Softscape

Publisher: Electronic Arts.

Platform: Atari 8-bit

Designed by Danielle Bunten Berry, M.U.L.E. is a single-player or multiplayer (up to four players), turn-based, land and resource-management strategy game. The aim of the game is to amass more wealth than your opponents. Up to four players can partake in the game. Any player's place that is not taken by a real person is controlled by the computer. Players can choose their race, all of which have different strengths and weaknesses. The game takes place on the planet Irata (Atari spelt backwards). Each M.U.L.E. (Multiple User Labour Element), after and which look like the four-legged Imperial Walkers from the movie *Star Wars: The Empire Strikes Back*, is modified to either gather energy, food or Smithore, which the M.U.L.E.s are made of. Players must balance buying and selling, and even use more advanced strategies like withholding resources to inflate prices, or broker deals with other players, making it more difficult for their opponents to boost their own economies. Random events, such as weather and space pirates, add another interesting element to the game. Many of the game's mechanics were inspired by the board game Monopoly.

Even though M.U.L.E. only sold around 30,000 units, it was highly regarded by critics and is often cited as one of the most important video games of its time because of its depth of gameplay. M.U.L.E. won Best Multiplayer Video Game in the 1984 Arcade Awards.

Major Havoc

Date of release: 1983

Region: USA

Developer: Atari

Publisher: Atari

Platform: Arcade

Designed by Owen Rubin and Mark Cerny, Major Havoc, is a single-player, vector based shooter and platform game. The aim is to destroy the Vaxxian robot army reactors and liberate the humans from the now-dead Vaxxian race. The player controls Major Havoc, a clone of a great hero. Gameplay starts with a standard space fixed shooter: enemies must be destroyed to gain access to the space station. Once this is done, the player must land on the white platform of the space station in the same vain as a Lunar Lander game. Finally, the game switches to a platformer, where the player is depicted as a figure moving around the station avoiding enemies in search of the reactor. Major Havoc only has a limited amount of oxygen. If the oxygen reaches zero a life is lost. More oxygen can be found in the station to buy more time. A mini-map at the top of the screen helps the player orientate themselves. Once the reactor is reached Major Havoc must set it to overload and escape the station before a counter reaches zero and it explodes. The game starts again with the space shooter section. Major Havoc also contained a game within a game. While waiting between levels, the player had a short amount of time to play a mini version of the game *Breakout* (1976) in the bottom right part of the screen. Completing that game earns even more points.

The original Major Havoc featured a trackball controller. The later editions used a dial instead. It is thought about only 300 of the trackball versions were ever made.

Manic Miner

Date of release: 1983

Region: UK

Developer: Mathew Smith

Publisher: Bug-Byte

Platform: ZX Spectrum

Manic Miner is a single-player, platform game and was originally programmed on a TRS-

80. Inspired by *Miner 2049er* (1983), the aim is to control Miner Willy and collect all the flashing objects on the screen, then reach the flashing portal to move onto the next level before the player's air runs out. Willy must avoid a different kind of enemy on each screen, including killer penguins, seals, toilets, PacMen, teddy bears/Ewoks and giant telephones. Each screen offers a different challenge with moving and disintegrating platforms. If not tackled correctly, the player may find a level impossible to complete. A certain amount of strategy and forethought is required to complete each screen, which is one of the many reasons why Manic Miner is such a compelling game. When the player reaches the flashing portal at the end of a level, the remaining air is converted into points. There are twenty self-contained screens to complete, each with a unique name. When the final screen is complete, the game starts again at the first screen.

Mathew Smith accomplished something thought impossible on the ZX Spectrum: having in-game music, in this case being Edvard Grieg's 'In the Hall of the Mountain King'. This could drive you a bit crazy as it was on about a thirteen-second loop. (I used to just turn the sound down a bit.) The music which plays on the title screen is Johann Strauss's 'The Blue Danube'. Manic Miner has become a cult game and certainly had plenty of personality with its uniquely identifiable British charm, from killer toilets to the giant boot that descends from above to squash Miner Willy upon losing his final life, straight out of *Monty Python's Flying Circus*.

It is also known for being a very difficult game to complete. This was the first game in the Miner Willy series and was followed by *Jet Set Willy* (1984) and *Jet Set Willy II: The Final Frontier* (1985). Manic Miner received high praise from critics and consumers alike and was quickly ported to many platforms of the day. Not only that, such was the impact of the game on the gaming community that clones of Manic Miner have been developed by enthusiasts throughout the decades since its initial release in 1983. Manic Miner won Best Arcade Style Game at the 1983 Golden Joystick Awards.

Pinball Construction Set

Date of release: 1983

Region: USA

Developer: BudgeCo

Publisher: BudgeCo

Platform: Apple II

Designed by Bill Budge, Pinball Construction Set does exactly what it says on the tin.

Players can create their own virtual pinball machine with flippers, bumpers and all kinds of other features; even setting up things like gravity. Creators could save their virtual machines on floppy disks and freely distribute them.

Pinball Construction Set is one of the first construction simulation games and inspired a generation of them. Pinball Construction Set was highly praised and sold well over 300, 000 units.

Atic Atac

Date of release: 1983

Region: Worldwide

Developer: Tim and Chris Stamper

Publisher: Ultimate Play the Game

Platform: BBC Micro and ZX Spectrum

Atic Atac is a single-player, action and adventure maze game. The aim is to escape the castle by finding the three pieces of a golden key within a maze of rooms. The player begins the game by choosing to play as a knight, serf or wizard. Each of these has a different attack. The game is viewed from an above perspective, one room at a time. There are colour coded keys that open their respective coloured doors. Only three items can be carried at any one time. Enemies drain your health (depicted as a cooked chicken) on contact. Players can collect food to replenish their health. The player has three lives.

The game was highly praised by critics and consumers alike. Atic Atac was Ultimate's third consecutive number one hit, firmly establishing them as a successful publisher/developer.

Spy Hunter

Date of release: 1983

Region: USA

Developer: Bally Midway

Publisher: Bally Midway

Platform: Arcade

Designed by George Gomez, Spy Hunter is a single-player, top-down, vertical-scrolling, vehicular combat game. The aim is for the player to amass as many points as possible. Points increase as long as the car is in motion. Bumping into civilian vehicles causes points to pause momentarily. Enemies also hinder the player's motion. Bullet-proof cars will try to bump you off the road, causing you to crash. The switchblade car has blades protruding from its wheels, and the Enforcer drives up beside you and shoots until your car explodes. The Mad Bomber is a helicopter that flies in front, dropping bombs in your path. Some enemies can be dispatched with the twin machine guns which fire from the front of your 'G-6155 Interceptor Car'. Other weapons can be called upon in later sections of the game, such as smoke screens, oil slicks and a missile for taking out the helicopter. These can be collected from the truck which pulls up in front of you. The steering control was rather sleek and hi-tech, looking as if it were designed more for an aircraft rather than a car. From time to time the player's car will enter a water section and promptly turn into a boat. Enemy boats need to be dodged or destroyed during this stage. It is easy to see how the gameplay was inspired by the James Bond movies of the time. The *Peter Gunn* theme music by Henry Mancini plays throughout the game.

Spy Hunter was a popular game in the arcades and was soon ported to most platforms of the day. Several sequels have cropped up over the years, including *Spy Hunter II* (1987) and *SpyHunter* (2001).

Mr. Do's Castle

Date of release: September 1983

Region: Japan

Developer: Universal

Publisher: Universal

Platform: Arcade

Mr Do's Castle, known as 'Mr. Do vs. the Unicorns' in Japan, is a single-player platform game. The aim of the game is to dispatch all the unicorn monsters, usually by knocking a block on top of them and then proceed to the next level. There are six floors in the castle. Ladders, some of which can be moved, link the platforms which are themselves made up of blocks with cherries or keys on them. These can be knocked out with Mr.

Do's hammer. Cherries earn points and the keys, if all knocked out of place, will make the door open at the top of the screen and give Mr. Do access to a shield, which must be collected, whereupon the unicorns turn into letters which the player must hit before the time runs out. The aim of this is to collect as many letters as possible. The letters spell out 'EXTRA', for an extra life. If too much time passes during gameplay the unicorns become more aggressive, in time splitting into two and moving faster about the screen to hunt you down. The game is a worthy sequel and has fantastic music.

The game was ported to most of the major consoles and home computers of its day.

Libble Rabble

Date of release: October 1983

Region: Japan

Developer: Namco

Publisher: Namco

Platform: Arcade

Designed by Toru Iwatanni (*Pac-Man* and *Pole Position*), Libble Rabble is an action-puzzle game, where the aim of the game is to harvest mushrooms by encircling them using a stretched-out line around the pegs laid out on the screen in a grid. Once a group of mushrooms is surrounded, the shape is filled in with a colour and the mushrooms disappear, giving points to the player. Hidden chests can also be revealed, opened and the creatures within harvested in the same manner for bonus points. Various enemies attempt to prevent the player from completing their task.

Libble Rabble was ported to the Sharp X6800 Home Computer (1987) and the Super Famicom (1990).

First Golden Joystick Awards

The first Golden Joystick Awards ceremony took place in London in November 1983. The Golden Joystick Awards are the second oldest video game awards ceremony, yet the longest-running due to the Arkies taking several years out.

Manic Miner (1983) wins Best Arcade-Style Game of the Year

The Hobbit (1982) wins Best Strategy Game of the Year

Ah Diddums (1983) wins Best Original Game of the Year

JetPac (1983) wins Game of the Year.

Punch Out!!

Date of release: December 1983

Region: Japan

Developer: Nintendo

Publisher: Nintendo

Platform: Arcade

Designed by Genyo Takeda and Shigeru Miyamoto, Punch Out!! is a single-player boxing game. The aim is to defeat all of your opponents: Glass Joe, Piston Hurricane, Bald Bull, Kid Quick, Pizza Pasta and Mr. Sandman. If the player can defeat all the other boxers, then the game begins again with Glass Joe, working through the rest at a higher degree of difficulty. The player is viewed from behind as a green-haired, wireframe character, so as to be able to see your opponent. Attacks can be made to the head and body. The player can defend his head and body. The opponent's eyes flash to cue when an attack will be made.

Punch Out!! was one of the few arcades to utilise two screens, one on top of the other, similar to Nintendo's first Vertical Multi-Screen Range Game & Watch Model (1982). The top screen displayed portraits of the fighters and information, such as score and time. The bottom screen displayed the gameplay.

Punch Out!! was rather successful and spawned several sequels including *Super Punch Out!!* (1984) and *Mike Tyson's Punch Out!!* (1987). Punch Out!! Won Most Innovative Coin-Op Game in the 1985 Arcade Awards.

Track & Field

Date of release: 1983

Region: Japan

Developer: Konami

Publisher: Konami

Platform: Arcade

Track and Field is a single-player or multiplayer athletics game. The aim is to beat the qualifying time for each event and move onto the next. Failing to beat the qualifying time means losing a life. Each player has three lives. The events are 100 meter dash, long jump, javelin throw, 110 meter hurdles, hammer throw and high jump. The control system involves alternately tapping two buttons to run or move and either tapping the jump button to jump or, in other events, holding the jump button momentarily to attain a good angle for the jump or throw and then letting go. Each event requires different timing and skill. If the player/s complete all the events, then the events begin again from the start with more demanding qualifying times. There are two sets of controls on the consoles and it is possible to have four players compete together by having two players on and then swapping between events or qualifying times.

Track & Field was well received and ported to most platforms of the time. Its popularity inspired a host of other sports games such as *Hyper Sports* (1984), *Summer Games* (1984), *Daley Thompson's Decathlon* (1984), *Winter Games* (1985), *California Games* (1987) and *International Track & Field* (1996).

Tapper

Date of release: December 1983

Region: Worldwide

Developer: Marvin Glass and Associates

Publisher: Bally Midway

Platform: Arcade

Tapper is a single-player action game. The aim is to halt the oncoming patrons by serving them drinks. There are four bars for the player to cover. As patrons move across the bar from left to right, you must fill a glass of beer from the barrel on the right and slide it down the bar. The empty glasses must be caught when the patrons slide them back or the player loses a life. A life will also be lost if any patron makes their way to the other side of the screen: the bartender (Tapper) is thrown across the bar by the unhappy patron if this happens. Occasionally the player will receive a tip for bonus points. From time to time, when a tip is picked up, a group of female dancers will appear, pausing those patrons without a drink and giving the player a chance to catch up. There are four different bar levels, each with its own theme: Western, sports, punk rock, and outer space. A bonus round involves choosing one of six cans to find which one hasn't been shaken. Choose the correct one and receive bonus points: choose one of the five incorrect ones and the bartender gets sprayed with beer. Digitised in-game music features Stephen Foster's 'Oh! Susanna'.

The original Tapper cabinets featured a brass rail footrest, drinks holders, actual Budweiser beer tap handles as part of the control system and Budweiser logo graphics in the game. The concept behind Tapper was later changed to root beer as it was believed it may have a bad influence on children.

Tapper was ported to most platforms of the day with some versions having the in-game logo changed to Mountain Dew or Pepsi.

Video Game Crash of 1983

The Video Game Crash of 1983 was a video game industry recession that mainly affected the USA, although repercussions were felt in other parts of the world.

Video games had experienced unprecedented popularity for the last several years. With the *Space Invaders* phenomenon, *Pac-Man* fever and the popularity of home consoles such as the Atari 2600 in the late 1970s, it appeared that the video games industry would continue to grow throughout the 1980s year on year, and nothing could stop it.

However, some saw video games as nothing more than a fad. As with any other 'toy', it was a passing phase that would soon be gone. More portentously there were those who had analysed the growing industry and foresaw what was to come. Expectation is what drove the industry, and expectation would be its downfall. The Atari 5200 had been a failure and the manufacture of 12 million underwhelming ports of *Pac-Man* (1982) were also selling poorly. The rushed *E.T. The Extra-Terrestrial* (1982) was another title that went largely unsold. Atari had a huge library of third-party games that lacked serious quality control. By December 1982 Atari realised they were in serious trouble. In desperation to acquire high-quality intellectual properties, the company paid extortionate amounts to develop games from which they saw little return. At the end of 1983, Atari were $536 million in debt.

Many entrepreneurs had invested heavily in amusement arcades, expecting the upward trend to continue. The market became saturated with too many arcade outlets. To make matters worse, interest in video games, in general, seemed to be waning. Whether this was indeed true or only appeared to be the case due to an over-saturated market is debatable.

The home computer was also seeing a surge in popularity. Prices had dropped with the incredibly popular ZX Spectrum and Commodore 64 entering households and offering not only games but also word processing and a multitude of other software. Even though games were now getting a bad reputation, the public still knew that computers were the future. They were also a gateway to coding. Consumers were also more likely to spend their hard-earned money on another exciting new invention. That of the VCR or home video recorder. The novelty of watching a movie in the home or recording the television involved the whole family and was growing in popularity.

After so many companies had gone bankrupt and amusement arcades closed, it seemed that those who had predicted video games as being just a passing craze had indeed been correct. This lack of confidence in the industry created a snowball effect and resulted in the crash.

However, in other parts of the world, such as the United Kingdom and Japan, this was not the case. The video game industry barely missed a beat and many companies, such as Sinclair, Nintendo and Sega, would prosper even more in these next two years than ever before.

The USA Video Game Crash would end with the introduction of Nintendo's reinvented Famicom, the Nintendo Entertainment System (1985), however, this did not happen overnight rather over the next few years. But for now, 'video game' was still a dirty word with a lot of retailers and Nintendo were careful to introduce their product as a toy rather than a video game console. The release of the Nintendo Entertainment System (NES) would kick-start the video game industry in America and become the best-selling console of the decade.

1983 Notable Omissions

Ah Diddums. Antarctic Adventure. Arcadia. Apocalypse. Beach Head. Bega's Battle. Bokosuka Wars. Blagger. Blaster Blaster. Bruce Lee. Cliff Hanger. Congo Bongo. Cube Quest. Chequered Flag. Crossbow. Demon Attack. Digger. Discs of Tron. Dreadnaught Factor. Excalibur. Food Fight. Hard Hat Mack Hunchback. Hungry Horace. James Bond 007. Juno First. Kagirinaki Tatakai. Krull. Lunar Jetman. Mad Planets. Metagalactic Llamas Battle at the Edge of Time. Murder on the Zinderneuf. Nobunaga's Ambition. Pac & Pal. Penetrator. Phozon. Pole Position II. Portopia Serial Murder Case. Q-bert's Qubes. Rescue at Rigel. Roc'n Rope. Scepter of God. Space Shuttle: A Journey into Space. Stonkers. Super Action Baseball. Suspended. Texas Chainsaw Massacre. Thunder Force. Tomytronic 3D handhelds. The Witness. World Series Major League Baseball.

1984

The Black Onyx

Date of release: January 1984

Region: Japan

Developer: Henk Rogers

Publisher: Bullet-Proof Software

Platform: NEC-8801

The Black Onyx was released in Japan in January 1984 by Bullet-Proof Software for the NEC-8801. Designed by Henk Rogers, The Black Onyx is an RPG where the aim is to explore the dungeons beneath the town Utsuro and obtain the Black Onyx, thus lifting the curse which has plunged the town into eternal night. The Black Onyx is very much like *Wizardry I* (1981) in the way that the screen is split into a first-person perspective, character portraits, enemy portraits and current status. It too has a party system, allowing you to control five different characters. It was also one of the first RPG video games to feature a health bar, a staple of many games since.

Henk Rogers, an American from Hawaii, grew up playing classic D&D. The West already had a rich history of RPG video games, such as *Ultima 1* (1980) and *Wizardry I* (1981), and these games did indeed have some influence on Japanese game development. Rogers moved to Japan and wanted to bring another such game to the Japanese market. Rogers had great difficulty getting his game off the ground. At the time RPGs weren't that big in Japan. He got his break after promising numerous Japanese games magazines that he would include their names in the game if they would spend a short amount of time playing it and write a simple review. The idea worked. The reviews turned out favourable and The Black Onyx went on to sell over 150,000 units.

It is now cited as one of the key video games that spurred Japan's interest in the RPG genre. Many developers who went on to work on games such as *Dragon Quest* (1986) and *Final Fantasy* (1987) were inspired by The Black Onyx. The game was ported to most Japanese home computers and consoles of the time.

Apple Macintosh

The Apple Macintosh, also known as the Macintosh 128K, was released in the USA in January 1984. Launched with the now-famous Ridley Scott '1984' television advert, the Macintosh 128K was a 16/32-bit home computer that shipped with 128 KB RAM and had a built-in floppy drive and black and white 512 x 342 resolution monitor, priced at $2,495.

The platform wasn't that renowned for its games. However, it was the first home computer to popularise the Graphical User Interface (GUI), which inspired Windows and every other GUI interface: the fundamental interaction between the player and the technology running our modern-day video games.

Sabre Wulf

Date of release: 1984

Region: UK

Developer: Ultimate Play the Game

Publisher: Ultimate Play the Game

Platform: ZX Spectrum

Sabre Wulf is a single-player action adventure game and the first in the Sabreman series. You control Sabreman, who must collect all the amulet pieces in a two-dimensional jungle maze, made up of 256 screens, and use it to get past the guardian at the exit. As with most computer games of the time, the game is presented in flip-screens rather than scrolling, meaning that when Sabreman reaches the edge of one side of the screen he appears on the next connecting part of the maze. Objects can be collected for more points. Enemies spawn randomly, and at any time. These can be dispatched head-on with your sword, except for the infamous Sabre Wulf, who will chase after you. Enemies can kill you if you are attacked from behind. Different coloured flowers can be consumed for different effects for a short time. These include invulnerability, significantly increased movement, impaired movement, and reversed controls. Once all the pieces of the amulet have been collected, you can exit the jungle maze through a cave. The game cuts to some text which tells you that the next adventure of Sabreman will be continued in the *Underwurlde* (1984), the next game in the Sabreman series.

Sabre Wulf was and still is considered one of the ZX Spectrum's best games and was soon ported to the other 8-bit platforms of the day. *Sabre Wulf* (1984), *Underwurlde* (1984), *Knight Lore* (1984) and *Pentagram* (1986) were all part of the Sabreman series. The first three games were all released in quick succession in 1984, giving the series high exposure and great success. *Pentagram* was released in 1986.

Adventure Construction Set

Date of release: 1984

Region: USA

Developer: Stuart Smith

Publisher: Electronic Arts

Platform: Commodore 64

Adventure Construction Set is a tile-based, menu-driven, adventure game creation system. The software came with a game example called *Rivers of Light* (1984).

ACS features included: combat system, random encounters, spells, shops, game logic, monster AI, multiplayer, music and sound. Games could be saved to disc and freely distributed among other users.

ACS was one of EA's best-selling titles of the time and was soon ported over to other home computers.

Ballblazer

Date of release: March 1984

Region: USA

Developer: Lucasfilm Games

Publisher: Atari

Platform: Atari 8-bit

Ballblazer is a single-player or two-player, first-person, 3D futuristic sports game. The aim of the game is to be the first player to score ten points. Each player controls a craft called a Rotofoil which glides along a chequered field. You must capture the ball in your force field, carry it and fire it into the goal. Carrying it through moving goal posts scores 1 point. Firing the ball and scoring from a close distance scores 2 points, while firing the ball and scoring from a long-distance scores 3 points. Your opponent can fire at the ball, and if hit you will lose possession.

Ballblazer was praised for its 3D graphics and its quick, exciting gameplay. It was soon ported to most platforms of the day. Looking back at Ballblazer today, it has similar elements to Psyonix's highly successful *Rocket League* (2015).

H.E.R.O.

Date of release: March 1984

Region: USA

Developer: Activision

Publisher: Activision

Platform: Atari 2600

Designed by John Van Ryzin, H.E.R.O. is a single-player, action platformer. You play as Roderick Hero. The aim of H.E.R.O. is to descend into the mines and rescue all the miners trapped in Mount Leone. Roderick is equipped with a helicopter backpack to hover and navigate the network of caverns, a laser helmet to deal with enemies such as spiders and bats, and a limited supply of dynamite to blow holes through cave-ins or magma. Some caverns are in complete darkness and revealed only for an instant when a stick of dynamite explodes. The player must find each miner before his power runs out, otherwise, he will lose a life. Magma, water and the creatures in the cavern can also cause H.E.R.O. to lose a life. Once a miner has been found, the player is instantly dropped into another part of the mine to rescue another miner. There are 20 levels to complete, after which it becomes a lot more difficult in pro mode.

H.E.R.O. is considered one of the better games for the Atari 2600. It was nice to see that some good games were still being made for the platform, even seven years after its initial release.

Duck Hunt

Date of release: April 1984

Region: Japan

Developer: Nintendo R&D1

Publisher: Nintendo

Platform: Famicom

Duck Hunt is a single-player, light-gun-shooter, sports game. The aim is to shoot the number of ducks required in order to proceed to the next round. At the beginning of the game, a hunting dog walks along the screen sniffing the ground, then he jumps into the grass to flush the ducks out. The player has only three shots to shoot either one or two ducks. The dog will pop up, revealing the shot ducks he's retrieved. When he pops back down, the ducks will be flushed out once more. Duck Hunt has three game modes to choose from. Game A requires the player to shoot one duck at a time. Game B requires the player to shoot two ducks at a time, and Game C requires the player to shoot at clay pigeons. The NES Zapper accessory is required to play Duck Hunt.

Duck Hunt was a launch title for the Nintendo Entertainment System (NES) in America in October 1985. The game received fair reviews, noting it was fun but lacked the depth and longevity of some games. It is one of the most common games for the NES, played by possibly every owner of the system. The game was ported to the arcade in the form of *Vs. Duck Hunt* (1985).

King's Quest 1

Date of release: May 1984

Region: USA

Developer: Sierra On-Line

Publisher: Sierra On-Line

Platform: IBM PCjr

Designed by Roberta Williams, King's Quest 1 is a single-player text and graphic adventure game. It is the first official game in the King's Quest series, discounting *Wizard and the Princess* (1980). You play as Sir Grahame and must save the Kingdom of Daventry by collecting three treasure. If Sir Grahame accomplishes this, he becomes king and the game ends.

King's Quest 1 was the first text adventure game to feature animations rather than a static image. This made for a level of immersion previously not experienced in this genre as environments came alive and characters moved and interacted with objects and each other. The game displayed 16-colour graphics. However, the illusion of more colours was possible using dithering. This is a process of chequer-boarding two colours which, when seen from a slight distance, gives the illusion of mixing them to create a new colour. King's Quest 1 was a technical leap in the text-adventure genre and a real showpiece at the time. It was one of IBM's launch titles for its new PCjr. Unfortunately, this platform didn't sell very well. Though Sierra On-Line did have great success with King's Quest 1 on other platforms.

King's Quest 1 was re-released in 1987 with a greatly expanded story. One of the treasures that must be retrieved is a magic mirror which becomes a significant plot device in the other games of the series. Other remakes were *King's Quest 1: Quest for the Crown* (1990) and *King's Quest 1: Quest for the Crown* (AGD Interactive, 2001, unofficial remake). There are eight other King's Quest games, the last episodes being *King's Quest VIII Mask of Eternity* (1998) and *King's Quest* (2015-16).

Bank Panic

Date of release: 1984

Region: Japan

Developer: Sanritsu

Publisher: Sega

Platform: Arcade

Bank Panic is a first-person, single-player, cowboy-themed shooting game. You play as a town sheriff in the Old West. Standing in the centre of a bank, you must shoot any robbers and allow customers to deposit their money. People enter through any of the twelve doors. Only three doors may be viewed at any time on screen. Being shot by a robber or shooting an innocent civilian loses a life. Bombs placed at doors must be shot before they explode. If they explode the player loses a life. More points can be earned by shooting the five hats that a boy is carrying. Shooting a robber when he is about to draw earns more points. Shooting a red-shirted robber when he is about to draw earns one letter in the word 'EXTRA'. Acquire all these letters for an extra life. The level ends when deposits are made through all twelve doors. The player then moves onto the next level.

Bomb Jack

Date of release: 1984

Region: Japan

Developer: Tehkan

Publisher: Tehkan

Platform: Arcade

Designed by Michitaka Tsuruta and Kazotoshi Ueda, Bomb Jack is a single-player platform game. The aim is to collect all the bombs on-screen, thus accumulating points and moving onto the next level. You play as Bomb Jack, a cute cape-wearing superhero who can jump very high and hover for short periods of time. You do not have to collect bombs in any particular order but collecting the ones that have their fuse currently lit earns more points. Enemies float around the screen attempting to hamper your progress. From time to time, different spinning icons appear and move around the screen. For example, the P icon (which appears when the bonus metre is filled) turns all the enemies into coins to be collected. The B icon increases the score multiplier. The E icon gives the player an extra life. The rarely seen S icon gives the player a free game. There are five different screens with five different locales from around the world. For example, the first screen shows the iconic Sphinx and one of the ancient pyramids of Egypt in the background. If all five screens are completed the player starts again on the first screen, only now the platform layout is different, and the difficulty increases.

Bomb Jack became a firm favourite in the arcade and then on the many platforms, it was ported to. Sequels include *Bomb Jack II* (1986), *Mighty Bomb Jack* (1986) and *Bomb Jack Twin* (1993).

Tower of Druaga

Date of release: June 1984

Region: Japan

Developer: Namco

Publisher: Namco

Platform: Arcade

Designed by Massanobu Endo, Tower of Druaga is a single-player, side-scrolling, action, role-playing maze game. The aim is to collect the key within the maze and use it to access the next level, ascend through all 60 floors of the tower, find the stolen blue crystal rod and rescue the Maiden Ki from the demon Druaga. You play as the golden-armoured knight Gilgamesh and must avoid or defeat multiple different kinds of enemies, such as slime, knights, wizards and dragons, with your sword. Gilgamesh may also use his shield to repel projectiles. Hidden treasure and items can be found on each floor: some of these are crucial if the player hopes to finish the game. There is also a timer that runs down on each floor.

Massanobu Endo was greatly inspired by the table-top RPG D&D and *Wizardry* (1981) as well as the mythical texts of *The Epic of Gilgamesh* and *The Tower of Babel.*

Tower of Druaga was incredibly popular in Japan, attracting millions of fans who shared tips and tricks on how to play and beat the game. In the West, the game did not prove to be as appealing. Many cited its clunky gameplay and high level of difficulty. Finding all the hidden items required to complete the game made it almost impossible. However, in

Japan, this seemed to make the game even more alluring. Interestingly, both East and West have had their share of difficult games. Since the turn of the century, though, the majority of difficult games do tend to come from the East. Tower of Druaga is said to be one of the main sources of inspiration for games like *The Legend of Zelda* (1986) and *Dragon Quest* (1986).

Tower of Druaga was ported to a handful of Japanese-made home computers and consoles. It also spawned the huge franchise known as the Babylonian Castle Saga which includes nine video games, Manga, two anime series and soundtrack albums.

Karate Champ & Karate Champ Player vs Player

Date of release: June 1984

Region: Japan

Developer: Technōs Japan

Publisher: Data East

Platform: Arcade

Karate Champ is a single-player, fighting game. The aim of the game is to successfully hit your opponent, earning a point. The first to two points wins the match. However, your opponent is also trying to land a blow, so defence is as important as attack. Each fighter has twenty-four moves he can perform using two joysticks.

Karate Champ Player vs Player, released later in 1984, is essentially the same game but this time it is a two-player version. The players are fighting for the adoration of a girl. The game features twelve unique locations and different bonus rounds.

Karate Champ Player vs Player would go on to establish the two-player fighting genre which gave rise to games such as *International Karate +* (1987), *Street Fighter II* (1991) and *Mortal Kombat* (1992).

CD-ROM

The CD-ROM (Compact Disc Read-Only Memory) was introduced at the Japanese Computer Show in 1984 by Denon and Sony. First conceived by James Russel in 1965 and developed by Denon in 1982, the CD-ROM was able to store large amounts of data that could be read by a drive installed in a computer or games console.

The Manhole (1988) was the first video game to be released on a CD-ROM in 1989. A great many games would be released on CD-ROM throughout the nineties and at the beginning of the twenty-first century.

Boulder Dash

Date of release: 1984

Region: North America

Developer: Peter Liepa and Chris Gray

Publisher: First Star Software

Platform: Atari 8-bit

Boulder Dash is a puzzle game where the player controls a character called Rockford. The aim is to collect all the diamonds and gems and reach the exit before the timer runs out. You must avoid enemies and falling rocks or lose a life.

Boulder Dash became extremely popular and was ported to all the major platforms of the time. It is still being ported to more modern platforms, such as Nintendo 3DS and mobile phones. It was also one of the few games to be ported to the arcade, in 1985, rather than the other way around. Boulder Dash had many sequels, such as *Boulder Dash II* (1985), *Boulder Dash 3* (1986), *Rockford* (1988), *Boulder Dash Part 2* (1990), and *Boulder Dash: Rocks!* (2007).

Daley Thompson's Decathlon

Date of release: 1984

Region: UK

Developer: Ocean Software

Publisher: Ocean Software

Platform: Multiple 8-bit home computers

Daley Thompson's Decathlon is a single-player, athletic sports game, inspired by *Track & Field* (1983). You play as Daley Thompson, a British athlete who won the gold medal in the 1980 and 1984 Olympics' Decathlon. The ten events take place over two days. The events are: 100 metres, long jump, shot put, high jump and 400 metres on Day 1. On Day

2 the player takes part in the 110 metre hurdles, pole vault, discus, javelin and 1500 metres. As in *Track & Field*, players must meet qualifying times or distances to carry on to the next event. Daley Thompson's Decathlon also carried on the tradition of alternatively tapping (or in some people's case, bashing) keys. A joystick could be used, but due to the punishment, it took from moving it vigorously left and right, games such as this became infamous for breaking them.

Daley Thompson's Decathlon was ported to other 8-bit platforms sold in the UK and went onto sell over a million units. Daley Thompson's Decathlon had one sequel with *Daley Thompson's Super Test* (1985). Daley Thompson's Decathlon won Best Arcade-Style Game of the Year at the 1984 Golden Joystick Awards.

1984 Arcade Awards

Electronic Games Magazine hosts the 1984 Arcade Awards.

Pole Position wins Best Coin-op Game of the Year.

Ms Pac-Man for the Atari 2600 wins Best Video Game of the Year.

Lode Runner for the Apple II wins Best Computer Game of the Year.

Skool Daze

Date of release: 1984

Region: UK

Developer: David Reidy and Helen Reidy

Publisher: Microsphere

Platform: ZX Spectrum and Commodore 64

Designed by husband and wife team David and Helen Reidy, together with Keith Warrington, Skool Daze is a single-player, simulation, platform, sandbox game. The player controls a schoolboy called Eric. The aim of Skool Daze is for Eric to steal his report card from the safe in the staffroom. To do this, various tasks must be accomplished around the school. The player must attend classes or risk getting caught. If caught Eric is given lines. If he receives 10,000 lines or more, he is expelled and the game ends. As well as many of the numerous pupils going about their business, three other characters feature prominently in the game: Angelface (the bully), Einstein (the swot), and Boy Wander (the tearaway). Each behaves in ways that fulfil their stereotype.

These pupils can also be renamed at the start of the game. Four teachers also feature Mr Wacker (the headmaster), Mr Rockitt (the science teacher), Mr Withit (the geography teacher), and old Mr Creak (the history teacher).

Even though the player has specific tasks to perform within the game, many players found they had more fun throwing the rule book out of the window, skipping classes, punching other pupils and teachers, and generally causing chaos. This is why Skool Daze is recognised by some as being a pioneer of the sandbox genre. It is also considered by some to be one of the ZX Spectrum's best games. Skool Daze had one sequel, *Back to Skool* (1985), which offered a larger game world and more features.

I, Robot

Date of release: June 1984

Region: USA

Developer: Dave Theurer

Publisher: Atari

Platform: Arcade

Designed by Dave Theurer (*Missile Command* (1980) and *Tempest* (1981)), I, Robot is a science fiction, third-person, multi-directional, 3D shooter. You play as robot1984 fighting against 'Big Brother'. The aim of the game is to move along 3D platforms, turning them from red to blue in a similar game mechanic to *Q*bert* (1982). This in turn allows the player to shoot a laser at the enemy's shield and ultimately the eye, destroying it. You then move onto the next level. There are 126 levels. Some levels are platform levels, while others have the robot flying through space and shooting at enemies. I, Robot also had an alternative mode called Doodle City where the player could freely draw with 3D objects on the screen.

Despite its technical achievement, I, Robot was poorly received. Only 750-1000 cabinets were ever produced, making it extremely rare and valuable today. I, Robot was one of the first arcade games to feature 3D polygonal graphics with flat-shading, as opposed to games that used wireframe to depict 3D graphics, such as *Battlezone* (1980) and *Star Wars* (1983).

Tetris

Date of release: June 1984

Region: USSR

Developer: Alexey Pajitnov

Platform: Electronika 60

Designed by Alexey Pajitnov, Tetris is a single-player or multiplayer puzzle game. The name comes from a combination of the word 'tetra', the Greek numerical prefix for the number four, and tennis. The aim of Tetris is to place the current puzzle piece, falling down into, what is sometimes referred to as the 'well', as best you can to ultimately create one or several solid horizontal lines without any gaps. At such point, the line/s are removed from the well. Removing four lines at once is called 'Tetris'. The more lines a player can clear with a single puzzle piece, the more points are awarded. A piece can be rotated or forcibly moved down rather than letting it fall naturally. The game is over when the current falling puzzle piece cannot fall because the well is full.

There are seven different kinds of puzzle pieces in Tetris. Pajitnov's first version of the game used only a monochrome text-based display and so the graphics were represented by letter characters. In 1986 he developed a full-colour graphical version of the game for the IBM PC and in no time it had been copied and spread throughout the Soviet Union. In 1987 Tetris was finally released in Europe and America for various 8-bit and 16-bit home computers and the home consoles. Tetris was marketed with a strong emphasis on its place of origin. The Soviet Union was a mysterious place and the idea of a video game being developed there was a novel one. Soviet imagery featured heavily on the packaging and in the game. Tetris was a hit. Yet this had all happened years before the Soviet Government agreed to license the game. Henk Rogers (developer of *The Black Onyx* 1984) made a deal for the rights to publish the game for Japanese consoles. Tetris became one of the Nintendo Famicom's most successful games, selling over two million units. The game would go on to sell around eight million units worldwide on the NES. Yet even more significant was the deal Rogers brokered directly with the Russians for the handheld rights. This led to Nintendo bundling Tetris with the Game Boy in 1989. This version of Tetris went on to sell thirty-five million units, making the game a true phenomenon. It also had what became one of the most identifiable pieces of music (a Russian folk tune called 'Korobeiniki') in video game history, becoming synonymous with the game. People of all ages and from all walks of life were playing Tetris, yet Pajitnov himself had received little to no money for his creation. The game belonged to the Russian people. However, this changed in 1996 when the rights were transferred from the Russian State to Pajitnov. He founded The Tetris Company to claim copyright registrations for the game in all formats. Any version or clone of Tetris now had to have a license agreement with The Tetris Company.

Almost every video gaming platform in history has its version or versions of Tetris. Over the years, many new features have found their way into the original game's fundamental mechanics, such as varying the size of the well, player vs player, sprint (first to complete 40 lines), and marathon (games lasting several hours). Other changes are purely aesthetical, such as animated backgrounds, sound and music. Psychologists have said that Tetris strikes the perfect balance between challenge and reward, putting players in a state of what is termed 'flow' (a state that many video games can induce) where the player is so focused and absorbed that the world around seems to melt away. It has also been proved that playing Tetris can increase cognitive function. However, it has also been noted for its addictive nature. Many critics and consumers cite Tetris as a perfect video game and one of the greatest ever made. To date, Tetris is estimated to have sold over 500 million units, making it one of the best-selling video games of all time. There are too many variants of the game to mention here. However, some milestones in the game's history would be *Tetris* (IBM PC (1986)), *Tetris* (Famicom (1988)), *Tetris* (Game Boy (1989)), *Tetris Plus* (Gameboy, PS1, Saturn (1996)), *Tetris DS* (Nintendo DS (2006)), *Tetris Effect* (Playstation 4, PC (2018)) and *Tetris 99* (Switch (2019)).

Hyper Sports

Date of release: 1984

Region: Worldwide

Developer: Konami

Publisher: Konami

Platform: Arcade

Hyper Sports is a single-player or multiplayer sports game and is the sequel to the successful *Track & Field* (1983). The aim is to qualify for each event and successfully move onto the next one. If the qualifying time or value isn't achieved, the player loses a life. As with its predecessor, Hyper Sports features two buttons for movement and an action button. The events featured in Hyper Sports are swimming, skeet shooting, vault, archery, triple jump, weightlifting and pole vault – a real juxtaposition of events. The fact that each event was very different from the last added to the game's appeal.

Hyper Sports was popular in the arcade, but possibly even more popular on the home computers it was soon ported to.

Impossible Mission

Date of release: 1984

Region: USA

Developer: Epyx

Publisher: Epyx

Platform: Commodore 64

Designed by Dennis Caswell, Impossible Mission is a single-player platform game. You play as a secret agent who has gained access to the lair of the evil genius, Professor Elvin Atombender. The aim is to move from screen to screen, searching every object or piece of furniture in an attempt to uncover the password puzzle pieces to gain access to the control room. The game begins with what would become the well-known speech-synthesised voice of the professor saying, "Another visitor. Stay a while. Stay forever!" The player must avoid enemy robots by either moving to different platforms or performing a somersault over them. However, you choose to do it, it's best to keep moving and searching the objects: each has a bar that decreases while you search. The player can also access computer terminals to freeze robots (temporarily) and reset moving platforms. You are given a time limit of six hours to collect all 36 password pieces. Ten minutes are removed every time you die. The game world is procedurally generated and so the layout and the locations of the password pieces are different every time. If the player can collect all the pieces and solve the password puzzle at the end, they gain access to the control room. The game cuts to the professor turning around as he says "No, no, no!" A female voice then says, "Congratulations. Mission Accomplished." The game ends displaying your statistics.

Impossible Mission is considered one of the best games for the Commodore 64. It was ported to most 8-bit machines of the time as well as the Sega Master System and NES. There are two Impossible Mission sequels: *Impossible Mission II* (1988) and *Impossible Mission 2025* (1994).

Jet Set Willy

Date of release: 1984

Region: UK

Developer: Software Projects

Publisher: Software Projects

Platform: ZX Spectrum

Designed by Matthew Smith, Jet Set Willy is a single-player platform game and the sequel to the popular *Manic Miner* (1983). Again, you play as Miner Willy, who is now filthy rich and wants to go to bed after a debauched party. However, his housekeeper will not let him until he tidies up all the objects strewn around the house. As with Manic Miner, Willy must avoid touching enemies or falling too far, otherwise, he will lose a life. The elongated foot of the maid will descend upon him if all lives are lost. There are 60 screens to explore which are all connected rather than being self-contained screen/levels to complete. The original mix of the weird and elements of humour are still here, with strange creatures and everyday inanimate objects moving about the screen in pre-determined patterns as if possessed. Each room has a unique name, and if Manic Miner was thought to be a hard platformer, Jet Set Willy ventured into new realms of difficulty that only the most dedicated gamer could hope to overcome. However, there was a problem. The first release of the game was impossible to complete due to a bug initiated once entering the 'attic room'. This was rectified later on. The game finishes when Willy returns to bed after collecting all the objects in the mansion, at which point the game goes to a cut-scene of Willy running to be sick in the toilet. The music played on the title screen is Beethoven's 'Moonlight Sonata', and during gameplay, there is an 8-bit rendition of Sheldon Harnick's 'If I were a Rich Man'.

Jet Set Willy was considered one of the most successful computer games of the 1980s and was ported to almost all the major 8-bit machines. Both Manic Miner and Jet Set Willy inspired a whole generation of platform games.

Karateka

Date of release: 1984

Region: USA

Developer: Jordan Mechner

Publisher: Broderbund

Platform: Apple II

Karateka is a single-player, karate-themed fighting game. The aim is to fight your way past several guards until you reach the master of the fortress Akuma, whom you must defeat to save Princess Mariko who is being held captive. The game begins with a cut-scene of the Princess being sent to a cell by Akuma. You must use a series of punches and kicks to defeat each enemy you encounter. Health bars for you and your current opponent are marked at the bottom of the screen. Health decreases with each blow landed and slowly recovers over time. From time to time the game cuts to the Princess in her cell. Also, Akuma's hawk will fly onto the screen and attack the player. When Akuma is finally defeated, the player enters Princess Mariko's cell and they leave the fortress together.

However, if you approach the Princess in a fighting stance, she will kick you once, knocking you unconscious and the game will end: a nice twist in the tail.

The fighting in Karateka may be a bit slow for some, yet there is something appealing about being tactical when wearing down an opponent. The minimalistic art style is beautiful and the rotoscoping animation of the characters is very well done, considering the limitations of the then seven-year-old Apple II technology. Jordan Mechner, a Yale student at the time, was influenced by Japanese woodblock print art, animation and silent movies.

Karateka is one of the first beat' em up video games – a game where there is a narrative and the protagonist must move through the level fighting different enemies. Critics praised Karateka's graphics and animation but were less impressed with the controls and some mechanics. Karateka was ported to most 8-bit home computers, as well as the Famicom. A remake was released in 2012, online-only, for the PS3, Xbox 360 and Wii U.

The Lords of Midnight

Date of release: 1984

Region: UK

Developer: Mike Singleton

Publisher: Beyond Software

Platform: ZX Spectrum

The Lords of Midnight is a single-player, role-playing, strategy game. The aim is to defeat the evil witch king, Doomdark, who has locked the land of Midnight in eternal winter. To do this you must either destroy the source of his power, which is the Ice Crown or raise an army strong enough to destroy Doomdark's forces. The player starts with four characters and can recruit a further twenty-eight. You move through the land of Midnight as seen from a first-person perspective. Each move redraws the screen, which changes the player's location significantly as buildings and the landscape alter drastically. The effect of pre-scaled images in the game, which could be viewed from any eight points of the compass and varying distances, was called 'landscaping' by Singleton. At the time this was enough for players to feel completely immersed in this world. Many enthusiastically felt compelled to draw maps containing the mountains, forests and landmarks of Midnight.

The game was an enormous success and was quickly ported to most of the other home computer platforms. It was also, much later, ported to mobile devices in 2012 and 2013. The Lords of Midnight had two sequels: *Doomdark's Revenge* (1985) and *Lords of Midnight: The Citadel* (1995). The Lords of Midnight won Best Strategy Game at 1984 Golden Joystick Awards. It is often cited as one of the most significant RPGs of the 1980s.

Spy vs. Spy

Date of release: 1984

Region: USA

Developer: Michael Riedel

Publisher: Beyond Software

Platform: Commodore 64

Spy vs. Spy is a single-player or multiplayer, split-screen, action strategy game, based on the *Mad Magazine* cartoon strip of the same name. The aim of the Spy vs. Spy is to find all the items hidden in the interconnected rooms and exit the building before the other player, or before the timer runs out. Players can lay a limited number of traps to try and kill their opponent. When all the items have been collected, the player can then exit the building and head to the airport, thus completing the level. This then begins the next level. Later levels have larger buildings, meaning more rooms to search and thus a higher difficulty level.

Spy vs. Spy was highly praised for its innovative game mechanics. It was released on the Atari 8-bit at the same time as the C64 version and was soon ported to other 8-bit and 16-bit home computers of the decade, as well as some home and handheld consoles.

Summer Games

Date of release: 1984

Region: USA

Developer: Epyx

Publisher: U.S. Gold

Platform: Commodore 64

Summer Games is a single-player or multiplayer sports game. The aim of Summer Games is to beat your opponents by gaining points at each event: a score of 5 for gold, 3 for silver and 1 for bronze. The game can accommodate up to eight players by each taking turns at the computer. This is sometimes referred to as 'hot seat' or 'hot seat multiplayer mode'. The game begins with a cut-scene of an athlete lighting the Olympic torch, played to a rendition of John Williams' 'Olympic Fanfare and Theme'. The player then chooses their name and country. The events in which the player/s partakes are pole vault, diving, sprinting, gymnastics (vault), swimming, skeet shooting and rowing.

Summer Games was rather successful, selling over 250,000 units. Summer Games was Epyx' first sports game in a very popular series. The others were *Summer Games II* (1985) (which had the novel feature of being played in conjunction with the original, carrying players; scores over from SG to SGII), *Winter Games* (1985), *World Games* (1986), *California Games* (1987) and *California Games II* (1990).

The Ancient Art of War

Date of release: 1984

Region: USA

Developer: Dave Murry and Barry Murry of Evryware Inc

Publisher: Broderbund

Platform: Apple II and MS-DOS

The Ancient Art of War is a single-player, real-time strategy (RTS) game. The title comes from the classical strategy text of the same name written by Chinese General Sun Tzu around the 5th century BC. The aim of The Ancient Art of War is to defeat your opponents or fulfil the criteria of the chosen campaign. There are eleven campaigns to choose from. The player can also change certain parameters or 'rules' of the game, such as food supply, supply lines, training and condition of your men, and terrain settings. The player can choose one of eight opponents, some real, others mythical. Some examples are Athena, Alexander the Great, Crazy Ivan and Sun Tzu. Each has a portrait, and description including strengths and weaknesses. Some are easy and others are more difficult. Sun Tzu is the most difficult. The player is presented with a map showing rivers, forests, mountains, settlements and forts. You can create squads of up to 14 units, consisting of archers, barbarians, knights and spies. Each type of unit is strong against certain units, but weak against others. For example, archers are strong against knights, barbarians are strong against archers, and knights are strong against barbarians. Spies aren't worth using in direct confrontation, but they can see twice as far as the other three and move much quicker. Elevation, food supply and condition of your squad also plays a part in whether you win or lose a battle. The player can also issue commands and create specific formations which can decide the outcome of an engagement. Battles can be fought on bridges, in forests, outside or inside forts. You may need to attack a fort or defend one. Again, using the right kind of units is vital. Barbarians are useless at defending when positioned on the fort wall. However, archers can easily pick off an ill-conceived attack from the enemy.

The Ancient Art of War allowed players to create their own maps and campaigns, making it possible to re-create well-known historical battles. This was a huge draw for some people. The game was highly praised and described as possibly the best strategy game ever made at the time of its release. The Ancient Art of War is one of the first RTS games and a milestone in the genre. The Ancient Art of War was ported to a handful of home computers. The game went onto spawn two sequels, *The Ancient Art of War at Sea* (1987) and *The Ancient Art of War in the Skies* (1993).

Vectrex 3D Imager

The Vectrex 3D Imager was released in the USA in 1984 by General Consumer Electronics.

Developed by John Ross, the Vectrex 3D Imager was a peripheral for the Vetrex home console that created a sense of depth when strapped on the head. A spinning disc in the headset gave the illusion of distance when playing certain games.

The device is not really a precursor to virtual reality (VR). The image does not change when the user moves their head to simulate a virtual world: it merely conveys a sense of primitive three-dimensions to the gaming experience. However, it is interesting to note that the aesthetic design of the Vectrex 3D Imager is precisely the same as current VR headsets.

The Hitchhiker's Guide to the Galaxy

Date of release: September 1984

Region: USA

Developer: Douglas Adams (author of *The Hitchhiker's Guide to the Galaxy*) and Steve Meretzky

Publisher: Infocom

Platform: multiple 8-bit home computers

The Hitchhiker's Guide to the Galaxy is a single-player, sci-fi, text-based adventure game based on the popular novel and radio serial of the same name. You play as Arthur Dent who escapes the Earth with his alien friend Ford Prefect moments before it is destroyed by a Vogon constructor fleet. The player navigates his way through the plot and solves puzzles. Later, the game's protagonists set out to discover the secrets of the mythical planet of Magrathea. The game ends when you land on the planet. However, this is only part of the story. A second game was meant to continue the story, but unfortunately, it was never made.

The game shipped with several feelies including a pin-on button, an order for the destruction of Arthur Dent's house, a Vogon order for the destruction of Earth, Persil-sensitive sunglasses, and other silly paraphernalia. The Hitchhiker's Guide to the Galaxy was known for its difficult puzzles, which some players found a hindrance, yet it was highly praised for its writing style and humour. The Hitchhiker's Guide to the Galaxy sold over 400,000 units after it was ported to most home computers of the time. Even though the sequel never materialised, two remakes were made: *The Hitchhiker's Guide to the Galaxy 20th Anniversary* (2004) and *The Hitchhiker's Guide to the Galaxy 30th Anniversary* (2014). Both added graphics to the text-only original.

Dragon Slayer

Date of release: September 1984

Region: Japan

Developer: Nihon Falcom

Publisher: Nihon Falcom

Platform: NEC PC 8801

Designed by Yoshio Kiya, Dragon Slayer is a single-player, fantasy, action RPG and the first in the Dragon Slayer series. The aim of the game is to slay several dragons. The player needs to discover crystals and take them to a house within the dungeon, and in doing so strengthen your character. You must do this until you can defeat a dragon. Dragon Slayer has such features as items, puzzles, chests and gold coins. It is the first RPG to feature hack and slash, real-time combat a feature, which would be greatly popularised two years later with *The Legend of Zelda* (1986)

Dragon Slayer was ported to several Japanese home computers as well as the Gameboy and Sega Saturn. Some of the most notable games in the Dragon Slayer series are *Dragon Slayer II: Xanadu* (1985), *Dragon Slayer IV: Sorcerian* (1987), *Dragon Slayer: The Legend of Heroes* (1989), *Lord Monarch* (1991) and *The Legend of Xanadu II* (1995).

Elite

Date of release: September 1984

Region: UK

Developer: David Braben and Ian Bell

Publisher: Acornsoft

Platform: BBC Micro

Elite is a first-person, space-trading and combat simulation game. The aim is to achieve the combat level of 'Elite', though the player can continue and play the game indefinitely. In this respect, Elite is one of the first open-world, sandbox video games. Players take control of a Cobra Mark III spacecraft and travel through hyperspace to different star systems trading goods, carrying out missions and taking down pirates. Each of the thousands of stars within the eight galaxies has a unique planet and orbiting space station to dock with. Here you can buy numerous items, including food, textiles, liquor and computers, to name but a few, and also more nefarious things such as narcotics and slaves. Elite was one of the first games to offer moral choice. Would you stay within the law? Or risk it and possibly make a lot more money trading illegal goods, or even turn to pirating, attacking other craft and stealing their cargo? It was a tempting choice, especially when the game offered you so many appealing yet expensive upgrades for your spaceship, like a larger cargo bay, a docking computer, fuel scoops, military lasers or an energy bomb. The gameplay can be very slow as you navigate your way to the space station and finally dock. Other times the tempo can step up, such as when an alien spacecraft might pull you out of hyperspace and suddenly you are in a dogfight to the death. Being caught between star systems without enough fuel can lead to being stranded. However, there is the ability to save your game.

Elite was one of the first 3D procedurally-generated game worlds. It was also the first home computer game to use 3D wireframe with hidden line removal. At the time of its release most games, especially in the space genre, were twitch, bullet hell games. Yet Elite offered so much more, and while it took some time for people to grasp just what it was all about, its appeal was undeniable. Players sunk hours into this sandbox universe amassing wealth and trying to be the best they could be. Critics could not help but admire its technical achievement, for the game world was so vast and the mechanics so intricate that some could not fathom how such a game could have come into existence; a credit to both Braben and Bell.

Acornsoft spent a lot of money marketing the game and the physical game itself was rather special. The box was bigger and the art highly polished. Included with the cassette or disk were a novella by Robert Holdstock, a 64-page *Space Trader's Flight Training Manual*, a reference card and a poster.

Elite was ported to pretty much every computer platform of the time. Each port had subsequent additions or variations. Official sequels to Elite were *Frontier: Elite II* (1993), *Frontier: First Encounters* (1995) and *Elite Dangerous* (2014). Elite has been cited as the game which established the open-world space-trading and combat genre. It provided the foundation from which all similar games have drawn inspiration: games such as *Wing Commander* (1990), *The X Series* (1999-2018), *Freelancer* (2003), *Eve Online* (2003), *Star Citizen* (2015), *No Man's Sky* (2016) and many others. Elite won Best Original Game at the 1984 Golden Joystick Awards. It also won multiple awards from the current games magazines of the time.

Deus Ex Machina

Date of release: October 1984

Region: UK

Developer: Automata

Publisher: Automata

Platform: ZX Spectrum.

Designed by Mel Croucher, Deus Ex Machina is a single-player action game, comprised of a series of simple yet strange mini-games. It was the first (and few) video games to be played with an accompanying soundtrack and narration on a tape recorder that was synchronised with the game. The game's concept is based on what is referred to as the 'Seven Ages of Man' from Shakespeare's *As You Like It*. The player nurtures a 'defect' in the machine which grows from conception, through the seven ages, and finally to death.

The game, lasting less than an hour, feels more like a multimedia experience than a typical video game. It was highly praised by some critics for its departure from traditional gaming conventions and has gained a cult following for much the same reason. There was nothing quite like it around at the time. The mix of narration, art and 1980s synthesised music is reminiscent of Jeff Wayne's Musical Version of *The War of the Worlds* (1978).

The game was ported to the C64 and MSX. A remake of the game called *Deus Ex Machina 2* was released in 2010.

Pac-Land

Date of release: October 1984

Region: Japan

Developer: Namco

Publisher: Namco

Platform: Arcade

Pac-Land is a single-player, side-scrolling platformer. The aim is to deliver the fairy to Fairyland and return home to Ms. Pac-Man and Baby Pac-Man. Ghosts and obstacles hinder Pac-Man's progress. As with other Pac-Man games, if Pac-Man eats a power pellet then he can eat the ghosts who are momentarily vulnerable. However, unlike previous games, Pac-Land is a platformer. Pac-Man now runs and jumps. There is also a timer at the bottom of the screen. Once the timer runs out the ghosts' movement increases. Any time left at the end of a level is converted into points. Fruit also appears and can be eaten for further points.

Pac-Land was never popular enough to warrant any sequels, but it adds an interesting change of pace to the Pac-Man series. Pac-Land was ported to most home computer and console platforms of the time.

Bounty Bob Strikes Back!

Date of release: 1984

Region: USA

Developer: Big Five Software

Publisher: Big Five Software

Platform: Atari 8-bit

Designed by Bill Hogue, Bounty Bob Strikes Back! is the single-player platform sequel to *Miner 2049er* (1982). Bounty Bob Strikes Back! is almost the same as its predecessor in that Bob must cover all the platforms on the screen before the timer runs out. However, there are a few differences. The platforms have a three-dimensional look and there are twenty-five mines to complete. Recurring game mechanics were elevators, matter transporters, slides, moving platforms, TNT and cannons, while new features introduced travel by suction tubes, a grain elevator, and pulverisers.

Bounty Bob Strikes Back! was another popular video game for the Atari 8-bit and was soon ported to most of the popular platforms of the time.

Excitebike

Date of release: November 1984

Region: Japan

Developer: Nintendo R&D1

Publisher: Nintendo

Platform: Famicom

Designed by Shigeru Miyamoto, Excitebike is a single or multiplayer, side-scrolling, motocross racing game. The aim is to qualify for each race by finishing in any of the first three places. The player begins the game by choosing any one of five tracks. Position and pitch of the bike are controlled by the d-pad, and with a bit of practice, the bike can perform somersaults. Acceleration must be used carefully so as not to overheat the engine, the temperature of which is shown at the bottom of the screen. The player must avoid obstacles and other players, as well as taking ramps at the correct speed.

Excitebike has a design mode where players can create their own tracks. In the Japanese version with the Famicom Data Recorder, tracks could be saved and loaded from a cassette. The design mode was certainly a great feature and a big draw for the game; it's a great shame that players in the West couldn't save their creations. Despite this, Excitebike was well-received in both the East and the West where it was released in 1985.

Excitebike has been ported to only a handful of other platforms, including the arcade in the same year. There are several games in the Excite series including *Excitebike 64* (2000), *Excite Truck* (2006), *Excitebots: Trick Racing* (2009), and *Excitebike: World Rally* (2009).

Knight Lore

Date of release: November 1984

Region: UK

Developer: Ultimate Play the Game

Publisher: Ultimate Play the Game

Platform: multiple 8-bit home computers

Designed by the Stamper Brothers, Knight Lore is a single-player, isometric action-adventure platformer and is the third game in the Sabreman series. You play as Sabreman and have been bitten by a Sabre Wulf in the previous game Sabre Wulf (1984). You must search through the 128 rooms and find 14 items that must be added to a cauldron in sequential order. The rooms contain dangerous enemies and hazards. Objects such as stone blocks and furniture can be moved about to reach the items you require. The game has a night and day cycle and you have forty days to complete your task. At night, Sabreman transforms into a werewolf. During this time the player can jump higher. However, certain enemies will only attack you as a werewolf. At sunrise, the player turns back into Sabreman.

The Stamper Brothers developed a revolutionary technique of overlaying sprites by creating a mask. They copyrighted this as the filmnation engine. Not wanting other developers to copy this technique before release (it was inevitable that others would), they were rather secretive about Knight Lore, which is regarded as something of a breakthrough in video game graphics. There was nothing new about isometric games: however, this was a virtual three-dimensional world in which the player could walk through, in front of and behind other objects seamlessly.

Knight Lore released to critical and consumer praise and sold well over a million copies (any game selling over a million units in the eighties was considered a hit) across the different platforms it was ported over to. The Stamper Brothers went onto release other games using their revolutionary filmnation engine, such as *Alien 8* (1985), *Nightshade* (1985), *Gunfight* (1986) and *Pentagram* (1986). Knight Lore has inspired so many games since its release, such as *Batman* (1986), *Head over Heals* (1987), *Cadaver* (1990), *Syndicate* (1993), *UFO: Enemy Unknown* (1994) and *Baldur's Gate* (1998). Even the most modern isometric games owe their roots to Knight Lore. Knight Lore won Game of the Year in the 1985 Golden Joystick Awards.

1942

Date of release: December 1984

Region: Worldwide

Developer: Digital Eclipse

Publisher: Capcom

Platform: Arcade

Designed by Yoshiki Okamoto, 1942 is a single-player, vertical-scrolling, World War II shooter. The aim of the game is to destroy the enemy planes and score as many points as possible. The player begins and ends each level by taking off from and landing on an aircraft carrier in their American Lockheed P-39 Lightning plane. Destroying specific enemy squadrons produces a 'Pow', which, if collected, gives the player additional firepower. The maximum firepower adds two additional planes to fly and shoot by your side. The player can perform a loop or vertical roll to avoid the hail of bullets on screen. However, this can only be done a limited number of times. At the end of each stage, the player must destroy a large boss plane to continue.

1942 was very popular in Japan and the West. It was one of Capcom's biggest hits. It began a whole series of similar games which include *1943: The Battle for Midway* (1987), *1941: Counter Attack* (1990), *19XX: The War Against Destiny* (1996) and *1944: The Loop Master* (2000).

Marble Madness

Date of release: December 1984

Region: USA

Developer: Atari Games

Publisher: Atari Games

Platform: Arcade

Designed by Mark Cerny, Marble Madness is a single-player, isometric, racing platform game. The aim is to guide a marble down through a course while avoiding obstacles and enemies in order to reach the finish line before the time expires. Any time left at the end of the run is added onto the next level. On a typical course, a player must guide the marble along the pathway being careful not to fall off the edge. Other mechanics involve pipes, a catapult and objects which protrude from the course that can help or hinder your progress. There are six courses in total, which does not sound like many, but the courses are rather challenging. The player uses a trackball to control the direction of the marble.

Marble Madness was the first arcade game to be written in the C programming language.

Marble Madness was praised by critics and consumers alike for its unique look and style as well as its gameplay, mechanics and sound. Marble Madness has many clones where you control a marble, or something similar, along a course. Some of the most notable are *Spindizzy* (1986), *The Super Monkey Ball Series* (2001-2019) and *Mercury Meltdown* (2006).

1984 Golden Joystick Awards

The 1984 Golden Joystick Awards were hosted in London.

Daley Thompson's Decathlon (1984) wins Best Arcade-Style Game of the year.

Elite (1984) wins Best Original Game

Lode Runner (1983) wins Best Computer Game of the year.

Knight Lore (1984) wins Best Game of the year.

Kung-Fu Master

Date of release: December 1984

Region: Japan

Developer: Irem

Publisher: Irem

Platform: Arcade

Designed by Takashi Nishiyama, Kung-Fu Master (originally released as Spartan X) is a single-player, side-scrolling beat 'em up. You control Thomas and must make your way through all five floors of the Devil's Temple, ultimately defeating the crime chief Mr X and saving your girlfriend, Silvia. Each level has hordes of enemies to punch and kick your way past. If mistimed then the player gets caught in a grapple and their health drops. To get out of the grapple you must wiggle the joystick left and right as if wriggling to break free. The player must also contend with falling objects and deadly creatures. The player has a limited amount of health, which drops every time he is hit or grappled. At the end of each floor, the player must defeat a boss before climbing up to the next level. When Mr X is defeated and you are reunited with your loved one, the game begins again only this time the difficulty is increased.

Kung-Fu Master is considered the first true beat 'em up because its pace and numerous enemies are akin to that of the traditional shoot 'em up. The original arcade version of the game was a success. Perhaps more significant was the success of the ported versions of the game to all the major home computers and consoles. Indeed, the NES version under the title *Kung Fu* went on to sell over 3.5 million units.

1984 Notable Omissions

Alien. Amstrad CPC 464. Attack of the Mutant Camels. Avalon. Balloon Fight. Booty. Circus Charlie. Cloak & Dagger. Cobra Command. Core War. Cutthroats. Demolition Derby. Dimension X. Donkey Kong 3. Do! Run Run. Dragon Buster. Drug Wars. Eureka! F-15 Strike Eagle. Flicky. Gaplus. Gilligan's Gold. Girl's Garden. Hareraiser. Hover Attack. Hydilde. Ice Climber. Jake Tramiel buys Atari. Kung-Fu Heroes. Mandragore. Mr Do's Wild Ride. Ocean is founded. Peter Pepper's Ice Cream Factory. Pitfall 2: The Lost Caverns. Pirate Ship Higemaru. Plasma Line. Psygnosis is founded. Raid on Bungeling Bay. Raid over Moscow. Rescue on Fractalus. Roland in Time. Roland on the Ropes. Seastalker. Seven Cities of Gold. Skyfox. Sorcerer. Space Ace. Star Force/MegaForce. Star Trek: Strategic Operations Simulator. Star Wars: Return of the Jedi. Super Bagman. Super Punch Out!! Super Xevious. Thayer's Quest. The Nintendo Vs Arcade video games. The Three Stooges. Tornado Low-Level. Underwurlde.

1985

Yie Ar Kung-Fu

Date of release: January 1985

Region: Japan

Developer: Konami

Publisher: Konami

Platform: Arcade

Yie Ar Kung-Fu is a single-player fighting game. You play as Oolong and can perform sixteen different moves. Health bars appear at the top of the screen for you and your opponent. Several blows must be landed for either fighter to be defeated. The player has three lives. One of the main features of the game was the variety of opponents the player faced. Different tactics were needed to defeat each one. The eleven opponents in order were, Buchu: big and strong, yet slow. Star: throws shuriken (throwing stars). Nuncha: uses nunchaku (two sticks connected at one end by a chain or rope). Pole: uses a pole. Feedle: An enemy who can replicate himself. Chain: uses a chain with a claw on the end. Club: a large man armed with a spiked club and a shield. Fan: throws steel fans. Sword: uses a sword. Tonfun: uses tonfa (sticks with a perpendicular handle). Blues: Blues is the same character as Ooling, but without his top off. If the player can defeat all eleven opponents, he then becomes the 'Grand Master'. The player can then begin again, only this time the opponents are more difficult to defeat.

The game was soon ported to home computers and consoles of the time. However, the number of opponents varies between platforms. The game spawned two sequels, *Yie Ar Kung-Fu II* (1986) and *Martial Champion* (1993). Yie Ar Kung-Fu went on to become the second best-selling game in the UK in 1986 and is often cited as one of the games to popularize the fighting genre.

1985 Arcade Awards

Electronic Games Magazine hosts the 1985 Arcade Awards.

Star Wars wins Best Coin-op Game of the Year.

Space Shuttle for the Atari 2600 wins Best Video game of the Year.

Ultima III: Exodus wins Best Computer Game of the Year.

Ninja Princess/Sega Ninja/The Ninja

Date of release: March 1985

Region: Japan

Developer: Sega

Publisher: Sega

Platform: Arcade

Ninja Princess is a single-player, vertical-scrolling, run and gun game. Set in Japan in 1630 during the Edo period, the aim of the game is to defeat the evil tyrant Gyokuro and his numerous lackeys. You play as the Princess Kurumi and run towards the top of the screen dispatching a variety of enemies with your throwing knives or shuriken.

Ninja Princess is cited as being one of the first video game to feature a female protagonist. Most video game protagonists of the day were either male or a non-gendered character such as a robot. The game was well-received in Japan and the west. It was ported to the Sega SG-1000 and later to the Sega Master System where the player's character was changed to a male ninja.

Commando

Date of release: April/May 1985

Region: USA/Japan

Developer: Capcom

Publisher: Capcom

Platform: Arcade

Designed by Tokuro Fujiwara, Commando is a single-player, vertical-scrolling, run and gun game. The player controls an army commando called Super Joe. The ultimate aim of the game is to reach the enemy HQ and destroy it. Joe must work his way through a multitude of enemy soldiers to reach his goal. The player has a machine gun with infinite ammunition and a limited number of grenades that can kill multiple enemies or destroy obstructions. More grenades can be picked up during gameplay. At the end of each stage, the player must face and defeat a wave of enemies who attack all at once in order to continue to the next level. When the enemy headquarters are reached and destroyed, a helicopter picks up Joe and the player is congratulated. The game begins again at the first stage, only this time the difficulty is increased.

Commando was fairly well-received by critics and consumers. Commando won Best Arcade-Style Game of the Year at the 1985 Golden Joystick Awards. The game was released on most 8-bit and 16-bit consoles and home computers of the time. Commando saw several sequels including *Mercs* (1989) and *Wolf of the Battlefield: Commando 3* (2008). In the West, Super Joe was marketed as being the main character in *Bionic Commando* (1987), making it an unofficial sequel to Commando.

Little Computer People

Date of release: 1985

Region: USA

Developer: Activision

Publisher: Activision

Platform: Commodore 64

Designed by David Crane and Rich Gold, Little Computer People is a single-player, life simulation game. The premise is that actual little people are living in your computer. The game starts with the player entering their name, the date and the time. This will then 'bring out' the little computer person, although this does take some time. The entire game takes place in a cutaway illustration of a three-storey house. The Little Computer Person (LCP) is randomly generated and is therefore unique. They will explore the house, watch TV or read, and the player can have somewhat limited interaction with them.

Some have suggested that LCP is not a game at all, only a simulation. It is very slow-paced and not much happens. The game was packaged with a magazine that carried on with the narrative about these little people inside your computer and how it all came about. Accompanying the magazine was an instruction booklet, a deed of ownership for the house and the game itself.

LCP is rather a niche game and it would be almost fifteen years until such concept would be fully realised by Will Wright, who cited LCP for one of several inspirations for his hit game, *The Sims* (2000). Little Computer People was awarded Best Original Game of the Year in the 1985 Golden Joystick Awards.

Paperboy

Date of release: April 1985

Region: USA

Developer: Atari Games

Publisher: Atari Games

Platform: Arcade

Designed by John Salwitz, Russel Dawe and Dave Ralston, Paperboy is a single-player, isometric, action game. The aim is to deliver newspapers to subscribers' homes. These are previewed on a map before the paperboy sets off. Subscribers' houses can be identified as brightly coloured houses on-screen, while non-subscribers have drab-coloured houses. Extra points can be scored by damaging non-subscribers property. Numerous obstacles must be avoided on the way. At the end of the street, there is an obstacle course to complete and more points can be earned here. Hitting any obstacle loses a life. The game starts on Monday and finishes on Sunday.

The original arcade version of Paperboy is a stand-up cabinet with bicycle handlebar controls. Paperboy is one of a unique breed of games in that it is neither science-fiction, war nor fantasy themed. Instead, it takes something every day and makes it into a fun, challenging game. Certainly, one of its appeals is its signature theme music and quirky sounds. Paperboy featured a screen resolution of 512 x 384, far larger than most other arcades of the time where a typical screen resolution would have been 320 x 224. Yet it is worth noting that the player had freedom of movement only within the bottom right area of the screen during the delivery stage. The entire screen didn't open for player movement until the obstacle course stages.

Paperboy was ported to just about every home computer and console of the time. It had one sequel, *Paperboy 2* (1991).

Gradius

Date of release: May 1985

Region: Japan

Developer: Konami

Publisher: Konami

Platform: Arcade

Designed by Hiroyaso Machiguchi, Gradius is a single-player, side-scrolling shooter. The player controls the *Vic Viper* spacecraft and must defeat waves of enemies. At the end of each stage, a boss must be destroyed before moving onto the next stage. The final stage boss is a giant brain that is rather easy to destroy when compared to the high difficulty of the rest of the game. Once finished, the game begins again at the first stage.

One of Gradius's most prominent features is its power-up system. Destroying a squadron of enemies drops a power-up that can be picked up. Highlighted at the bottom of the screen is the current power-up which the player can select. Power-ups include speed-up, missile, double and laser. Players can select the power-up or hold off for when something more useful to their environment or playstyle is available. This game mechanic introduces another level of strategy to the game and would be imitated by other shooters.

Gradius was ported to most of the home computers and consoles of the time. Gradius was the spiritual successor to *Scramble* (1981). Due to its popularity, there were many Gradius sequels, most notably *Salamander* (1986), *Gradius II: Gofer's Revenge* (1988), *Gradius Gaiden* (1997) and *Gradius V* (2004). Gradius inspired the mother of all side-scrolling shooters – *R-Type* (1987), a game that would define the genre thereafter.

Atari ST

The Atari ST (also known as The Atari 520ST) Personal Computer was released in North America in June 1985. The Atari ST was a 16-bit home computer that shipped with 512 KB of RAM and supported a colour palette of 512 colours. A 3.5-inch DD floppy disk drive was sold separately. It was one of the first home computers to use a colour GUI (Graphical User Interface) called GEM. The Atari ST sold for $799.99 with a monochrome monitor or $999.99 with a colour monitor.

The ST models flourished in the CAD and desktop publishing industries. The Atari 520ST was followed by the Atari 1040ST (1986), Atari TT (1990) and Atari Falcon (1992). The Atari ST's main competitor was the Amiga 1000, which it managed to undercut in price.

Notable games on the Atari St family were as follows: *Starglider* (1986), *Oids* (1987), *Dungeon Master* (1987), *Carrier Commander* (1988), *Blood Money* (1989), *Xenon 2: Megablast* (1989), *Lemmings* (1991), *Sensible Soccer* (1993), *Cannon Fodder* (1993) and *Civilisation* (1993).

Commodore Amiga 1000

Released worldwide in July 1985, the Amiga 1000 was a 16-bit home computer that shipped with 256-512 KB of RAM and supported a 12-bit colour palette of 4,096 colours and 4 x 8-bit pulse code modulation (PCM) audio channels. It also included a 3.5-inch DD floppy disk drive. The Amiga 1000 sold for $1,295 for the 256 KB model and $1,495 for the 512 KB model. The machine was renowned for its graphical prowess. Many people were stunned by photograph-like digital stills, multi-tasking graphical user interface (Workbench 1) and the famous bouncing ball demo, which was a spinning chequered red and white 3D ball that bounced around the screen casting a shadow. In 1985 this was all incredibly impressive and beyond anything seen before. Later the machine was used extensively in video editing and 3D Graphics.

The Amiga 1000 was the first in the Amiga family, followed by the Amiga 2000 (1987), Amiga 500 (1987), A3000 (1990), A600 (1992), A1200 (1992) and A4000 (1992).

This remarkable machine was built for games, its capabilities surpassing all of its 16-bit contemporaries. Unfortunately, it seemed to take a while for this fact to sink in for the company. Once gaming on the Amiga finally took off it went into the stratosphere and few other platforms could touch it, although this would not happen until the release of the Amiga 2000 and Amiga 500 in 1987.

Tales of the Unknown: Volume I. The Bard's Tale

Date of release: 1985

Region: USA

Developer: Interplay Productions

Publisher: Electronic Arts

Platform: Apple II

Tales of the Unknown: Volume I. The Bard's Tale, usually referred to as just The Bard's

Tale, was Designed by Michael Cranford. The Bard's Tale is a single-player, turn-based, first-person RPG. Long ago the evil wizard, Mangar, froze the lands surrounding the town of Skara Brae. The aim of The Bard's Tale is to explore the dungeons and to acquire several items found in the dungeons, levelling up in order to reach Magnar's Tower and defeat him. The player begins by choosing a party of six warriors from specific classes such as bard, hunter, magician, monk, paladin, rogue and warrior. Each class has the usual skill set. However, the bard, in particular, was rather interesting. He played magical songs that could affect the entire party over a period of time, acting to increase attack speed or adding to all characters' defences against attacks.

The Bard's Tale was renowned for its exceptional 3D graphics and animated characters. Another noteworthy feature was the facility for the player to import characters from the games *Wizardry* (1981) and *Ultima III* (1983), both very similar games to The Bard's Tale. This feature was very rare and quite revolutionary at the time.

The Bard's Tale was ported to most home computers of the time, as well as an NES version. Due to its popularity and healthy sales, The Bard's Tale spawned three sequels: *The Bard's Tale II: The Destiny Knight* (1986), *The Bard's Tale III: Thief of Fate* (1988) and *The Bard's Tale IV: Barrow's Deep* (2018). A game creation system was also sold called *The Bard's Tale Construction Set* (1991), where players could develop their own adventures. The Bard's Tale was one of the best-selling RPG video game of the 1980s, selling over a million units.

The Way of the Exploding Fist

Date of release: June 1985

Region: Worldwide

Developer: Gregg Barnett

Publisher: Melbourne House

Platform: Commodore 64

The Way of the Exploding Fist is a single-player or two-player, karate fighting game. The aim is to defeat your opponent by delivering two blows. Each time an opponent is defeated, the player must defeat another, more difficult opponent. The characters can perform eighteen different movements including high and low punches and kicks, a jumping kick and a roundhouse kick. The player must also contend with a bonus round which involves knocking out a charging bull with a single blow.

The Way of the exploding Fist was a great success and was one of the best-selling games for the ZX Spectrum and Amstrad CPC series. It spawned two sequels: *Fist 2: The Legend Continues* (1986) and *Exploding Fist +* (1988). The Way of the Exploding Fist was awarded Game of the Year in the 1985 Golden Joystick Awards.

Baraduke

Date of release: July 1985

Region: Japan

Developer: Namco

Publisher: Namco

Platform: Arcade

Baraduke is a standard single-player or two-player, scrolling shooter, where the aim is to destroy all the aliens with the ultimate goal of defeating the big boss at the end of the game. The player controls a figure in a biohazard suit, who can fly around with a jet-pac and holds a laser rifle as a weapon. Destroying enemies, the Octy, makes them drop power-up items. The player has a limited amount of shield. However, some of this can be regained through a game of chance played between levels.

Baraduke is significant because it is revealed at the end of the game that the character in the game is female. *Metroid* (1986) famously did the same reveal one year later. The game also has a two-player option where both players work together on screen to banish your enemies and progress through each level.

Baraduke spawned one sequel with *Bakutotsu Kijūtei: Baraduke II* (1998), released only in Japan for the arcade.

Tau Ceti

Date of release: 1985

Region: UK

Developer: CRL Group PLC

Publisher: CRL Group PLC

Platform: ZX Spectrum

Designed by Peter Cooke, Tau Ceti is a single-player, space simulation and first-person shooter game. It is set on the planet Tau Ceti III where a meteor has crashed into it, causing a major malfunction of the colony's systems and turning them rogue. The aim of Tau Ceti is to collect all of the reactor rods scattered amongst the planet's towns and shut down the planet's main reactor. The player controls a ship and must shoot and destroy robotic enemies and find the control rods to complete the mission.

Considered ground-breaking in its day, Tau Ceti is renowned for its 3D graphics that pushed the limits of what was thought possible on the 8-bit home computers.

The game was soon ported to other home computers of the time. An expanded, enhanced version was released for the 128K Spectrum. Tau Ceti spawned one sequel, *Academy* (1986).

Where in the World Is Carmen Sandiego?

Date of release: 1985

Region: USA

Developer: Broderbund

Publisher: Broderbund

Platform: Apple II

Where in the World Is Carmen Sandiego? is a single-player, educational game. The aim is to find and apprehend one of the game's 'thief' characters, one of whom is Carmen Sandiego, who has stolen anything from a valuable painting to (somehow) an entire monument. There are many different thieves and it is your job to travel the world and investigate, gathering clues as to their identity. Once you have enough clues, you can issue a warrant and, if you can, catch the suspect and arrest them. The player has one week of in-game time to fulfil their mission. Players can use *The World Almanac* book supplied with the game or their own knowledge to solve the geographical clues. If the suspect is caught, the player's rank increases. The proceeding cases become more difficult with the final case pitting you against Carmen Sandiego herself.

The game was immensely popular in schools in the USA, where it was used as a fun educational tool. This user-base rocketed the game's sales into the millions, creating an entire franchise, consisting of a television show and many re-releases and sequels which branched out to other areas of education. Some examples of these sequels are: *Where in the U.S.A. Is Carmen Sandiego?* (1986), *Where in Europe Is Carmen Sandiego?* (1988), *Where in Time Is Carmen Sandiego?* (1989), *Where in Space Is Carmen Sandiego?* (1993) and *Where on Google Earth Is Carmen Sandiego?* (2019), which uses satellite imagery integrated into the game. Where in the World Is Carmen Sandiego? is the best-selling educational video game in the USA.

Buggy Boy/Speed Buggy

Date of release: 1985

Region: Japan

Developer: Tatsumi

Publisher: Tatsumi

Platform: Arcade

Buggy Boy is a single-player, third-person, off-road racing game. The aim is to complete each course in the fastest time possible. Each course is made up of five legs. The player must also avoid obstacles, such as logs, by manoeuvring around or jumping over them. The player can also collect flags or go through gates for extra points or extra time.

The original arcade cabinet of Buggy Boy comprised three screens to create an amazing panoramic view, a rare feature in 1985.

Buggy Boy was ported to a handful of 8-bit and 16-bit home computers popular at the time.

Hang-On

Date of release: July 1985

Region: Japan

Developer: Sega

Publisher: Sega

Platform: Arcade

Designed by Yu Suzuki, Hang-On is a single-player, third-person, motorcycle racing game. The aim is to complete all five stages in the quickest times possible. A timer runs down throughout the stages. If the timer reaches zero before the player passes a checkpoint, the game ends. Each stage features a different environment.

Billboards in the game featuring cigarette ads became a point of controversy as they were thought to encourage young people to smoke. Hang-On was one of the first video games to use Sega's 'Super Scaler' technique. This technique involved sprite scaling at high-frame rates to give the illusion of riding at great speed down the track, passing competitors' bikes. Three types of arcade cabinet were manufactured for Hang-On: a stand-up cabinet with handlebars, a similarly upright cabinet with a seat, and finally a bike cabinet, where the player would sit on a model bike on which they would need to lean left or right to control the bike on-screen.

Hang-On was only ported to Sega's consoles and to some Japanese home computers of the time. Many systems struggled to perfect the arcade's 'Super Scaler' technique on their limited hardware. Hang-On spawned two sequels: *Super Hang-On* (1987) and *Hang On GP '95* (1995).

Green Beret/Rush 'n Attack

Date of release: 1985

Region: Japan

Developer: Konami

Publisher: Konami

Platform: Arcade

Green Beret, known as Rush 'n Attack in America, is a single-player, side-scrolling, run and gun game. The aim is to rescue the hostages held on a Russian military base. You control a lone soldier who must defeat waves of enemies to achieve the objective. The game is broken down into four stages: missile, harbour, bridge, and the final camp. There are a multitude of enemies to deal with, and each uses a specific weapon. Some will use a melee attack while others use guns, mortars and even flamethrowers. There are also dogs to deal with. The player has only his trusty knife with which to defend themselves. However, by killing specific enemy soldiers he can pick up a flamethrower with limited ammunition. The player must think ahead, deciding whether to fight on ground level or climb up ladders to fight on one of the higher levels. The player can duck under or jump over enemy fire. Yet timing is essential as enemies are coming from all directions, and a badly-timed jump, for example, can have you landing on a waiting live grenade. At the end of each stage, an alert sounds and you must defeat a huge wave of enemies. Green Beret is very much the side-scrolling version of *Commando* (1985). At the end of the final stage, the player must defeat a bunch of flamethrower enemies to finally reach and free the hostages, which plays out in a quick cut-scene.

Eggerland Mystery

Date of release: 1985

Region: Japan

Developer: HAL Laboratory

Publisher: HAL Laboratory

Platform: MSX home computer

Eggerland Mystery is a single-player, puzzle maze game. The aim is to collect all the jewels in the maze and then make it to the open door to the next level. Each level presents the player with a different enemy: some enemies chase you while others will shoot at you. There are some who won't activate until the final jewel is collected. The player's character, Lolo, a blue blob with eyes, can move certain blocks in the maze. This mechanic is essential when particular enemies are activated, otherwise, the player cannot make it to the exit. Lolo is also given a limited number of fireball-like projectiles to deal with enemies.

There are thirteen games in the Eggerland series, and as the game series has evolved, new mechanics and gameplay features have been introduced. Some of the most notable games in the Eggerland Series are *Eggerland: Revival of the Labyrinth* (1988), *Eggerland: Departure to Creation* (1988), *The Adventures of Lolo 2* (1990), *The Adventures of Lolo 3* (1991) and *Eggerland Episode 0: Quest of Lala* (1996).

Ghost 'n Goblins

Date of release: September 1985

Region: Japan

Developer: Capcom

Publisher: Capcom

Platform: Arcade

Known as Makaimura (which translates to 'Demon World Village') in Japan, Ghost 'n Goblins was designed by Tokuro Fujiwara. Ghost 'n Goblins is a single-player, side-scrolling platformer. The aim is to work your way through the different levels, avoiding obstacles and defeating enemies to ultimately rescue Princess Prin Prin from Satan. Enemies along the way include zombies rising from the ground, deadly plants that spit poisonous projectiles, bats and dragons. The game opens with a quick cinematic of the knight Sir Arthur sitting with the Princess. Satan appears and kidnaps the Princess. Arthur dons his armour, and you begin your quest. The player begins the game with the default weapon, which is the lance. This can be fired at a rapid rate horizontally across the screen. Other weapons can be acquired, such as the dagger (knife), torch, and shield (cross). It is generally agreed that the dagger or the shield are the most efficient weapons when it comes to disposing of enemies. The player can take only two hits before losing a life. The first hit disposes of Arthur's armour, whereupon the player must continue fighting in his underwear. A second hit turns the player into a pile of bones. Armour can be reacquired as a pick-up item. Arthur can duck, jump and climb ladders. There are six levels to the game to complete until the player must face and destroy the demon lord, Astaroth. However, once defeated, a message informs the player that the room is an illusion, a trap devised by Satan. The player finds themselves back at the beginning of the game and must complete the whole thing again. If the player has the determination to do such a thing and defeat Astaroth, the princess kisses the knight and the badly translated text reads *Congratulation. This Story is Happy End. Being the wise and courageous Knight that you are, you feel strength welling in your body.*

The game is renowned for its graphics, atmosphere, humour, music and sound. Above all, though, it is well-known for its high level of difficulty. It presents a challenge that is both intimidating and appealing, in a similar way to the Souls series of games which began with *Demon Souls* (2009). After its success in the arcade, it was ported to most home computers and consoles, the Amiga version being the closest in recreating the arcade experience at the time. Ghost 'n Goblins is the first Famicom game to use the 128 KB Cartridge.

Ghost 'n Goblins had many sequels, some of the most notable are *Ghouls 'n Ghosts* (1988), *Super Ghouls 'n Ghosts* (1991), *Maximo: Ghosts to Glory* (2001), *Ultimate Ghosts 'n Goblins* (2006) and *Ghost 'n Goblins Resurrection* (2021).

Super Mario Bros.

Date of release: September 1985

Region: Japan

Developer: Nintendo E&D

Publisher: Nintendo

Platform: Famicom and NES

Designed by Shigeru Miyamoto (Donkey Kong and Mario Bros.), Super Mario Bros. is a single-player, side-scrolling, platform game. The aim is to reach the end of each stage with the ultimate purpose of rescuing Princess Toadstool from the game's main antagonist, Bowser. As Mario (or his brother Luigi, if playing in multiplayer mode) runs through the level, he must avoid numerous enemies, or deal with them by jumping on top of them, or he can also jump up, hitting a brick that an enemy is standing on. The game has several power-up items. Collecting the Super Mushroom makes Mario grow to twice his original size. Collecting the fire flower from specific '?' bricks gives Mario the ability to throw fireballs at his enemies. Collecting the starman power-up, which is only gained by hitting hidden invisible bricks, gives Mario temporary invincibility. Mario can collect coins during each level. Coins are lying around in the level, while others can only be collected after they are released by hitting the '?' brick or hidden invisible bricks. If the player collects 100 coins, he receives an extra life. If Mario collects the green-spotted orange 1-up mushroom, released by hitting a specific brick, he can also gain an extra life. Mario will lose a life if touched by an enemy, falls down a pit, or fails to finish a level before the timer runs out. There are eight worlds each containing four stages, some of which are underground or underwater. In the final level, Mario must defeat Bowser to at last be reunited with Princess Toadstool.

Koji Kondo wrote six pieces of what has now become some of the most iconic and easily identifiable music in video game history. It was one of the first times where music was composed to specifically cater to the game's differing levels. More elaborate than most repetitive tunes of the time, Kondo's work inspired a whole generation of developers to enhance the music in their games.

Super Mario Bros. has sold over 40 million units in total. It is cited by some as the game that kick-started the home video game industry in the USA in 1985 and 1986, after the crash of 1983. Some cite it as one of the greatest video games of all time. Certainly, it was the game that made many in the USA fall in love with video games, if not for the first time, then possibly again. It is the game that truly popularised Mario as a character on the home systems. Since Super Mario Bros., further Mario games throughout the years are often seen as examples of perfecting the craft of video game design.

Nintendo Entertainment System

The Nintendo Entertainment System or NES, known as the Famicom in Japan, was released in the USA in New York City in October 1985 and the rest of the USA in February 1986. The NES is an 8-bit, cartridge-based, third-generation video game console. It shipped with two controllers and could display a total of 25 colours on screen. The NES had 17 launch games including *Duck Hunt* (1984), *Exitebike* (1984) and *Super Mario-Bros.* (1985). The NES is responsible for kick-starting the video game industry in the USA after the crash of 1983. However, it is worth noting that this did not happen overnight. Instead, it took years for the home video game industry to once again gain traction in the USA and, ultimately, succeed.

Nintendo was careful as to exactly how they marketed the redesigned Famicom for the American audience. Retailers had experienced the crash first-hand and were wary of investing in anything to do with consoles or video games. Nintendo pitched their machine as an entertainment system: a toy for children with strict censoring policy and quality control. This concept was reinforced with the introduction of the optional Robotic Operating Buddy, or ROB peripheral. The marketing ploy worked. The NES and its recognisable game characters, such as Mario and Donkey Kong, soon worked their way into the hearts and minds of American children, becoming a mainstream part of their culture. It became not only the bestselling third-generation gaming platform but would go on to become the most successful home console of all time up until the mid-nineties.

The NES was the best-selling video game console of the 1980s, and along with the Famicom has sold around 62 million units. Some of the most notable games for the NES were *Mario Bros.* (1983), *Castlevania* (1983), *The Legend of Zelda* (1986), *Metroid* (1986), *Final Fantasy* (1987), *Contra* (1987), *Mega Man 2* (1988), *Tetris* (1989), and *Super Mario Bros. 3* (1990).

Sega Master System or Sega Mark III

The Sega Master System, also known as the Sega Mark III, was released in Japan in October 1985 by Sega. The Sega Master System was an 8-bit, cartridge- and card-based, third-generation video game console. It was capable of 256 x 192 resolution and could display a total of 32 colours from a possible 64 colour palette. Two accessories were available for the Master System: a light gun and 3D Glasses, each designed to work with specific games.

The Master System launched in the USA in September 1986, and in Europe in 1987. Despite featuring more powerful hardware, it could not dethrone the immensely popular NES, which saw unprecedented success in the USA and Japan. Yet the Master System did very well in Europe and had its strongest following in South America. Its following in Brazil was and remains so strong that the Master System is still in production in Brazil at the time of writing, making it the longest-lived console in the history of video games. Many people in other parts of the world hold the Master System in high regard in precisely the same manner as North Americans do with the NES.

It is estimated that the Sega Master System has currently sold 13 million units. Even though the Master System played second fiddle to the NES when it came to sales, many of its games were graphically superior. Some of them were the best arcade ports of the time. A few of the most notable games for the Master System were *Alex Kidd in Miracle World* (1986), *Phantasy Star* (1987), *R-Type* (1987), *Shinobi* (1988), *Wonder Boy in Monster Land* (1988), *Psych Fox* (1989) and *Operation Wolf* (1990).

Dragon Slayer II: Xanadu

Date of release: October 1985

Region: Japan

Developer: Nihon Falcom

Publisher: Nihon Falcom

Platform: PC-8801

Designed by Yoshio Kiya, Dragon Slayer II: Xanadu, often referred to as simply Xanadu, is a single-player, action RPG, and the sequel to the successful *Dragon Slayer* (1984). At the beginning of the game, the aim of the game is rather vague, although being called Dragon Slayer gives the player a general idea. You begin as a potential hero who visits the king. He gives you some food and gold and simply wishes you good luck. From here you explore the game. The player moves around the game-world like a platform game, moving left to right, up and down, climbing ladders and jumping. The player fights monsters, buys items, solves puzzles and levels up. The character's point of view will shift from a third-person side-view perspective to first-person when interacting with the many beautifully drawn characters. Xanadu had many great features, such as a karma meter and character statistics, which could be affected depending on what the character had equipped themselves with. The appearance of the character was also dependent on equipped items.

Xanadu was immensely popular in Japan and inspired Nintendo's *The Legend of Zelda* (1986). At the time it was the best-selling PC video game in Japan, with over 400,000 units sold in just a few months.

Xanadu set itself up as one of the foundations of real-time action RPGs and went onto spawn many sequels, such as *Xanadu Scenario II* (1986), *Faxanadu* (1987), *Revival Xanadu* (a remake of the original Xanadu (1995), *Xanadu Next* (2005), and *Tokyo Xanadu* (2015).

Gauntlet

Date of release: November 1985

Region: USA

Developer: Atari Games

Publisher: Atari Games

Platform: Arcade

Designed by Ed Logg, Gauntlet is a single-player or multiplayer, hack and slash, dungeon crawl game, heavily inspired by *Dandy* (1983). The aim of Gauntlet is to defeat hordes of enemies and find the exit in each dungeon, taking the player to the next level. The maze, being much larger than the screen size, scrolls with the player's movement seen from a top-down perspective. Players may move around independently. However, if one player attempts to move to one edge of the screen and another player to the other edge then the screen will cease scrolling, meaning that cooperation is vital to successfully navigate each labyrinthian dungeon. One of the main appeals of Gauntlet is that four players can play simultaneously. Each player can choose one of four characters: Warrior – who has the strongest melee attack but a weak use of magic, Valkyrie – who has the strongest armour, Wizard – who has a very strong use of magic but has the weakest armour, and Elf – who has a good-ranged bow and arrow attack and fast movement. Players must decide who they are going to be as there can only be one of each character. This was to change in the sequel *Gauntlet II* (1986), where the same character could be chosen multiple times. Enemies spawn from monster generators and home-in on the players. There are several different enemy types: some use a melee attack, while others have a ranged attack. Enemies include ghosts, grunts, demons, lobbers, sorcerers, thieves and Death, who is by far the most dangerous enemy as he can only be destroyed with a magic potion. If the player doesn't possess one, it is best to run! Death's touch will quickly drain your life away. A player's health slowly ebbs away over time and can only be topped up with food, or by inserting more coins. Other players can insert coins and join at any point in the game. However, if the final player dies and no one inserts any coins before the countdown ends, all progress is lost. I wonder if the developers foresaw how strong peer pressure would ensure that players would keep inserting coins to stay in the game and not let their friends fight alone in the dungeon? Probably. Gauntlet involves a fair amount of strategy. Players must work together or risk getting spilt up and over-run by hordes of monsters. Warrior and Valkyrie should take the brunt of the attack and eat most of the food. It is best if the Wizard collects and uses potions for when things get dire. Music and sound featured heavily in Gauntlet. The game would frequently inform players with helpful information, for example, "Elf needs food badly," "Warrior is about to die," "Don't shoot food."

Gauntlet was a very successful and incredibly popular video game and was quickly ported to most home computers and consoles of the time. It inspired a whole generation of multiplayer, usually four-player, video games including *Golden Axe* (1987), *Teenage Mutant Ninja Turtles* (1989) and *The Simpsons* (1991). Gauntlet popularised the multiplayer dungeon crawl video game and spawned several sequels, including *Gauntlet 2* (1986), *Gauntlet* Legends (1998), *Gauntlet: Dark Legacy* (2002) and *Gauntlet: Seven Sorrows* (2005). Gauntlet was awarded Game of the Year at the 1986 Golden Joystick Awards. It is also cited as one of the greatest video games of all time

Mercenary: Escape from Targ/ Mercenary: A Flight Simulator Adventure

Date of release: 1985

Region: UK & USA

Developer: Novagen

Publisher: Novagen

Platform: Atari 8-bit

Mercenary: Escape from Targ, known as Mercenary: A Flight Simulator Adventure in the USA, often referred to as just Mercenary, was designed by Paul Woakes, Bruce Jordan and Mo Warden. Mercenary is a single-player, first-person, action-adventure game. You have crash-landed on the planet Targ and must find a means of escape. You can move around on foot or fly around in an aircraft, partake in combat and build up wealth by taking on missions.

The graphics were a big draw for some players: a mix of 3D flat-shaded and wireframe environments, which back in 1985 made for quite an immersive experience, especially considering that the game ran on 8-bit home computers.

Mercenary was highly praised for its graphics and absorbing gameplay. However, it was noted that making a map was advised as players could get lost in the rather immense game world. Mercenary was soon ported to several 8-bit and 16-bit home computers. The other games in the Mercenary series were *Mercenary: The Second City* (1986), *Damocles* (1990) and *Mercenary III: The Dion Crisis* (1992).

Paradroid

Date of release: 1985

Region: UK

Developer: Graftgold

Publisher: Hewson Consultants

Platform: Commodore 64

Designed by Andrew Braybrook, Paradroid is a single-player, shoot 'em up, puzzle game. The aim of Paradroid is to destroy or convert a host of droids that have been turned against their human masters, all aboard a fleet of spaceships. The game is viewed from a top-down perspective as the player controls a special droid called the 'Influence Device'. Throughout the ship, players encounter multiple droids which they can either destroy or take over by subverting their systems. This is done through a mini-puzzle game with a time limit. If successful, the player then controls this droid and can continue to subvert other droids. There are several different kinds of droids in the game. If the player loses the mini-game, then either the droid they were inhabiting is destroyed or they are returned to the Influence Device. Each droid is represented as a sphere with a three-digit number on it. The higher the number, the more powerful the droid and therefore the more difficult it is to destroy or subvert. The player can access computer terminals to view the ship's map as well as information about the different droids. The ship is comprised of twenty decks, and each deck is made up of a series of connected rooms. Lifts transport the player to different decks. There are eight ships in the fleet. If the player completes all eight ships, the game begins again, however the difficulty increases.

Paradroid is considered by some to be the best game released for the Commodore 64. It was later ported to a handful of 16-bit home computers.

Ultima IV: Quest of the Avatar

Date of release: November 1985

Region: USA

Developer: Origin Systems

Publisher: Origin Systems

Platform: Apple II

Designed by Richard Garriot, Ultima IV: Quest of the Avatar is a single-player RPG. It was the first game in the 'Age of Enlightenment' trilogy. The gameplay has less emphasis on hack and slash and more on building your stats by practising the eight virtues during gameplay, with the ultimate aim of becoming the Avatar. The eight virtues are honesty, compassion, valour, justice, sacrifice, honour, spirituality and humility. The player must also find certain items and gain access to the Codex of Ultimate Wisdom to become the Avatar. This instalment of the Ultima series also offered its players a significantly larger game world to explore, around sixteen times larger than its predecessor, Ultima III.

This change in direction for the Ultima series was partly because Garriot received mail from parents informing him how his violent games were corrupting and adversely affecting their children. Garriot decided to create an ethical framework that would encompass the game's mechanics and narrative. Garriot managed to succeed in creating one of the best games in the Ultima series. There is anecdotal evidence that the lessons learnt in how a person might conduct themselves in Ultima IV, made them a better and more virtuous individual in real life.

Ultima IV was ported to most home computers of the time.

Roller Coaster

Date of release: 1985

Region: UK

Developer: S. Brocklehurst

Publisher: Elite Systems

Platform: ZX Spectrum

Roller Coaster is a single-player, puzzle platformer. The aim of Roller Coaster is to collect all the money bags left scattered throughout the amusement park by a disgruntled employee. You play as the owner, Colonel G. Bogey, and must avoid the many perils of the park.

The game was highly praised by critics and sold very well on the Spectrum platform.

Roller Coaster is the first video game to simulate amusement rides.

Windows 1.0

Windows 1.0 was released worldwide in November 1985.

Developed by Microsoft, Windows 1.0 was Microsoft's first graphical user interface (GUI). It was not that well-received at the time due to a few teething problems. However, it is worth noting here as Windows is, broadly speaking, the base Platform/Operating System for most PC games.

Déjà Vu

Date of release: 1985

Region: USA

Developer: ICOM Simulations Inc

Publisher: Mindscape

Platform: Macintosh

Déjà Vu is a single-player, point-and-click adventure game in the style of the 1940s detective genre. At the beginning of the game, the player finds that he has no memory of who he is. The aim of Déjà Vu is to find out who was responsible for the dead body found in the office while trying to avoid being framed for the murder. The player must interact with a range of colourful characters and solve puzzles to succeed.

Déjà Vu was successful enough to be ported to many home computers and consoles over the proceeding years, quite often with improved graphics.

Lord of the Rings: Game One

Date of release: 1985

Region: Worldwide

Developer: Beam Software

Publisher: Melbourne House

Platform: Commodore 64

Lord of the Rings: Game One is a single-player text adventure with graphics. The player takes the part of Frodo and must take the one ring to Mount Doom and destroy it, defeating Sauron and his armies.

Despite being based on the ever-popular fantasy novel/s of the same name, and despite the previous success of *The Hobbit* (1982), Lord of the Rings: Game One wasn't well-received by Critics, and players complained about many aspects of its often-broken game mechanics.

Suffice it to say, Game Two was never made.

Space Harrier

Date of release: December 1985

Region: Worldwide

Developer: Sega

Publisher: Sega

Platform: Arcade

Designed by Yu Suzuki, Space Harrier is a single-player, third-person, rail shooter. The aim is to destroy as many enemies as possible and dodge any obstacles in your path. The player is seen from behind holding a laser cannon under their arm that enables them to fly and shoot. Moving at great speed above a chequerboard landscape, all manner of enemies coming toward you in different attack patterns, from flying heads made of stone (similar to the stone heads on Easter Island), robots and Cycloptic woolly mammoths. Bosses at the end of each level are usually a Chinese dragon that must be destroyed in order to continue to the next stage. There are eighteen stages. When the final boss is destroyed the game displays 'The End.' The player can begin again if they have any credits left. The game is terrifically fast-paced and can feel incredibly immersive and chaotic. At times the player must desperately find the next safe area of the screen which isn't filled with either obstructions, enemies, or enemy fire. The play area feels even smaller when the sky is replaced by a chequerboard ceiling, making it feel as if the player is flying down a horizontal cavern.

Space Harrier had two other features that made it an unforgettable arcade experience. First of all, was its incredible soundtrack composed by Hiroshi Kawaguchi and its integration of sound. When the game begins, a synthesized voice utters the immortal words, "Welcome to the Fantasy Zone. Get Ready!" When you complete a stage a voice says, "You're doing great!" Space Harrier's second feature was its arcade cabinet. The player would sit in the cockpit-like cabinet which used an analogue flight stick with a trigger as its controller. The entire cabinet would move, dependent on the stick's movement, making for an unprecedented immersive and thrilling experience.

Space Harrier was one of the first 16-bit arcade games to be released. Its incredible graphics as well as the aforementioned features made it a huge hit. Yu Suzuki designed several well-received games using this effective sprite-scaling technique, including *Hang-On* (1985), *Out Run* (1986) and *After Burner* (1987). Space Harrier was ported to most home computers and Sega consoles. However, many of these platforms, especially the 8-bit ones, struggled to recreate the graphics of the original arcade game. Space Harrier also spawned two home console sequels: Space Harrier 3-D (1988) and *Space Harrier II* (1988).

1985 Golden Joystick Awards

The 1985 Golden Joystick Awards were hosted in London.

Commando (1985) wins Best Arcade-style Game of the Year.

Little Computer People (1985) wins Best Original Game of the Year.

The Way of the Exploding Fist (1985) wins Game of the Year.

1985 Notable Omissions

Airwolf. Alien 8. Alpha Attack. A Mind Forever Voyaging. Balance of Power. Battle City. BMX Racers. Boulder Dash II. Cauldron. Caves of Doom. Chaos: The Battle of the Wizards. Daley Thompson's Super Test. Dynamite Dan. Citadel. City Connection. Clu Clu Land. Codemasters is founded. Commodore 128. Dynamite Dan. Fairlight. Gun smoke. Gridiron Fight. Hogan's Gun. Jet Set Willy II: The Final Frontier. King's Valley. Legendary Wings. Mercenary. Metro-Cross. Monty on the Run. Motos. MSX2. Nightshade.

Nonterraqueous. Racing Destruction Set. Rare is founded. Return of the Invaders. Ring King. Saboteur. Section Z. Silent Service. Soul of a Robot. Sky Kid. Starquake. Star Wars: The Empire Strikes Back. Summer Games II. The Eidolon. The Legend of Kage. The pawn. The Rats! Thexder. Thing on a Spring. Twinbee. Who Dares Wins II. Winter Games. Wrecking Crew.

1986

Ikari Warriors

Date of release: February 1986

Region: Japan

Developer: SNK

Publisher: Tradewest

Platform: Arcade

Simply known as Ikari in Japan, Ikari Warriors is a single-player or multiplayer, vertical-scrolling, run and gun shooter with very similar gameplay and mechanics to *Front Line* (1982). The aim is to reach the village of Ikari and free Colonel Cook. Players can collect power-ups for their guns and grenades. They can also use tanks and helicopters against the hordes of enemies sent against them. This game, influenced by *Commando* (1985), became one of the most popular arcades of 1986 due to its two-player co-op feature and the rotary joystick, which allowed the player to shoot in any one of eight different directions.

It was soon ported to most home consoles and home computers of the time. Ikari Warriors spawned two sequels: *Victory Road* (1986) and *Ikari III: The Rescue* (1989).

The Famicom Disk System

The Famicom Disk System, or FDS for short, was released in Japan in February 1986 by Nintendo. The FDS is simply a floppy disk drive system released exclusively for the Famicom. Floppy disks, called 'Disk Cards', were slower but cheaper than the traditional cartridges used by the Famicom. Floppy disks had a few other beneficial features, such as offering larger game worlds by using multiple disks, and the ability to save data. High scores saved on disk could be taken to a retailer's Disk Fax kiosk, downloaded and added to a nationwide leaderboard, offering prizes for the highest scores. These kiosks were the precursor to the online leader-boards of today. They could also be used to copy a new game from a library onto the rewritable disk for a very reasonable fee. This concept of purchasing new games became very popular in Japan and was still available up until 2003. It is certainly one of the lesser-known yet significant innovations connected with video games.

The Legend of Zelda

Date of release: February 1986

Region: Japan

Developer: Nintendo EAD

Publisher: Nintendo

Platform: Famicom Disk System

Designed by Shigeru Miyamoto, Takashi Tezuka and with music by Koji Knondo, The Legend of Zelda is a single-player, top-down, action-adventure game. The aim is to collect all eight fragments of the Triforce of Wisdom and rescue Princess Zelda from the evil Ganon. Taking place in the fantasy land of Hyrule, you play as the young hero, Link. The player can move around in any one of four directions, interacting with characters and objects, and using a sword and shield to dispatch monsters. You must find and then explore the game's dungeons which, feature hidden rooms, secret passageways and keys, in an attempt to discover the fragments of the Triforce. A more difficult mode of the game could be accessed upon completion called 'Second Quest'.

Miyamoto wanted to create a fantasy game that was in contrast to the D&D-inspired games in Japan, such as *The Black Onyx (1984)* and *Dragon Quest (1986)*. He drew inspiration from his childhood experiences of exploring of the countryside around Kyoto. It was this sense of wonder and discovery that Miyamoto wanted to bring to The Legend of Zelda. The Legend of Zelda was one of the first games to offer players a hard mode, where the design and layout of the game were significantly different. It was also one of the launch titles for the Family Computer Disk System. Being such a large game, for the time, it suited the platform perfectly as players could easily save their progress on disk, a relatively new concept in the eighties. When the game was ported over to the Famicom and the NES a year later, the cartridge included a built-in battery to facilitate the requirement of saved games. Included with the game were a fold-out map and a game guide. However, some players in the USA struggled with the game's hidden areas and clues. An 800-phone number was set up to offer any help needed. The four call-handlers were swamped, and soon the staff numbers were bolstered to 200 to take on the huge demand.

The Legend of Zelda became one of the most popular games for Nintendo, selling over 6.5 million units. It has become one of Nintendo's most beloved video game franchises, spawning a multitude of sequels. Some of the most notable are *The Legend of Zelda: A Link to the Past* (1991), *The Legend of Zelda: Link's Awakening* (1993), *The Legend of Zelda: Ocarina of Time* (1998), *The Legend of Zelda: A Link Between Worlds* (2013), *The Legend of Zelda: The Wind Waker HD* (2013), *The Legend of Zelda: Majora's Mask* (2015) and *The Legend of Zelda: Breath of the Wild* (2017).

Uridium

Date of release: March 1986

Region: UK

Developer: Andrew Braybrook

Publisher: Hewson Consultants

Platform: Commodore 64

Uridium is a single-player, horizontal-scrolling shoot 'em up. The aim of Uridium is to destroy enemy Super-Dreadnought ships, which are draining mineral resources from each planet. You control a Manta Class space fighter. The fighter can move in any one of eight directions, has twin lasers and can perform a quick 180-degree flip to attack enemies approaching from behind. The player must destroy all the enemy fighters in space and take out each Super-Dreadnought. There are fifteen levels or Super-Dreadnoughts to destroy, each named after the metal they are draining from the planet. Landing on its surface and then completing a quick mini-game will destroy the enemy ship. Each level ends with the Super-Dreadnought vaporised by the destruction of its nuclear reactor. The final level is named after a fictional metal called Uridium, although Braybrook believed this to be a real metal element when he developed the game.

Uridium was soon ported to the other popular home computer platforms of the day and was highly praised by critics and consumers alike. Uridium had one expanded re-release with *Uridium+* (1986) and one sequel, *Uridium 2* (1993). Uridium was voted Best Arcade-style Game of the Year at the 1986 Golden Joystick Awards.

Ubisoft Entertainment

Ubisoft Entertainment was founded in France in March 1986 by five brothers Christian, Claude, Gerard, Michael and Yves Guillemot.

Ubisoft is known for publishing such video games as the *Assassin's Creed* series, *Far Cry* series, *Tom Clancy's Rainbow Six*, *Ghost Recon* and *Splinter Cell* series.

Arkanoid

Date of release: July 1986

Region: Japan

Developer: Taito

Publisher: Taito

Platform: Arcade

Designed by Akira Fujita, Arkanoid is a single-player clone of *Breakout* (1976). However, Arkanoid offered enough new game mechanics to be more than a simple clone. The aim of Arkanoid is to destroy all the blocks by bouncing the ball off your paddle and then proceed to the next stage, with the ultimate goal of defeating the game's boss, a giant Easter Island-like stone head, at stage 33. If the ball gets past your paddle, you lose a life. The player's paddle is portrayed as a spaceship called the *Vaus*. Not all bricks have the same effect once hit, with some taking multiple hits to destroy. Power-ups can be released upon destroying some bricks. Power-ups include a twin laser to quickly decimate blocks, splitting the ball into three, a larger paddle, and even one that opens an exit that will instantly take you to the next level. Arkanoid used a dial to control the paddle's movement and a single button for the laser when required.

The game was well-received due to its simple-to-understand gameplay, yet varied, challenging and extremely engaging level design. It revitalised the Breakout genre for years to come, spawning several sequels and a great number of clones on all platforms of the time. Arkanoid sequels include *Tournament Arkanoid* (1987), *Arkanoid: Revenge of Doh* (1987), *Arkanoid: Doh It Again* (1997) and *Arkanoid Returns* (1997).

Wonder Boy

Date of release: April 1986

Region: Japan

Developer: Escape

Publisher: Sega

Platform: Arcade

Designed by Ryuichi Nishizawa, Wonder Boy, also known as Super Wonder Boy, is a single-player, horizontal-scrolling platform game. The aim is to rescue Wonder Boy's girlfriend, Tina, from the Dark King. Wonder Boy, wearing nothing but grass shorts, moves from left to right, jumping and using an inexhaustible supply of throwing axes to dispatch various monsters and break open eggs. The player can also ride a skateboard through certain parts of the game and release a fairy which offers temporary protection. Wonder Boy loses a life if he falls down a pit or his vitality drops to zero. Points and vitality are awarded for collecting fruit and hearts. At the end of the game, Wonder Boy must defeat the Dark King and is then reunited with his girlfriend.

Wonder Boy went on to be one of Sega's best-selling arcades. In the following year, It was ported to Sega's line of consoles and most popular home computers of the time. It has also seen ports to the mobile, Wii and Playstation platforms. There are five sequels in the Wonder Boy series: *Wonder Boy in Monster Land* (1987), *Wonder Boy III: Monster Lair* (1988), *Wonder Boy III: The Dragon's Trap* (1989), *Wonder Boy in Monster World* (1991), and *Monster World IV* (1994).

Dragon Quest/Dragon Warrior

Date of release: May 1986

Region: Japan

Developer: Chunsoft

Publisher: Enix

Platform: Famicom

Known as Dragon Warrior in the USA, Dragon Quest is a single-player, fantasy RPG. The aim is to retrieve the balls of light and rescue the princess from the evil dragon lord, thus saving the Kingdom of Alefgard. The game begins with the player being sent upon his quest by the king. The player must converse with NPCs to gather information, which allows them to access and discover new areas containing items and opportunities, fight monsters to gain XP (experience points) and level-up, increasing the player's character's strength, speed, agility and ability to use magic. Whereas the majority of the game is seen from a third-person overhead perspective, looking down on the characters and surrounding environment, combat takes place in a first-person turn-based mode. This change of game mode would become synonymous with JRPGs such as *Phantasy Star* (1987) and *Mother* (1989). Gold can also be acquired and used in shops selling goods, weapons and armour. It can also be used to stay at inns to recover HP (health points) and MP (Mana/Magic points).

Dragon Quest is sometimes referred to as the father of JRPGs. However, games such as *Adventure* (1979), *Ultima* (1981), *Wizardry* (1981), *The Black Onyx* (1984) and *Dragon Slayer* (1984) certainly paved the way for Dragon Quest. Dragon Quest became part of a trilogy, where *Dragon Quest II* (1987) is the sequel and *Dragon Quest III* (1988) is the prequel. The game series went on to inspire a manga series comprising 21 volumes, an anime movie and a television series. Dragon Quest was significant in that it created a foundation of game mechanics that most JRPGs are based on. Its popularity in Japan has become somewhat remarkable, to the point where it is ingrained in their culture. It is considered to be Japan's national game. Dragon Quest has become so popular that sequels have almost always been released at the weekend to avoid masses of workers and students taking time off to play it, as happened during the chaotic launch of *Dragon Quest III* in February 1988. There are currently eleven Dragon Quest games in the main series, at the time of writing. Cited by some as the best are *Dragon Quest V: Hand of the Heavenly Bride* (1992), *Dragon Quest VIII: Journey of the Cursed King* (2004) and *Dragon Quest XI: Echoes of an Elusive Age* (2017). Dragon Quest has also spawned several spin-off games with Dragon Quest Heroes series and Dragon Quest Builders series.

Leader Board

Date of release: 1986

Region: USA

Developer: Access Software

Publisher: Access Software

Platform: Commodore 64

Designed by Bruce Carver and Roger Carver, Leader Board is a single-player or multiplayer golf game. The aim is to complete each course with the least amount of swings. There are four courses in total. In multiplayer mode, players take turns at the computer to take their shots. This is sometimes referred to as 'hot seat' as the players are constantly getting off the seat to allow the next player to have their turn.

Leader Board was highly praised for its graphics with Bruce Carver receiving much acclaim for its technical achievement. Leader Board spawned several quick successive sequels which introduced some new courses. These were *Leader Board Tournament* (1986), *Leader Board: Executive Edition* (1987) and *World Class Leader Board* (1987).

Thrust

Date of release: May 1986

Region: UK

Developer: Jeremy Smith and Rob Hubbard

Publisher: Superior Software

Platform: BBC Micro

Thrust is a single-player, multi-scrolling, multi-directional shooter. The aim is to manoeuvre your spacecraft and use its tractor beam to collect the pod found on each level/planet. The pod is often found in subterranean caverns. Turrets shoot at your spacecraft; however, the player can use a shield to defend against attack and return fire, destroying the turrets. Reactors can be shot to stop the turrets from firing for a short amount of time, but if the player shoots the reactor too much, it will go critical and the player will see a countdown display before the current planet explodes. Fuel is consumed every time the ship's thrusters are used. Extra fuel can be collected using your tractor beam on fuel depots. Thrust features realistic physics such as gravity and inertia. If the player isn't careful, the weight and the swing of the pod can easily pull the ship into a wall of a cavern, causing both to explode. There are six initial levels where the gravity is normal, then another six where the gravity is reversed. The planet is invisible in the next six levels and can only be seen when the shield is used. The final six levels combine an invisible planet with reverse gravity. This makes twenty-four levels in total and Thrust an extremely gripping and difficult game to complete.

Thrust was well-received and soon ported to the popular 8-bit home computers of the day. It spawned many clones and one sequel, *Thrust II* (1987). Thrust was inspired by the arcade game *Gravitar* (1982).

Atari 7800

The Atari 7800 was released in the USA in May 1986 by Atari. The Atari 7800 is an 8-bit, third-generation, video game console with 4 KB of RAM and could output 256 colours. The graphics were a definite improvement on Atari's two previous home consoles: the

Atari 2600 (VCS) and the Atari 5200. Unfortunately, it still used the same sound chip as the old 2600. The joystick was an improvement on the terrible 5200 controllers and the console itself was a lot smaller. It seemed that Atari had learnt some lessons from 7800's direct predecessor.

The Atari was the first console to have backwards compatibility straight out of the box, in this case with most, but not all, of the extensive Atari 2600 game library. Despite this, game development was a slow trickle for the 7800 compared with that of the market leader – the NES. Consumers wanted to play new games. Thus, the Atari 7800 had sold around 100,000 units by the end of 1986, whereas the NES had sold well over a million.

Some of the most notable games for the Atari 7800 were *Xevious* (1986), *Ms. Pac-Man* (1986), *Ballblazer* (1987), *Food Fight* (1987), *Dark Chambers* (1988), *F-18 Hornet* (1988), *Alien Brigade* (1990) and *Motor Psycho* (1990).

Bethesda Softworks

Bethesda Softworks, also known simply as Bethesda, was founded in the USA in June 1985 by Christopher Weaver. Initially a video game publisher, Bethesda Softworks opened its own in-house development team in 2001, called Bethesda Game Studios.

Bethesda is best known for publishing/developing games such as *The Elder Scrolls* series (1994-present), *Fallout* series (2008-present), *Dishonoured* series (2012-2017), *Doom* series (2012-present) and *Wolfenstein* series (2014-present).

Famitsu

Famitsu was first published in Japan in June 1986 by Kadokawa Game Linkage. *Famitsu* is considered the predominant video game magazine in Japan.

Originally focusing on the Famicom, *Famitsu* soon expanded its content to other gaming platforms. Games are scored by a panel of four reviewers who give a score out of ten, giving a total score out of forty.

Super Mario Bros. 2/ Super Mario Bros.: The Lost Levels

Date of release: June 1986

Region: Japan

Developer: Nintendo

Publisher: Nintendo

Platform: Family Computer Disk System

Designed by Takashi Tezuka and Shigeru Miyamoto, Super Mario Bros. 2, later known as *Super Mario Bros.: The Lost Levels* (1993) in the west, is a single-player, side-scrolling platform game. Super Mario Bros. 2 is a direct sequel to Super Mario Bros. It is essentially the same game with some minor changes. However, these are enough to make the game exceedingly difficult. This was the main reason it was not initially released in the West: it was deemed too tough for Western audiences. The game contains bonus levels that can only be unlocked if the player completes the game eight times.

What is known as Super Mario Bros. 2 in Japan was not released in the USA until 1993 as the now-familiar Super Mario Bros.: The Lost Levels. Despite its frustrating difficulty putting some players off, it still sold 2.5 million units in Japan, making it the best-selling game on the Nintendo's Family Computer Disk System.

Solomon's Key

Date of release: July 1986

Region: Japan

Developer: Tecmo

Publisher: Tecmo

Platform: Arcade

Designed by Michitaka Tsuruta, Solomon's Key is a single-player, puzzle platformer. The aim is to retrieve Solomon's Key and return the world to light. Each room contains a key which the player-controlled sorcerer called Dana must collect and then escape to the next level through the door before the timer runs out. There are 50 levels in the game. The player can run, jump and create or demolish blocks. This game mechanic can be used in a few different strategies, such as creating a pathway to the key or blocking enemies. However, enemies can only be blocked once, and after this, they will destroy the block if they encounter the block again on their predetermined path. The player can also create fireballs to destroy enemies. Other features include hidden rooms, secret levels (there are 14 of these, thus making the total number of levels 64) and bonus points giving the game an element of replayability. Solomon's Key requires strategy and the ability to think on your feet, otherwise, players can find themselves being made short work of by the many different enemies in the game.

The game sold rather well and was ported to most of the popular home computers and home consoles. A prequel was released called *Fire 'n Ice*, also known as *Solomon's Key 2*, in 1992.

Imogen

Date of release: 1986

Region: UK

Developer: Micro Power

Publisher: Micro Power

Platform: BBC Micro

Designed by Michael St Aubyn, Imogen is a single-player, puzzle platform game. There are sixteen levels, each containing a spell fragment. The aim is to collect each spell fragment in the mountain's dungeon. Upon completion, you will then be able to escape to the world above. You play as the Wizard, Imogen, who saved his town from a dragon by transforming into a dragon himself. Unfortunately, he lost his mind and was taken to the dungeon. Once Imogen can escape the dungeon, he regains his sanity and can live once more in the town. Imogen has the ability to change his form, each with unique abilities. The player needs to utilise these abilities to solve puzzles and complete each level. The forms which the player can make use of are as follows:

- his human form, who can make use of various objects
- a cat, that can leap long distances
- a monkey, that can climb ropes
- a bird that can fly, though this is only available in one level.

The game is designed in such a way that Imogen cannot die, However, each play-through only allows 150 transformations. The game becomes unwinnable if Imogen hasn't escaped the dungeon by his final transformation.

Imogen, through its unique game mechanic, is often cited as one of the BBC Micro's best games.

Salamander

Date of release: July 1986

Region: Japan

Developer: Konami

Publisher: Konami

Platform: Arcade

Salamander, also known as Life Force: Salamander, is a single-player or cooperative-player, multi-scrolling shooter and is the third of the *Gradius* series of games after *Scramble* (1981) and *Gradius* (1985). The aim is to simply destroy waves of enemy aliens throughout the six stages of the game, with the ultimate aim of defeating the game's final boss and escaping the planet before it explodes. Salamander evolved the shoot 'em up genre with its rich alien graphics, power-up systems, featuring both horizontal- and vertical-scrolling stages and cooperative play.

Salamander has been ported to many home computers and home consoles over the years. It also spawned a three-volume anime series, first released in 1988. There are many games in the Gradius series. However, Salamander being a spin-off, strictly speaking, has only one sequel: *Salamander 2* (1996).

Metroid

Date of release: August 1986

Region: Japan

Developer: Nintendo R&D1

Publisher: Nintendo

Platform: Family Computer Disk System

Designed by Satoru Okada, Gunpei Yokoi, Hiroji Kiyotake and Yoshio Sakamoto, Metroid is a single-player, action-adventure, science-fiction themed, vertical- and horizontal-scrolling platform game. The aim of Metroid is to retrieve the parasitic Metroid organisms stolen by the space pirates. To fulfil this goal, the player must destroy 'Mother Brain', the biochemical life-form that controls the space pirate fortress located on the planet Zebes. You play as the bounty hunter Samus Aran, a space-suited figure with a laser beam weapon on their arm. Emphasis is placed on exploring the H.R. Giger-inspired environment and collecting power-ups. With these, the player can explore previously inaccessible regions of the game world. (This influenced many to adopt a similar game mechanic. This subgenre of games is sometimes referred to as Metroidvania games.) Power-ups increase the player's armour and weapons. Others allow the player to morph into a rolling ball, use bombs and perform a screw attack. These new abilities are used to defeat enemies and access new areas of the map. The game has multiple endings depending on the time of completion. It is only revealed that Samus Aran is female if the player completes the game in under five hours. Even though *Baraduke* (1985) had done a similar reveal one year earlier, Metroid still helped establish a strong female protagonist in a medium where the player usually took the part of a male.

The game was soon released for the NES. Metroid began one of Nintendo's most successful games franchises. Some of the most notable games in the Metroid series are *Super Metroid* (1994), *Metroid Fusion* (2002), *Metroid Prime* (2002), *Metroid Zero: Mission* (2004), *Metroid Prime 3: Corruption* (2007) and *Metroid Samus Returns* (2017).

The Sentinel/The Sentry

Date of release: 1986

Region: UK

Developer: Geoff Crammond

Publisher: Firebird

Platform: BBC Micro

The Sentinel is a single-player, first-person 3D puzzle game. The aim is to find the Sentinel in the three-dimensional, polygonal landscape, absorb it and take its place. You play as the Synthoid, a robot, whose only way to move around the self-contained environment is by absorbing the energy of objects, such as trees, and then using that energy to create another Synthoid into which the player transfers its consciousness. The player always begins somewhere on the lower part of the terrain and the Sentinel stands on the highest part of the terrain, slowly rotating 360 degrees, watching. If the Sentinel spots you, your energy begins to drain. If the player's energy drains completely, the game is over. However, if the player is desperate, they can use a hyperspace system which will jump them onto a random location of the map. Later levels contain Sentries which must be dealt with, as well as the ever-watchful Sentinel. The game has about 10,000 possible playable levels, due to the terrain being procedurally generated.

The Sentinel was one of the first home video games to fully feature 3D flat-shaded environments. Its unique game mechanics and graphics made it a cult favourite and it was soon ported to the other popular home computers of the time. It spawned one sequel, *Sentinel Returns* (1998), which was nowhere near as well-received as the original.

The Sentinel won Best Original Game in the 1986 Golden Joystick Awards.

Spindizzy

Date of release: 1986

Region: UK

Developer: Electric Dreams

Publisher: Electric Dreams

Platform: 8-bit home computers

Designed by Paul Shirley, Spindizzy is a single-player, isometric, puzzle platformer. The aim is to use the Gyroscopic Environmental Reconnaissance And Land-mapping Device, known as GERALD for short, to map every part of a strange artificial world discovered in a new dimension. There are 385 screens to map. GERALD can take the shape of a ball, gyroscope or an inverted pyramid. Unfortunately, these changes are purely cosmetic and play no part in the game's puzzles. The player must map the entire dimension in a set time. More time can be gained by collecting gems, but time will be lost if GERALD falls off the edge of the dimension. If your time runs out, the mission is aborted, you are pulled out of the dimension and the game is over. Success hinges on moving as quickly as possible over ramps, through mazes and up and down lifts, as well as overcoming other obstacles. The player can rotate the view in 90 degrees increments, giving them four different possible views to help navigate through some of the more tricky and precarious paths. The timer, jewels collected, and the number of screens left to map are all displayed on the screen.

Spindizzy was inspired by *Marble Madness* (1984), which shares many of the same game mechanics. Spindizzy had one sequel: *Spindizzy Worlds* (1990).

Super Sprint

Date of release: 1986

Region: USA

Developer: Atari Games

Publisher: Atari Games

Platform: Arcade

Designed by Robert Weatherby and Kelly Turner, Super Sprint is a single-player or multiplayer Formula One racing game. The aim is to be the first to finish the race. Each race requires three laps of the circuit, which is seen from an overhead perspective. There are eight circuits. When the game starts, the player can decide which circuit to race. The winner of each race continues onto the next circuit. There are many hazards for the player to avoid, including oil slicks and tornadoes. Super Sprint also features bridges, tunnels, shortcuts and ramps. If the player's car is destroyed it is quickly replaced on the track using a helicopter. The player can collect wrenches to customize their car between circuits. Customization choices include improved traction, better acceleration, or a higher top speed.

The arcade cabinet housed three sets of steering wheels and accelerator pedals. The screen didn't scroll but instead showed the entire circuit, and to accommodate this the screen resolution was 512 x 384, higher than many games of the time.

Super Sprint was ported to most popular home computers.

Out Run

Date of release: September 1986

Region: Japan

Developer: Sega

Publisher: Sega

Platform: Arcade

Designed by Yu Suzuki, Out Run is a single-player, third-person, racing game. The aim is to reach your finish line before the timer runs out. The player must pass checkpoints to refill their timer during the race or they will lose the game. The road forks numerous times, leading to one of five different finishing lines. Each one represents a different level of difficulty and cinematic. The player drives a Ferrari Testarossa Spider and must avoid other vehicles whilst driving through the countryside, deserts and by the ocean. Yu Suzuki was inspired by a trip to Europe for the game's locations.

Out Run was highly praised for its graphics (like two others of Suzuki's games – *Hang-On* and *Space Harrier* – it used the sprite-scaling technique), its music by Hiroshi Kawaguchi (featuring three different soundtracks selectable by the player), and its arcade cabinet. This was a sit-down cabinet in the shape of a car, with a steering wheel and pedals, which moved in sync with the game. All these features earned Out Run the reputation as a very cool game to play.

It was ported to most home computers and home consoles from 1986 to the current date. It also spawned several sequels, such as *Out Run 3-D* (1988), *Turbo Out Run* (1989), *Out Run Europa* (1991), *Out Runners* (1992) and *Out Run 2* (2003). Out Run was Sega's best-selling video game of the 1980s and won both Best Game of the Year and Best Arcade-Style Game of the Year in the 1987/1988 Golden Joystick Awards.

Dragon Ball: Dragon Daihikyo

Date of release: September 1986

Region: Japan

Developer: Epoch

Publisher: Epoch

Platform: Super Cassette Vision

Dragon Ball: Dragon Daihikyo is a single-player, vertical shoot 'em up.

There is nothing impressive about the game itself but Dragon Ball: Dragon Daihikyo is significant as it is the first video game based on the extremely popular Dragonball manga and then anime series. A few of the most notable of these are Dragon Ball Z: The Legacy of Goku 2 & Buu's Fury (2003), Dragon Ball Z: Budokai 3 (2004), Dragon Ball: Budokai Tenkaichi 3 (2007) and Dragon Ball FighterZ (2018).

Chiller

Date of release: 1986

Region: USA

Developer: Exidy

Publisher: Exidy

Platform: Arcade

Designed by Larry Hutcherson, Vic Tolomei and Ken Nicholson, Chiller is a single-player, horror-themed, light-gun game. The aim is to shoot (maiming or killing) various NPCs in each room for the most points possible. There are also eight hidden items in each of the rooms which give the player more points and a chance at a free game in the bonus round. The bonus rounds involve shooting at a one-armed bandit for extra points. There are four rooms in Chiller: torture chamber, backroom, hallway and graveyard. Chiller had extremely graphic violence compared to other video games of the time, with players able to blow flesh apart revealing bone underneath and witness as a hapless victim is slowly eaten, bit by bit, by an alligator, all accompanied by their tortured screams.

As with another Exidy game, *Death Race* (1976), Chiller was very controversial because of its violent content. Many amusement arcades wouldn't even buy it. Chiller was the most expensive arcade game at the time, able to output 256 colours to display its macabre bloody detail.

Bubble Bobble

Date of release: September 1986

Region: Japan

Developer: Taito

Publisher: Taito

Platform: Arcade

Designed by Fukio Mitsuji, Bubble Bobble is a single-player or cooperative platform game. The aim is to rescue the girlfriends of Bub and Bob, the cutesy dragon protagonists, from the Cave of Monsters. Bub and Bob must work through each level, tackling enemies by blowing out bubbles and trapping them inside. Once the trapped enemy is hit, it turns into fruit which the player can collect for points. Each stage is cleared once all the enemies are defeated. There are 100 stages in the game. The game had a number of different endings. If the game is completed with two players, it is revealed that Bub and Bob, and in turn their girlfriends, are human as they change back to their natural forms. Each screen of the game wraps around from bottom to top, meaning that if a player drops through a gap in the bottom of the screen they appear again at the top: handy for dodging monsters. There are several power-ups in the game. These include items that give the player increased speed or allow the player to blow bubbles faster. The umbrella, if collected, allows the player to skip some stages.

The game was immensely popular due to its fast and fun gameplay, not to mention its very catchy, and now classic, theme music by Tadashi Kimijima. It was soon ported to several platforms over the next several years.

There are dozens of games in the Bubble Bobble series. Here are just a few: *Rainbow Islands: The Story of Bubble Bobble 2* (1987), *Parasol Stars* (1991), *Bubble Bobble Part 2* (1993), *Puzzle Bobble* (1994), and *Bubble Memories: The Story of Bubble Bobble III (1996)*.

Castlevania

Date of release: September 1986

Region: Japan

Developer: Konami

Publisher: Konami

Platform: Family Computer Disk System

Castlevania is a single-player, action, horror-themed platformer. The aim is to seek out and destroy Count Dracula. You play as Simon Belmont and must enter Dracula's immense castle, avoiding obstacles and defeating various enemies that lurk within. The player can move left to right, jump, crouch and climb stairs to navigate their way around and avoid the many pitfalls they will encounter. Simon also has the use of a whip to destroy his enemies. The player has a health meter that depletes every time they take a hit from an enemy. Health can be restored by eating food scattered throughout the game world. When the player loses all their health, they lose a life. The player has four lives. More lives are granted when achieving a specific score. When all lives are lost, the game is over. However, the player can continue from the beginning of the current level.

Castlevania is renowned for its game design and music, as well as its difficulty.

It soon became a classic game for the Famicom and the NES in America, where it was released in May 1987. Castlevania was ported to a select few home computers, Gameboy Advance and, more recently, to mobile devices. The original Castlevania spawned a multitude of sequels over the years, some of the most notable being *Castlevania III: Dracula's Curse* (1989), *Super Castlevania IV* (1991), *Dracula X: Rondo of Blood* (1993), *Castlevania: Symphony of the Night* (1997), *Castlevania: Aria of Sorrow* (2003).

Akumajo Dracula, also known as *Vampire Killer*, was a Castlevania port. Released one month after the original Castlevania for the MSX2, Vampire Killer had improved graphics and alterations to some of its game mechanics yet is essentially the same game as Castlevania. An animated Castlevania Netflix series was first aired in 2017.

Square Co.

Square Co., also known as SquareSoft, is founded in Japan in September 1986 by Masafumi Miyamoto. Square Co. merged with Enix to form Square Enix in 2003.

Square Co. is best known for the *Final Fantasy* series (1987-current date), *Secret of Mana* (1993), *Chrono Trigger* (1995), *Super Mario RPG* (1996), *Bushido Blade* (1997), *Final Fantasy Tactics* (1997), *Xenogears* (1998), *Parasite Eve* (1998) and the *Kingdom Hearts* series (2002-present date).

Space Quest I

Date of release: October 1986

Region: USA

Developer: Sierra On-Line

Publisher: Sierra On-Line

Platform: DOS and Apple Computers

Designed by Mark Crowe, Scott Murphy and Sol Ackerman, Space Quest: Chapter I – The Sarien Encounter, or just Space Quest I, is a single-player, text-based adventure game. You play as Roger Wilko, the janitor on board the spaceship *Arcada*. The Sariens have killed the crew and stolen the experimental device known as the 'Star Generator'. The aim of the game is to retrieve the device. The player uses the arrow keys to control Roger's movement, and text commands to control his interaction with his environment. Space Quest I is full of puzzles, interesting characters and quirky humour, which would go on to define the series. There are many references to science-fiction movies and modern-day pop culture.

Space Quest I has many narrative similarities to *PlanetFall* (1983). However, that was a purely textual game. Space Quest I evolved this format with graphics and some fantastically designed characters. A remake with improved graphics was released in 1991.

Space Quest I went on to sell around 200,000 units. It was also ported over to the Amiga and Atari ST. There are six Space Quest games in the series, numbered 1-6, released between 1986-95.

Rampage

Date of release: 1986

Region: USA

Developer: Bally Midway

Publisher: Bally Midway

Platform: Arcade

Designed by Brian Colin, Jeff Nauman and Sharon Perry, Rampage is a single-player or multiplayer action game. The aim of Rampage is to destroy all the buildings. Each player controls a giant monster, either George the gorilla, Lizzie the 'Godzilla' or Ralph the werewolf. Each player must climb the buildings and bash them until they are reduced to rubble. Soldiers will attack from tanks and helicopters, or from the windows of the buildings, injuring the player's monster. Health can be restored by eating food found during gameplay or by simply eating a soldier. Civilians, waving their arms within the buildings, can be captured for more points. If the player's health is reduced to zero, they revert to their previous human form. Once the buildings are destroyed, the player proceeds to the next level, moving to different cities in the USA as they progress through the game. There are 768 levels or days in Rampage.

Even though the concept was rather common in the movie industry, giant monsters destroying cities was rather new to video games and controlling the monsters was great fun. The game was a success in the arcades, and Rampage was soon ported to most 8-

bit and 16-bit home computers and consoles. Many years later, Rampage spawned several sequels on numerous consoles. However, none of them was well-received. Rampage was released as a feature film in cinemas in 2018.

Defender of the Crown

Date of release: November 1986

Region: USA

Developer: Cinemaware

Publisher: Cinemaware

Platform: Amiga

Designed by Kellyn Beck and James D. Sachs, Defender of the Crown is a single-player strategy game. Set in England in the Middle Ages, the aim of Defender of the Crown is to gain control from your adversaries over all the territories and regain the lost crown. The player can choose between four different characters, each with different leadership qualities, jousting and swordplay abilities. The player also has an income and a sum of money in their treasury. This can be used to build your army, comprising, soldiers, knights and catapults, which are needed to lay siege to castles. The player can seek to conquer different territories in which case your army will be pitted against your enemies. Usually, the side with the biggest army will win. The player can also acquire territories by winning the jousting tournament. Random events occur, such as Norman rogues sabotaging your catapults and reducing them to piles of scrap, or a Saxon lady being kidnapped whom you can choose to rescue. If you do rescue her then a love scene is played out to add to the narrative that the player's character and the Saxon lady have fallen in love. When the final territory has fallen, you are declared king. It is revealed that Robin Hood has been holding onto the crown for safekeeping, which he now gives to you.

The game's graphics, created by James D. Sachs, were years ahead of anything else in the home gaming market and even surpassed a lot of what was in the arcade. Defender of the Crown was often used to showcase the Amiga's graphical prowess and potential as a platform for games. It influenced many game developers approach to art in video game graphics.

Defender of the Crown was Cinemaware's first game, each being based on various movie themes. These included *Rocket Ranger* (1988), *It Came from the Desert* (1989), and *Wings* (1990). Defender of the Crown sold over a million units. It was soon ported to the NES and most home computers of the time. However, most of these systems could not support the game's amazing graphics. Fortunately, Cinemaware expanded the gameplay to make up for this a little.

Alex Kidd in Miracle World

Date of release: November 1986

Region: Japan

Developer: Sega

Publisher: Sega

Platform: Sega Master System

Alex Kidd in Miracle World is a single-player, platform game. The villainous King Janken has taken over the kingdom and turned its citizens to stone. You play the young martial artist Alex Kidd. The aim is to defeat Janken and retrieve the crown. To do this the player must play through seventeen stages, defeating enemies and avoiding obstacles. Alex defeats enemies and breaks rocks, to collect money and other items, by punching with his mighty fists. Money can be spent at the shop to buy items, including vehicles such as a motorbike and helicopter, which can only be used during a specific part of the game. When Alex encounters Janken's Henchman he must play rock, paper, scissors to the death!

Alex Kidd in Miracle World was highly acclaimed by critics and consumers alike and spawned several Alex Kidd games. The other games in what is known as the Alex Kidd series are *Alex Kidd: The Lost Stars* (1986), *Alex Kidd BMX Trial* (1987), *Alex Kidd: High-Tech World* (1987), *Alex Kidd in the Enchanted Castle* (1989) and *Alex Kidd in Shinobi World* (1990).

Alex Kidd in Miracle World would go on to be built into many original Master Systems and Master System II consoles.

1986 Golden Joystick Awards

The 1986 Golden Joystick Awards were hosted in London.

Uridium (1986) wins Best Arcade-style Game of the Year.

Sentinel (1986) wins Best Original Game of the Year.

Knight Lore (1984) wins Best Game of the Year.

720°

Date of release: December 1986

Region: USA

Developer: Atari Games

Publisher: Atari Games

Platform: Arcade

Designed by John Salwitz and Dave Ralston, 720°, is a single-player, skateboarding game. The aim of 720° is to gain points to earn a ticket to the skate park and take part in the event there. The player starts the game in the streets and must avoid obstacles performing tricks to earn points. Once the timer bar runs out, the words 'Skate or Die!' appear. Killer bees are released (for some reason) and the player must reach the skate park before being intercepted by the bees. If the player is caught by the bees, they lose a life. At the park, the player gains points by doing tricks. Points mean money and medals; the money can be used to upgrade your equipment. There are four events in 720°. These are ramp, downhill, slalom and jump. There are four levels, in each event making up a total of sixteen events.

The screen size of 720° was larger than most arcades that preceded it. Whereas a typical arcade screen resolution would be something like 320 x 224, 720° was 512 x 384.

The game was ported to most 8-bit home computers and some home consoles.

Rolling Thunder

Date of release: December 1986

Region: Worldwide

Developer: Namco/Atari Games

Publisher: Namco/Atari Games

Platform: Arcade

Rolling Thunder is a single-player, side-scrolling, run and gun game. The aim is to save the female WCPO (World Crime Police Organization), Agent Leila Blitz. You play as Albatross, another WCPO agent, who must overcome a multitude of the hooded members of the secret society called Geldra. The player can duck or enter doors to take cover, jump and vault up to higher levels. You also have a pistol, and later an assault rifle. The game is split into stages, ten in total. At the end of each stage, you can see Agent Blitz being tortured on a large screen. At the end of the game, you must defeat the head of Geldra and rescue Agent Blitz.

Rolling Thunder was praised for its character design and animations.

Rolling Thunder was ported to most home computers and the NES. It spawned two sequels: *Rolling Thunder 2* (that offered cooperative play and the option to play as a female agent) (1990) and *Rolling Thunder 3* (1993).

Kid Icarus

Date of release: December 1986

Region: Japan

Developer: Nintendo R&D1

Publisher: Nintendo

Platform: Family Computer Disk System

Produced by Gunpei Yokoi, Kid Icarus, known as Light Mythology: Palthena's Mirror in Japan, is a single-player platform game with a Greek mythological theme. The aim is to recover three sacred treasures which are needed to save Angel Land and its ruler, the goddess Palutena. You control Pit, a winged boy with a bow and arrow, working your way through each level, jumping on platforms, killing monsters and collecting a variety of objects such as hearts. Hearts can be used to buy items at the shop. The player can enter through doorways into chambers containing different risks and rewards. Players can also increase their overall health and have the opportunity to enhance their bow and arrow in a number of ways, such as with increased range or flaming arrows, which can hit multiple targets. Pit can shoot arrows in four different directions. The screen scrolls vertically or horizontally with the player, dependent on the stage. There are three major stages within the game – the underworld, the overworld and Skyworld. A boss must be defeated at the end of each stage to gain a sacred treasure.

The game would be released a few months later in the rest of the world for the NES. Kid Icarus is renowned for its gameplay and music. It is considered a classic 1980s' platformer. Despite being so popular, the game only saw two sequels, and these were to come years later with *Kid Icarus: Of Myths and Monsters* (1991) and *Kid Icarus Uprising* (2012).

1986 Notable Omissions

Academy. Ace of Aces. Adventure Island. *Alex Kidd: The Lost Stars*. Alter Ego. Army Moves. Balloon Fight. Batman. BMX Simulator. Bomb Jack II. Boulder Dash 3. Chiller (same name, different game). Double Dribble. Druid. Fantasy Zone. Finders Keepers. Fist 2: The Legend Continues. Gauntlet II. Genpei Toma Den. Goody. Gunfight. Gunship. Habitat. Happing Mappy. Jackal/Top Gunner. King's Quest III. Knightmare. Labyrinth. Mappy-Land. Mercenary: The Second City. Mighty Bomb Jack. Mind Walker. Might and Magic Book One: The Secret of the Inner Sanctum (First Might and Magic game). Mobius: The Orb of Celestial Harmony. Mr. Goemon. Pentagram. Play Choice – 10. Plump Pop. Pro Baseball: Family Stadium. Rebelstar. Renegade. Side Pocket. Sky Kid Deluxe. Slap Fight. Starflight. Starglider. Super Hang-On. Super Mario Bros. The Lost Levels. The Goonies. The Return of Ishtar. Trap Door. Trinity. Victory Road. World Games. Yie Ar Kung-Fu II. Xanadu Scenario II.

1987

Darius

Date of release: February 1987

Region: Japan

Developer: Taito

Publisher: Taito

Platform: Arcade

Designed by Toshio Kohno, Darius is a single-player or multiplayer, side-scrolling shoot 'em up. The aim of Darius is to defeat waves of enemies and the boss at the end of each zone. The game is made up of 28 zones. After each boss, the player chooses one of two paths to take. Therefore, the player only plays 7 zones in a single run. Other zones can be explored in other play-throughs. Similar to many shoot 'em ups of the time, specific enemy types drop power-up items for the player/s to collect, such as bombs, missiles and shields.

Darius's stand-out feature was its three horizontal displays to make one huge panoramic view. To accomplish this, the left and right screen are reflected by a one-way mirror, in alignment with the display in the middle which is the only screen facing the player. The effect is an almost seamless view, three displays wide. Each display has a typical resolution of 288 x 224, giving an overall display of 864 x 224. This was very impressive in 1987.

Darius was ported to a few home computers and consoles of the time. However, due to display limitations, they could not emulate the arcade's unique three-screen experience. Darius spawned several sequels including *Darius II* (1989), the only sequel to feature the three-screen set-up, *Darius Gaiden* (1994) and *G-Darius* (1997).

Contra

Date of release: February 1987

Region: Japan

Developer: Konami

Publisher: Konami

Platform: Arcade

Designed by Koji Hiroshita, Contra, also known as Gryzor or Probotector, Contra is a single- or two-player, multi-directional, scrolling, run and gun game. The original arcade version is set in the year 2633 A.D. An alien entity has landed on Earth and taken control of the evil Red Falcon organisation. The player must take out waves of enemies and ultimately destroy the alien entity. The game switches from side-scrolling with upper and lower levels to a forward-facing 3D perspective. Players can move left, right, duck and jump, leaping to higher levels and dropping to lower levels. You can also fire in any one of eight directions. The player begins the game with a standard rifle. Other weapons can be acquired by destroying specific enemy types. These weapons include a machine gun, spread gun, laser gun and a fireball gun. Other power-ups include an increase in firing speed and a temporary impenetrable shield. There are seven levels in Contra, beginning outside in the jungle and ending up inside the enemy's base.

Contra continued the popular trend of having two players work together against a common foe, a trend that would continue for years to come. The game became renowned for its difficulty. It was ported to many different platforms under one of the three names previously mentioned. It spawned several sequels. Most notable of these are *Super Contra* (1988), *Contra III: The Alien Wars* (1992), *Contra: Hard Corps* (1994), *Neo Contra* (2004), *Contra 4* (2007) and *Hard Corps: Uprising* (2011).

Bionic Commando

Date of release: March 1987

Region: Japan

Developer: Capcom

Publisher: Capcom

Platform: Arcade

Designed by Tokuro Fujiwara, Bionic Commando, known as Top Secret in Japan, is a single-player, multi-directional-scrolling platform game, advertised in the USA as a sequel to *Commando* (1985). The aim is to defeat a multitude of enemies as you infiltrate their base in an effort to stop a missile launch and defeat their leader, who was originally a revived Adolf Hitler, although this was changed in the international version.

There are four levels: Forest, The Enemy Outpost, The Underground Base, and the Final Base. The player can use the character's bionic arm which has the ability to extend. This can be used to grab levels directly above or at a 45-degree angle, in which case the player can swing across a gap or swing and pull themselves up to a higher level. The arm can also be used to take out enemies, or the player can use their gun.

Bionic Commando was well received and soon ported to most of the popular home computers of the time. Bionic Commando spawned several sequels: *Bionic Commando: Elite Forces* (1999), *Bionic Commando* (2009) and *Bionic Commando Rearmed 2* (2011).

Operation Wolf

Date of release: 1987

Region: Japan

Developer: Taito

Publisher: Taito

Platform: Arcade

Operation Wolf is a single-player, first-person, on-rails shooter. The aim of the game is to rescue five hostages. You play as Special Forces Operative, Roy Adams. The player must dispatch numerous enemies who appear on-screen and try to eliminate you. Enemies attack with knives, guns, grenades, mortars, armoured vehicles and helicopters. The player's damage bar fills up whenever you're hit or if you shoot any civilians. Damage can be recovered with health power-ups, and ammunition can be replenished by shooting such things as barrels and crates. A special machine-gun power-up gives the player 10 seconds of unlimited fire and an increased rate of fire, allowing the player to lay waste to their enemies. There are six stages in the game, each with a different environment and bonuses after completion. For the most part, players can choose which stages to play. The final stage has the player shooting enemies while the hostages jump onto a moving rescue plane.

The arcade featured a mounted gun that would reverberate when the trigger was pressed. A red button on the side of the gun was used to throw a grenade. The game does not use light-gun technology, instead using spatial positioning within the mechanism of the gun to determine the rotation of the gun and where it is pointing on the screen.

Operation Wolf Began a new genre of rail-shooters featuring weapons as part of the cabinet. As well as spawning three sequels of its own – *Operation Thunderbolt* (1988), *Operation Wolf 3* (1994) and *Operation Tiger* (1998) – it influenced similar arcade rail-shooter games. Some of these were: *Terminator 2: Judgment Day* (1991), the *Virtua Cop* series (1994-2003), the *Point Blank* series (1994-2016), the *Time Crises* series (1995-2015) and *The House of the Dead* series (1996-2018).

Zarch/Virus

Date of release: 1987

Region: UK

Developer: David Braben

Publisher: Superior/Acornsoft

Platform: Acorn Archimedes

Zarch, also known as Virus, is a single-player, third-person, 3D shooter. The aim of Zarch is to prevent a virus from being spread across the landscape by destroying all the enemy vessels in each level. The player must shoot down all the seeder vessels spreading the virus, as well as taking on the more deadly attack craft supporting the seeder vessels. Once done, the player receives bonus points depending on how much of the landscape remains uninfected. Each stage gives the player a new landscape to protect. The player's position in the overall landscape is shown on a mini-map at the top left of the screen. An altimeter bar is also displayed at the top of the screen, giving the player an idea of how close they are to the ground. This is very useful after dogfighting high up in the air.

Zarch can be an extremely difficult game to play, like *Defender* (1980), only a small part of the game world is displayed at a time. Enemies can abruptly appear, requiring a little luck to defeat. Players also must contend with gravity and not crashing into the landscape while taking the fight to the enemy: game mechanics reminiscent of *Gravitar* (1982) and *Thrust* (1986).

Despite its difficulty, critics and consumers were taken by its gameplay and astonished by its 3D graphics. Most games were 2D and those that were 3D either used techniques such as sprite-scaling or were slow-moving. Zarch/Virus was a milestone in 3D video games. Its smooth, fast-moving gameplay featured shaded polygonal landscapes and ships, real-time 3D lighting effects and shadowing, and multiple particle generation for ships' thrust, fire and virus effects: even these particle effects had shadows! It was years ahead of its time. David Braben had done something ground-breaking with *Elite* (1984) and he did it yet again with Zarch/Virus. The game was ported to a handful of home computers and spawned a pseudo-sequel with *Conqueror* (1988).

Amiga 2000 and Amiga 500

The Amiga 2000 and Amiga 500 were released in the USA in April 1987.

Despite the release of the first Amiga model (1000) in 1985, it wasn't until the release of the more affordable Amiga 500 when games began to flourish on the platform. Ports of games between the 8-bit and 16-bit versions were noticeably different as far as graphics were concerned. Quite often the Amiga version of any given port from the Arcade was the closest version to the original. It was at this time when Nintendo attempted to release the NES into Europe. The Amiga's graphics and sound prowess made the ageing NES look like old news and Nintendo's console failed to get the same traction it had in Japan and North America.

As with Commodore's previous 8-bit machine, the Commodore 64, the 16-bit Amiga had a strong homebrew and demo scene, pervading the home computing culture and pushing the boundaries in terms of graphics and sound on this incredible machine.

The Amiga 500 was a huge success, selling over five million units. Notable games for it included *Defender of the Crown* (1986), *International Karate +* (1987), *F18 Interceptor* (1988), *Batman* (1989), *Shadow of the Beast* (1989), *Alien Breed* (1991), *Lemmings* (1991), *Turrican II: The Final Fight* (1991), *Cannon Fodder* (1993), *Dune II: The Fight for Arrakis* (1993) and *Speedball 2: Brutal Deluxe* (1993).

Wizball

Date of release: May 1987

Region: UK

Developer: Sensible Software

Publisher: Ocean Software

Platform: Commodore 64

Designed by John Hare, Chris Yates and Peter Johnson, Wizball is a single-player or two-player, side-scrolling, shoot 'em up. The aim of Wizball is to return all the colour, stolen by the evil Zark, to the now-grey Wizworld. You play the part of a wizard who has turned himself into a magical green ball, shooting enemies and collecting the three colours (red, blue and green) that they drop.

There is a total of eight levels in the game. The wizard can navigate through different levels using portals. These are limited to three levels, to begin with. However, more levels can be accessed as the player progresses. The player can acquire the assistance of his cat, Catellite, also in ball form which can be sent forth to collect drops, without any risk to the player, by merely holding down the fire button. Catellite can be controlled independently by a second player in two-player mode.

Wizball was highly praised and is considered one of the Commodore 64's best games. It was soon ported to other 8-bit and 16-bit home computers. Wizball spawned one sequel with *Wizkid: The Story of Wizball II* (1992).

The Ninja Warriors

Date of release: 1987

Region: Japan

Developer: Taito

Publisher: Taito

Platform: Arcade

The Ninja Warriors is a single-player, side-scrolling, action game. The aim is to defeat the corrupt forces of the President of the USA. In the year 1993, the tyrannical president has declared martial law. Only the female Ninja android 'Kunoichi' or the male ninja android 'Ninja' can stop him. The player must defeat waves of enemies using hand-to-hand combat or using limited shurikens. The game comprises of six levels. At the end of the game, the android must kill the president. However, the Ninja warrior is double-crossed as a General remote-detonates the android, taking the White House with it.

Like *Darius* (1987), The Ninja Warriors also featured three horizontal displays to make one huge panoramic view for the play area. To accomplish this, the left and right screen are reflected by a one-way mirror in alignment with the display in the middle, which is in actuality there, facing the player. The effect is an almost seamless view, three displays wide. Each display had a typical resolution of 288 x 224, giving the overall display an impressive 864 x 224 pixels.

The game received positive reviews and spawned one sequel on the SNES with the imaginatively titled *The Ninja Warriors Again* (1994).

Dizzy: The Ultimate Cartoon Adventure

Date of release: June 1987

Region: UK

Developer: Andrew Oliver and Philip Oliver (commonly known as the Oliver Twins)

Publisher: Codemasters

Platform: 8-bit home computers

Dizzy is a single-player platform game. The aim of Dizzy is to collect several items scattered around Katmandu and put them in a cauldron to create a potion to defeat the evil wizard Zaks. The items Dizzy needs to collect are a cloud's silver lining, a vampire dux feather, and a troll brew. Only one item can be carried at a time. The player controls Dizzy, a cute anthropomorphic egg, who tumbles through the air when he jumps, hence the name of the game. Various hazards must be avoided, or Dizzy will lose a life. The player has three lives.

Even though the original Dizzy was released on only three platforms, it was very well received, especially on the ZX Spectrum. The Oliver Twins knew their market well and focused on giving the consumer what they wanted: well-presented graphics and tight gameplay.

The Dizzy series became one of the most successful British video game franchises, publishing around 20 titles in total. Some of the most notable Dizzy games include *Treasure Island Dizzy* (1988), *Magicland Dizzy* (1990), *Spellbound Dizzy* (1991), *Fantastic Dizzy* (1991), *Dizzy: Prince of the Yolkfolk* (1991) and *Crystal Kingdom Dizzy* (1992).

Ys 1: Ancient Ys Vanished

Date of release: June 1987

Region: Japan

Developer: Nihon Falcom

Publisher: Nihon Falcom

Platform: PC-8801

Ys 1: Ancient Ys Vanished, also known as Ys: The Vanished Omens or The Ancient Land of Ys, was designed by Masaya Hashimoto and Tomoyoshi Miyazaki, with beautifully composed music by Yuzo Koshiro. Ys 1: Ancient Ys Vanished is a single-player, action RPG. The aim of Ancient Ys Vanished is to find all six books of the ancient land of Ys and, with the knowledge they reveal, banish the evil which has befallen the island. You play as Adol, who was swept up on the shores of the island. The player converses with NPCs of the various towns, can buy and sell at the shops and explore the land and dungeons, occasionally finding treasure chests. As with other JRPGs of the time, the game is played from a top-down perspective. However, Ys was unique from other JRPGs in that the view did not change when entering combat. The enemy encounters were not random: they could be seen in the game world, like the *Zelda* games. Even more unique was what was termed the 'bump attack' system, whereby the player automatically attacks the enemy on contact. Certain rules applied: if the player attacks the enemy dead-centre, the player receives the most damage. Off-centre, the enemy takes most of the damage. If the player can attack the enemy's side or back, then the enemy receives all the damage. This required a certain level of practice yet was very rewarding if mastered. It could be tough if the player ventured into areas with stronger enemies. However, the game balanced this out by having the character's health naturally recharge merely by standing still for a short amount of time. The player could also quickly level their character up and have them buy a better sword, shield and armour.

The game was ported to other Japanese home computers and consoles, as well as the Apple II and MS-DOS Platforms. Ancient Ys Vanished was the first game in what is now known as the Ys series. Some of the most notable of these games are *Ys IV: The Dawn of Ys* (1993), *Ys VI: The Ark of Napishtim* (2003), *Ys: The Oath in Felghana* (2005), *Ys Seven* (2009) and *Ys: Lacrimosa of Dana* (2016).

RoadBlasters

Date of release: June 1987

Region: USA

Developer: Atari Games

Publisher: Atari Games

Platform: Arcade

RoadBlasters is a single-player, third-person, vehicular combat game. The aim is to drive your armed car to the finish line before running out of fuel.

There are 50 levels/races to take part in. Enemy cars can be destroyed with the onboard cannon of the player's car, while indestructible obstacles must be avoided. Extra fuel can be picked up on the road and a fuel bonus is awarded, based on your score, at the end of each race. The game ends if the player runs out of fuel and therefore cannot continue.

RoadBlasters received medium to high praise from critics and consumers and was ported to various platforms of the time.

A.P.B.

Date of release: 1987

Region: USA

Developer: Atari Games

Publisher: Atari Games

Platform: Arcade

A.P.B. (All Points Bulletin) is a single-player, top-down view, vehicular combat game. You play as police rookie, Officer Bob. The aim is to fulfil your daily quota of giving out tickets or arrests. The game starts with a quick practice driving around a course. The player then moves onto handing out tickets to littering drivers by driving up to the perp's car and pressing the siren button. As the days (similar to stages or levels) go by, the crimes become more serious. The player must meet their quota before the day is out, displayed as a timer. Drive-thru donut shops give the player more time. The player can drive through the 'Speed Shop' to get high-performance equipment. When an A.P.B. is called, the player must catch the fugitive and take them back to the station. There they must force a confession before the chief enters the room. By alternatively tapping the fire and siren button, an amusing animation of the fugitive being shaken is played out. The game also has a demerit system. If you cause too much damage, don't meet your quota or falsely arrest someone, the player will receive demerits. Too many demerits and the game is over.

The cabinet came in two versions, one with a seat and one without. The controls comprised a steering wheel, pedal, fire button and siren button. When the siren button was pressed the red and blue lights at the top of the cabinet lit up and the siren sounded. A.P.B. was cited as being overly complex by some but uniquely refreshing by others. However, everyone enjoyed the humour injected into the game.

Digital Devil Story: Megami Tensei

Date of release: July 1987

Region: Japan

Developer: Atlus

Publisher: Namco

Platform: Famicom

Based on the Japanese Science Fantasy novels written by Aya Nishitani, Digital Devil Story: Megami Tensei, directed by Kouji Okada, is a single-player, first-person Role-playing game and one of the first games in the Megami Tensei series. The game is set in a high school where the main protagonists Akemi Nakajima and Yumiko Shirasagi summon demons using a computer program. To stop the demons, they must enter a dungeon and dispatch various monsters. The dungeon is also inhabited by NPCs whom the player can converse with, buy and sell goods, and replenish their health. After each turn-based combat encounter, Monsters/Demons can be negotiated with, and if successful, can be summoned to fight for you. This would become a hallmark game mechanic in the Megami Tensei series. The game is known for its difficulty partially due to its restrictions on saving the game and its tough enemies, especially bosses, which require the player to grind and level-up to beat.

Another game of the same name, also based on the novels, was released in 1987 for various Japanese home computers. This game was a top-down dungeon crawler, reminiscent of *Gauntlet* (1985). An Anime movie based on the first novel was also released earlier the same year. In 1995 Opera House developed an enhanced port of the original Famicom version for the Super Famicom. There are over a dozen games in the main Megami Tensei series, some of the most notable of these are: *Shin Megami Tensei III: Nocturne* (2003), *Shin Megami Tensei: Strange Journey Redux* (2009), and *Shin Megami Tensei IV* (2013).

Megami Tensei has also spawned several spin-off games. The most successful of these is the very popular Persona series. The first of which was *Revelations: Persona*, released in 1996.

Double Dragon

Date of release: July 1987

Region: Japan

Developer: Technōs Japan

Publisher: Taito

Platform: Arcade

Designed by Yoshihisa Kishimoto, Shinichi Saito and Koji Kai, Double Dragon is a single-player or two-player, side-scrolling beat 'em up, and the spiritual successor to *Renegade* (1986). One or two players control street tough guys, twin Brothers Billy and Jimmy Lee. The aim is to rescue Billy Lee's girlfriend by taking on waves of thugs, some of whom just use their fists while others wield weapons. Players can disarm enemies and use their weapons, which include a baseball bat, whip, knife and stick of dynamite. Certain objects in the environment can be picked up and thrown, dealing out damage to enemies, such as barrels, boxes and rocks. The staples of the player's attacks are using punches, kicks, jump kicks and throws to defeat the street thugs. Each player loses a life when their life gauge is depleted. This happens if you are hit too many times, or if you fall down a pit or into some other hazard. The player will also lose a life if the timer reaches zero. The timer restarts at the beginning of each stage. Each stage has a boss to defeat at the end if the player is to continue. There are four stages in the game. If the game is played with one player then once the final boss is defeated, the player rescues the girl. However, if the game is played with two players then the final boss must be defeated, after which the brothers fight one another for the girl's affections.

Double Dragon was a very popular game in the Arcade as well as on the home computer and home console ports. It was one of the best examples of the cooperative beat 'em up genre of the time. Double Dragon spawned several sequels including *Double Dragon II: The Revenge* (1988), *Double Dragon 3: The Rosetta Stone* (1990) and *Super Double Dragon* (1992).

Driller/Space Station Oblivion

Date of release: 1987

Region: Japan

Developer: Major Developments

Publisher: Incentive Software

Platform: 8-bit and 16-bit home computers

Known as Space Station Oblivion in the USA, Driller is a single-player, first-person, puzzle/shooter game. The aim is to drop a series of mining rigs on the abandoned moon of Mitral before the four-hour time limit is up. The mining rigs will vent the build-up of gas from within the moon. If the player fails in their mission, the moon will explode, taking with it the nearby inhabited planet. There are eighteen rigs to drop. The player must find these sites and deal with many obstacles, including an active security system that views the player as hostile.

Driller was one of the first home video games to feature flat-shaded 3D graphics from a first-person perspective (as opposed to wireframe, or a mix of both) using the Freescape game engine by Incentive Software. A nine-minute-long soundtrack by Matt Gray that plays during the loading screen establishes an atmospheric mood. It is considered by some as a classic piece in this era of home computer games.

Driller spawned one sequel with *Dark Side* (1988).

Leisure Suit Larry in the Land of the Lounge Lizards

Date of release: July 1987

Region: USA

Developer: Sierra On-Line

Publisher: Sierra On-Line

Platform: Apple II and PC DOS

Designed by Al Lowe, Ken Williams and Mark Crowe of Sierra On-Line, Leisure Suit Larry in the Land of the Lounge Lizards is a single-player, text and graphical adventure game. The aim is to ensure that Larry Laffer, the game's 38-year-old male protagonist, finally loses his virginity. The player must solve several puzzles to accomplish this goal. The player controls Larry using the directional keys and interacts with NPCs and objects by typing in text commands. Money must be won during games of Blackjack or on a slot machine game in order for the player to pay for taxis and buy drinks to essentially progress through the game. Larry attempts to woo several women yet is rejected until the end of the game, where he finally achieves his goal.

Leisure Suit Larry in the Land of the Lounge Lizards' cheesy, light-hearted, adult-themed premise set it apart from the crowd, making it a cult hit. A minority of people considered the game sleazy and tasteless. However, it wasn't long before initially slow sales suddenly rocketed, and the game sold over 300,000 units.

The game was re-released with improved graphics and sound in 1991 for the Amiga, DOS and Macintosh. A remake was also released with *Leisure Suit Larry: Reloaded* (2013). There are several Leisure Suit Larry games. Some of the most notable are *Leisure Suit Larry III: Passionate Patti in Pursuit of the Pulsating Pectorals* (1989), *Leisure Suit Larry 6: Shape Up or Slip Out!* (1993) and *Leisure Suit Larry 7: Love for Sail!* (1996).

Xybots

Date of release: 1987

Region: USA

Developer: Atari Games

Publisher: Atari Games

Platform: Arcade

Designed by Ed Logg and Bob Flanngan, Xybots is a single-player or two-player cooperative, 3D, third-person shooter. The aim is to infiltrate the fortress and destroy the robot enemies that have invaded the planet. You play as either Major Rock Hardy and/or Captain Ace Gunn, dependent on whether you are playing alone or in two-player cooperative mode. Each player possesses a laser gun to destroy the Xybots. Enemies will drop energy pods which are needed to top up your energy. Energy depletes from 100% to 0% as the player moves and shoots, acting as a timer. Enemies will also drop coins, which can be used at the shop between levels to buy power-ups, such as increased shot power, slow energy loss, enemy mapper, warning arrow, extra armour and increased speed. The screen is divided into multiple sections. The bottom half of the screen is split into two, showing a third-person, 3D view of the play area. The top left and top right of the screen show each player's respective status. The top middle part of the screen displays the map.

Xybots' controls were something of a rarity. To turn your character 90 degrees the player needed to twist the joystick left or right. It is easy to see how this was originally going to be a gauntlet game, only from a 3D third-person perspective, and it still maintains many of the same mechanics.

Even though Xybots wasn't exactly a resounding success, its uniqueness sets it apart from many other arcade games of the day, giving it something of a cult status. The game was ported to most 8-bit and 16-bit home computers as well as to the Atari Lynx (1989). Xybots is considered by some to be a precursor of the modern-day third-person shooter or action-adventure game.

R-Type

Date of release: July 1987

Region: Japan

Developer: Irem

Publisher: Irem

Platform: Arcade

R-Type is a single-player, science-fiction themed, horizontal-scrolling shooter. The aim is to defeat the Bydo aliens that are threatening to destroy humanity. The player controls the R-9a starship *Arrowhead* which is armed with a wave cannon. The player can tap the fire button to unleash multiple weak shots or hold the button down to increase the power of the beam. Enemies come in many different shapes and sizes. Destroying specific groups of enemy ships allows the player to collect power-ups, which add something to help the player defeat the host of alien enemies. These include diagonal lasers that bounce around the screen damaging/destroying enemies, an inexhaustible source of guided missiles, and speed boosts. The most significant of these power-ups is what is called a force. The force is an indestructible ball that can be attached to the front of the player's ship, acting as a shield. The player can detach the force at any point and attach it onto the back of their ship to act as a shield to the rear, or they can have the force floating free. The force also fires and destroys any enemies it comes into contact with. The player can acquire two forces that can wreak a lot of havoc when set free. R-Type comprises eight stages with a boss at the end of each stage. These bosses were unlike anything seen before in a video game: either huge animated, nightmare creatures, or an alien ship larger than the entire screen. After defeating the final boss, your ship is joined by the other R-9a's as you celebrate the destruction over the invading Bydo.

R-Type was highly praised for its graphics (heavily influenced by the alien movies and the work of H.R. Giger), its music by Masato Ishizaki and its game mechanics, as well as being renowned for its high difficulty.

The game was ported to most platforms of the time and was quite often seen as a benchmark for the said platform, with the ageing 8-bits falling short of the mark in terms of graphics, while the Amiga, PC Engine and TurboGafx-16 versions were pretty much close to arcade-perfect. R-Type is often cited for being one of the best arcades and the best shoot 'em up of all time. Even though some of its game mechanics had been seen before, R-type seemed to embody and perfect the genre in a way that has never been seen since. As with many games that become untouchable classics, it was all a case of timing and 1987 was the perfect time for R-Type. It was a forgone conclusion that R-Type would see numerous sequels. Some of the most notable are *R-Type II* (1989), *R-Type Leo* (1992), *R-Type III: The Third Lightning* (1993), *R-Type Delta* (1998) and *R-Type Final* (2003).

Metal Gear

Date of release: July 1987

Region: Japan

Developer: Konami

Publisher: Konami

Platform: MSX2

Designed by Hideo Kojima, who would go on to spearhead the development of the Metal Gear series, Metal Gear is a single-player, top-down, action-adventure, stealth game. The aim is to infiltrate the heavily armed country of Outer Heaven, rescue the captured members of FOXHOUND and destroy Metal Gear, a walking tank capable of launching a nuclear strike anywhere in the world. You play as Solid Snake, an operative of the Special Forces Unit FOXHOUND. The player is contacted by his handler Big Boss and other characters, who each supply useful tips on how to progress through the game. The emphasis in Metal Gear is on stealth as the player soon learns that direct confrontation with the enemy is best avoided. Sneak attacks from behind rather than frontal assault is the name of the game. Being spotted by enemies or cameras will raise an alarm, which can end things rather quickly for Snake. Key cards must be used to open doors to new areas. There are also items such as weapons, rations, a gas mask, cigarettes and a cardboard box that can be found and used in certain situations. Freeing prisoners increases Snake's rank, giving him increased maximum health and carrying capacity. The player must also deal with several bosses such as Shoot Gunner armed with a riot gun, 'Machinegun Kid armed with a machine gun (no surprise there), Fire Trooper armed with a flamethrower, Coward Duck armed with a deadly boomerang, and finally the end boss.

The game went onto enjoy a fair amount of success, selling well over one million units. Metal Gear was soon ported to the Famicom and NES. In 1990 it was also ported to MS-DOS and Commodore 64 platforms. Not until after 2004 would it see widespread ports to other consoles and even mobile devices.

Many of the plot devices, characters, emphasis on stealth, boss fights, twists in the narrative and even items such as the cardboard box would become regular features in future Metal Gear games. Some of the most notable of these are *Metal Gear Solid* (1998), *Metal Gear Solid 3: Snake Eater* (2004), *Metal Gear Solid 4: Guns of the Patriots* (2008), *Metal Gear Solid: Peace Walker* (2010) and *Metal Gear Solid V: The Phantom Pain* (2015).

After Burner

Date of release: July 1987

Region: Japan

Developer: Sega AM2

Publisher: Sega

Platform: Arcade

Designed by Yu Suzuki and music by Hiroshi Kawaguchi, who both worked on *Hang-on* (1985) and *Space Harrier* (1985) After Burner is a single-player, third-person, flight combat simulator. The aim of the game is to destroy as many of the enemy aircraft as possible. The player controls an F-14 Tomcat fighter jet. To dispatch enemy planes, the player must use their F-14's machine guns or a limited number of heat-seeking missiles.

There are eighteen stages in After Burner, featuring a variety of environments. The game is remembered for employing the same scaling-sprite technique used in *Hang-on* (1985) and *Space Harrier* (1985). It also used a rotating cockpit cabinet, requiring players to strap in, making for a thrilling arcade experience. Stereo sound and flashing lights inside the cockpit added to the intensity of the fast-paced gameplay – an intensity that was matched by only a few of its contemporaries.

After Burner spawned several sequels and spin-off games, such as *After Burner II* (1987), *G-Loc: Air Battle* (1990), *Strike Fighter/ After Burner III* (1991) *Sky Target* (1995) and *After Burner Climax* (2006).

Alien Syndrome

Date of release: 1987

Region: Japan

Developer: Sega

Publisher: Sega

Platform: Arcade

Alien Syndrome is a single-player or two-player, top-down perspective, multi-directional-scrolling, run and gun game. The aim of Alien Syndrome is to destroy the aliens within each ship or space station and rescue any captured crew. The player/s can choose between being Ricky or Mary. When the game begins, the player is informed of how many people must be rescued before the bomb goes off. Waves of aliens must be killed to find and free each of your comrades. Map terminals keep you updated as to where any remaining comrades are. Weapon depots give the player new weapons, such as a flamethrower, and robot depots give the player small accompanying attack robots. When the crew are rescued a door opens and the player must destroy the alien boss that waits inside. Once the boss is defeated, the ship explodes, and the player moves onto the next round. There are seven rounds and a final boss. The alien bosses are especially grotesque.

Alien Syndrome was heavily influenced by the *Alien* movies directed Ridley Scott and James Cameron, and John Carpenter's *The Thing*.

Alien Syndrome was ported to most of the popular home computers and consoles of the time. The game received a remake in 2004 and a sequel, *Alien Syndrome* (2007).

NetHack

Date of release: July 1987

Region: worldwide

Developer: The NetHack DevTeam

Platform: MS-DOS

NetHack is a single-player, fantasy, roguelike game. The aim is to retrieve the Amulet of Yendor. Similar to its predecessor *Hack* (1985), the player must traverse dungeons, encounter monsters and use items to stay alive. It displays the world using text-based characters, also known as ASCII characters.

Over the years updated versions were released. As of 1989, NetHack was also open-source, meaning that the code was available to anyone. People could develop their own version of it. There were also many software applications that would translate and enhance NetHack's ASCII look for 2D graphics, for those who didn't consider themselves purists. 'NetHack for Microsoft' and 'NetHack on OPENSTEP/NeXTSTEP' changed ASCII text to graphical tiles to represent the dungeons, while 'Vulture's Eye' created an isometric perspective of the game.

NetHack had a strong, faithful following.

Street Fighter

Date of release: August 1987

Region: Japan

Developer: Capcom

Publisher: Capcom

Platform: Arcade

Designed by Takashi Nishiyama and Hiroshi Matsumoto, Street Fighter is a single-player or two-player fighting game. You play as Ryu in the single-player game and Ryu or Ken in the two-player game. The aim is to defeat your opponents at an international martial arts tournament. The player can perform a series of different punches and kicks, defend, and use three special moves. These are Psycho Fire (Hadoken), Dragon Punch (Shoryuken), and Hurricane Kick (Tatsumaki Senpu Kayaku). These special moves are performed by quickly using a specific joystick and buttons combination. The moves were not displayed on the cabinet, only revealed by accident, familiarisation and eventually mastery. This knowledge, of course, can be passed onto other players.

Street Fighter was the first video game to introduce joystick/button combination special moves. The game itself was well-received; however, it will always live in the shadow of its sequel which refined the game perfectly. Nonetheless, the original Street Fighter did lay the groundwork for the many sequels that lay ahead, sometimes releasing multiple titles in a single year. Some of the most notable are *Street Fighter II* (1991), *Street Fighter II Turbo: Hyper Fighting* (1992), *Super Street Fighter II Turbo* (1994), *Street Fighter Alpha 2* (1996), *Street Fighter Alpha 3* (1998), *Street Fighter III: 3rd Strike* (1999),

Ultra Street Fighter IV (2014) and *Street Fighter V: Arcade Edition* (2018). Street Fighter was ported to most 8-bit and 16-bit home computers and consoles of the time.

The Guild of Thieves

Date of release: 1987

Region: UK

Developer: Magnetic Scrolls

Publisher: Rainbird Software

Platform: 8-bit and 16-bit home computers

Designed by Rob Steggles, The Guild of Thieves is a single-player, text and graphic adventure game. The aim is to ransack a castle and the surrounding area of all its valuables. You play as an aspiring member of the Guild of Thieves. The game is essentially text-based with rendered images, which looked beautiful on the 16-bit computers.

Guild of Thieves was not only known for its outstanding graphics; it also had intriguing puzzles and well-written narrative. As was popular with such games of the time, it came packaged with several items, or feelies, to evoke a more in-depth experience. Included with the game were a map, a contract of service, thief's newsletter, adventure guide, and Bank of Kerovnia account card.

The Guild of Thieves takes place in the same world as a previous text-based game *The Pawn* (1985). The Guild of Thieves won Best Adventure Game at the 1987/1988 Golden Joystick Awards.

Head Over Heels

Date of release: 1987

Region: UK

Developer: Ocean Software

Publisher: Ocean Software

Platform: ZX Spectrum

Designed by Jon Ritman and Bernie Drummond and with music by Guy Stevens, Head Over Heels is a single-player, isometric, action-adventure, platform game. The aim of Head over Heels is to find the stolen crowns of each planet, thus liberating them and ultimately defeating the Emperor. The player can control two characters: Head, who has the ability to jump higher than Heels and can fire doughnuts from his Hooter (nose) to paralyze his enemies, and Heels, who can run faster than Head and, unlike him, can climb staircases and carry items in his bag. A player must use each character's abilities separately or together to solve puzzles and make their way through the game world, which features conveyor belts, switches, teleporters, moving platforms, springy platforms and destructible platforms. The game comprises 300 rooms.

Head over Heels was considered a big game at the time, expanding on the popular isometric genre in home computers that had begun with *Knight Lore* (1984). Head Over Heels' other stand-out features were its graphics, and wacky sense of humour, which had a strong appeal for children and some adults. Head Over Heels' surreal environments featured such strange things as the Reincarnation Fish which, once eaten, can bring the player back to life after death at the location where it was eaten, and Killer Daleks with the head of an elephant or Prince Charles. There were also Cuddly Stuffed White Rabbits which give a multitude of power-ups, while Hush Puppies are creatures that never wake up and thus are often used as tables or steps.

Head Over Heels was very highly praised by critics and loved by gamers. It was soon ported to other 8-bit and 16-bit home computers, where it had similar success. Head Over Heels was subject to a remake in 2003.

Nebulus

Date of release: 1987

Region: UK

Developer: Hewson Consultants

Publisher: Hewson Consultants

Platform: 8-bit and 16-bit home computers

Designed by John M. Philips, Nebulus is a single-player, platform game. The aim of Nebulus is to destroy eight towers that have been built in the sea. To accomplish this the player must ascend the towers and plant bombs at the top. You play as a small, bipedal frog-like creature called Pogo. Pogo can walk left and right, jump and shoot bubbles at the varied enemies on the tower. The game's most distinctive feature is its gameplay. As Pogo moves the camera orbits around the outside of the cylindrical tower keeping Pogo in the centre of the screen. The player moves along ledges, stairs and elevators, and enters and exits doorways on his way to the top of the tower. If Pogo touches an enemy, then he drops down to the next available ledge, hindering his progress.

Nebulus was ported to most 8-bit and 16-bit home computers as well as the NES and Gameboy. There was one sequel, *Nebulus 2* (1991). Nebulus was also known as Castelian, Kyorochan Land, Subline or Tower Toppler. Nebulus was awarded Best Original Game of the Year at the 1987/1988 Golden Joystick Awards.

Rastan Saga

Date of release: 1987

Region: Japan

Developer: Taito

Publisher: Taito

Platform: Arcade

Designed by Yoshinori Kobayashi and Toshiyuki Nishimura, Rastan is a typical side-scrolling, single-player, hack and slash platform game, where the player controls a Barbarian who must defeat hordes of enemies on his quest to slay a dragon. The player must also avoid obstacles, many of which can kill instantly. There are six levels in Rastan Saga, each set in a different environment and with a boss at the end of each. Rastan Saga was originally going to be a 'Conan the Barbarian' game. However, Taito could not secure the rights and thus the game was named Rastan Saga.

Rastan Saga was ported to many home computers and home consoles, but most could not recreate the graphics of the arcade. Rastan Saga spawned two sequels: *Rastan Saga II* (1989) and *Warrior Blade: Rastan Saga Episode III* (1991).

Sid Meier's Pirates!

Date of release: 1987

Region: USA

Developer: MicroProse

Publisher: MicroProse

Platform: Commodore 64

Designed by Sid Meier, Sid Meier's Pirates! is a single-player, open-world, action/adventure, strategy game and is the first Sid Meier game to include his name in the title. At the start of the game, the player chooses an era to play in between the 16th and 18th centuries. This sets the economic and political conditions of the game world. The player receives a letter of marque to work as a privateer for either the English, French, Dutch or Spanish. The power play between the four different countries is always shifting and the player must be flexible to take advantage of certain situations and not get caught out. As an open-world game, the aim varies dependent on the player: you may stay legal and loyal to whomever you wish or become a pirate. Features in the game include exploration of the Caribbean, trading, attacking enemy ships or towns, hunting for buried treasure, rescuing long-lost family members and getting married. Sid Meier's Pirates! is rather unique in that your character ages during the game, affecting overall gameplay. The player must ensure that they have accumulated enough wealth during the game to retire comfortably. Ending up as a beggar on the streets would be considered a fail, whereas becoming the king's advisor would be considered a success.

With its absorbing open-world gameplay, it could easily take up many hours of a player's time. Such games are all too common today but in 1987 it was rather unique and ground-breaking.

Sid Meier's Pirates! was ported to most 8-bit and 16-bit home computers, as well as the NES. The game never saw any sequels. However, it has been subsequently re-released three times with improved graphics and a few tweaks here and there, in 1993, 2004 and mobile versions from 2008.

International Karate +/Chop N' Drop

Date of release: October 1987

Region: UK

Developer: System 3

Publisher: System 3

Platform: 8-bit and 16-bit home computers

International Karate +, usually referred to as IK+ and known as Chop N' Drop in the USA, was designed by Archer MacLean with music by Rob Hubbard. IK+ is a single-player or two-player PvP (player versus player) fighting game. The aim is to defeat all your opponents and accumulate as many points as possible. Three players fight all at the same time: either a single player and two computer-controlled opponents, or two players and one computer-controlled opponent. Players must knock out their opponents thus accumulating knock-out points. The winner of each round is the player who has the most knock-out points within the 30-second time limit. If a player comes last in this scoring system, they are eliminated and cannot continue. After every two rounds, the player must compete in a bonus round involving fending off bouncing balls from both the left and right sides of the screen. IK+ introduced several new moves to its predecessor *International Karate* (1985). These include somersault, backflip and split kick, which if timed perfectly could take down two opponents simultaneously.

IK+ had some other quirky features. If the T key was pressed, the fighters' trousers would all fall down. Typing in a curse word would receive a rebuke from the game or even reset the game if the player continued to do it.

For some, IK+ would come to represent the pinnacle of the first generation of home PvP fighting games based around karate, which began with *Karate Champ Player vs Player* (1984). Soon the fighting genre would evolve away from this theme with games like *Street Fighter* II and *Mortal Kombat*. IK+ won the Best 16-bit Soundtrack of the Year at the 1988/1989 Golden Joystick Awards.

Rainbow Islands: The Story of Bubble Bobble 2

Date of release: 1987

Region: Japan

Developer: Taito

Publisher: Taito

Platform: Arcade

Designed by Fukio Mitsuji, Rainbow Islands is a single-player, vertical-scrolling platform game. The aim is to defeat Super Skull Monsta, the boss of Shadow who has transformed your friends into dragons and has them kept prisoner.

The player must clear seven islands, each with four rounds. There are also secret rooms along the way. The player must make their way to the top of the screen to clear it. The player can run left, right, jump and shoot rainbows to kill their enemies by hitting them with the rainbows or crushing the rainbow above their head. The enemies turn into goodies to collect for points, some of which are coloured jewels. Collect all the coloured jewels and you will be rewarded with the use of an extra rainbow. You can climb the rainbows along the floor and, if you keep pushing the jump button, you can jump a rainbow without crushing it. Each island is sinking, and the player must climb to the top of the level to receive a chest full of goodies. If the player lingers too long, they will fall into the sea, killing the player and losing a life. Like Bubble Bobble the controls are very smooth and responsive, and the action is fast-paced. Also, like its predecessor, Rainbow Islands has multiple endings.

Hisayoshi Ogura composed a variation of 'Over the Rainbow' from the movie *The Wizard of Oz* for the game's main theme music. The game was highly praised by critics and consumers alike and was soon ported to the 8-bit and 16-bit home computers and home consoles of the time.

PC Engine/TurboGrafx-16

The PC Engine, known as the TurboGrafx-16 in the rest of the world (except France), was released in Japan in October 1987 by NEC Home Electronics. The PC Engine is a fourth-generation, cartridge-based, 8-bit console capable of displaying 482 colours simultaneously due to its 16-bit video display controller and 16-bit video encoder, making for some beautiful graphics for the time. It was very popular in Japan when it launched, outselling the ageing Famicom. Yet this trend would not be repeated in the USA. The PC Engine received some criticism in the West since the console alluded to the fact that it was a 16-bit console with the name TurboGrafx-16. The fact was that it had an 8-bit CPU. Despite this, the console was able to display similar graphics to a 16-bit machine due to the aforementioned reasons.

The PC-Engine was the first video game console to play games on a CD-ROM format when NEC launched a CD-ROM add-on. The console was subject to many variations and add-ons over the years to increase performance and longevity.

Being a pseudo-16-bit machine, the PC Engine has some great-looking games, some of the most notable being *Military Madness* (1988), *Blazing Lazers* (1989), *Bonk's Revenge* (1989), *Neutopia II* (1991) and *Splatterhouse* (1990).

Maniac Mansion

Date of release: October 1987

Region: USA

Developer: Lucasfilm Games

Publisher: Lucasfilm Games

Platform: Apple II and Commodore 64

Designed by Ron Gilbert, David Fox and Gary Winnick, Maniac Mansion is a single-player, graphical adventure game. The aim is to help Dave Miller rescue his girlfriend Sandy Pantz from a mad scientist whose mind has been enslaved by a sentient meteor, which is seen falling to Earth in the game's opening cut scene. In fact, Gilbert coined the word 'cut-scene', many of which were created in Maniac Mansion to advance the narrative. The player can choose two other friends to join Dave, each based on a typical 1980s archetype, such as the geek, rock chick, surfer dude, etc. The player can control their characters, exploring the mansion and solving puzzles. Maniac Mansion is a non-linear game, meaning a lot of puzzles and interactions with other characters can be done at any time and don't necessarily rely on each other to progress through the game. There are many different outcomes depending on what you do and which characters you play with. There are also multiple endings to the game. On the downside, though, there is an awful amount of backtracking, which can be rather tiresome at times.

Ron Gilbert and Gary Winnick wanted to create a game that was a mesh of comedy and horror/science-fiction B-movie tropes. The game features a multitude of interesting characters, beginning with the Edison family who have all been influenced by the meteor, and two disembodied talking tentacles: Purple Tentacle and Green Tentacle. Each of these NPCs has distinctive characteristics and purpose within the game. Gilbert created the Script Creation Utility (SCUMM) game engine for Maniac Mansion to allow players to point and click on specific words on-screen and then places in the game world to interact with. SCUMM would be used for other LucasArts graphical adventure games, for example, *The Secret of Monkey Island* (1990).

Maniac Mansion was popular with fans of the genre at the time, but it took years to attain the cult status that it enjoys today. The game was ported to other home computer platforms and the NES. The NES port had some of its mild sexual and horror content cut, diminishing the character of the game somewhat. A television series loosely based on the game was produced and first aired on Canadian TV in 1990. Maniac Mansion spawned one sequel with the highly acclaimed *Day of the Tentacle* (1993). Maniac Mansion is often referred to as a milestone in text/graphical adventure games as it allowed players to focus more on the game itself rather than worrying about inputting the correct syntax.

Atari XEGS

The Atari XE, or Atari XEGS, was released in the USA in 1987 by the Atari Corporation. The Atari XEGS was an 8-bit home computer that shipped with 64 KB of RAM and supported a 256-colour palette. Priced at $159 for the base unit, the Atari XEGS was intended as a cheaper, entry-level computer, being just a fraction of the price of their Atari ST (1985). The base unit was in essence a console. The idea was that the XEGS keyboard could be bought separately and attached to the console, essentially changing the console into a computer. Other peripherals included the XEGS joystick and XG-1 light gun. The XEGS also had backwards compatibility with previous Atari 8-bit games, as well as its own library.

The Atari XEGS was a modest venture and managed to sell over 100,000 units. It was never going to make a dent in the NES sales in North America and Japan or affect the momentum of the 16-bit home computers in Europe.

Some notable games on the AtariXEGS were *Battlezone* (1987), *Crystal Castles* (1987), *Flight Simulator II* (1987), *Lode Runner* (1987), *Star Raiders II* (1987) and *Airball* (1988).

Pac-Mania

Date of release: November 1987

Region: Japan

Developer: Namco

Publisher: Namco

Platform: Arcade

Designed by Toru Iwatani and Akira Usikura with music by Yuriko Keino and Yoshito Tomuro, Pac-Mania is a single-player, isometric, maze game. Pac-Mania is essentially an isometric version of Pac-Man. The player can only see a portion of the maze, making it more difficult to avoid the ghosts. However, Pac-Man can now jump over ghosts to counterbalance this handicap. The ghosts are also very fast, numerous and aggressive after the first level. Pac-mania also continued the theme of inter-level cutscenes.

The game was well-received. Critics and consumers loved its smooth gameplay and the effortless way it seemed to translate the much-loved Pac-Man game to the 3D world.

Pac-Mania was ported to almost all the popular home computers and home consoles of the time. Some of the 16-bit conversions were very faithful to the original. It is worth noting that this was one of the first times a 2D video game and character had first been translated to the realms of 3D, albeit an isometric one.

Shinobi

Date of release: November 1987

Region: Japan

Developer: Sega AM1

Publisher: Sega

Platform: Arcade

Designed by Yutaka Sugano with music by Yasuhiro Kawakami, Shinobi is a single-player, side-scrolling, hack and slash platformer. The aim of Shinobi is to stop Zeed, a criminal organization that is kidnapping children. You play a ninja called Joe Musashi rescuing the child hostages and dispatching numerous different enemies, some of whom are ninjas themselves. The player has an unlimited supply of shuriken with which to accomplish this goal: these get upgraded to exploding bullets when a certain number of children are saved. He can also use punches or kicks if an enemy gets too close. This attack is upgraded to a katana attack when enough children are saved. Higher levels or background levels can be reached to ensure all the children are saved. A special ninjutsu attack can be performed once per stage. These are thunderstorm, tornado or doppelganger attack. This will clear the screen of all enemies or inflict high damage if fighting a boss. These bosses are encountered at the end of each mission. At this point, the player partakes in a bonus round. The bonus round is played from a first-person perspective. Ninjas jump towards you and you must dispatch them with your shuriken.

Shinobi was well received, and it was soon ported to the home computers and consoles of the time.

The game has many sequels, most notably *Shadow Dancer* (1989), *The Revenge of Shinobi* (1989), *Shinobi III: Return of the Ninja Master* (1993) and *Shinobi 3D* (2011).

Galaga '88

Date of release: December 1987

Region: Japan

Developer: Namco

Publisher: Namco

Platform: Arcade

Galaga '88 is a single-player, fixed shooter. As with previous Galaga games, the aim is to destroy as many enemy ships as possible and to accumulate the highest score possible, ultimately defeating the game's final boss. The player has an option at the beginning of the game to play with one ship with two lives in reserve or to play with two ships side by side thus doubling the player's firepower but with the trade-off of presenting a larger target and having only one life in reserve. Compared with previous Galaga games, the sprites, effects and backgrounds are much more advanced. There are many different enemy types. Some combine into larger enemies, some feature armour taking multiple hits to take out, while others spawn smaller craft. Capsules can be collected from specific enemies. These can allow the player to skip stages and advance further in the game. When a stage is cleared of alien ships, the player automatically warps to the next stage. There are also bonus stages called Cha Cha Stages, in reference to the music played while the player attempts to destroy all forty enemies which dance around on the screen. There are multiple stages within each dimension, of which there are five. Each dimension consists of different backgrounds, enemy types and behaviours, and an end-of-level boss. The game consists of 29 stages in total.

Galaga '88 has been ported to many consoles since its first release in 1987. Galaga '88 is the fourth game in the Galaga series.

Dungeon Master

Date of release: December 1987

Region: USA

Developer: FTL Games

Publisher: FTL Games

Platform: AtariST

Designed by Doug Bell, Dungeon Master is a single-player, first-person, party-based, fantasy RPG, dungeon crawling game. The aim is to recover Librasulus' firestaff. Thus, Librasulus can take physical form and defeat Lord Chaos. The player resurrects four champions of their choice to take on the quest. Within the dungeon, the player encounters traps, items such as weapons and armour to equip their character with, food to replenish health and keys to open gates. Dungeon Master was the first first-person RPG to feature real-time combat rather than turn-based. It also used a unique technique to cast spells. Players would click a series of runes to cast specific spells giving them a more immersive interaction with how magic worked within the game. This game also popularised the paper doll interface used in many dungeon crawl games to this day such as the *Diablo* series. The paper doll interface typically displays parts of the body where the player can click and drag found items such as helmets, body armour, gauntlets and boots and weapons to increase a player's statistics.

Because of the game's well-designed features, it soon became incredibly popular and was highly praised by critics.

Ported to several other platforms, it spawned four sequels with *Dungeon Master: Chaos Strikes Back* (1989), *Dungeon Master: Theron's Quest* (1992), *Dungeon Master II: The Legend of Skullkeep* (1993) and *Dungeon Master Nexus* (1998). Dungeon Master was the Atari ST's best-selling game of all time with over 40,000 units sold.

Mega Man

Date of release: December 1987

Region: Japan

Developer: Capcom

Publisher: Capcom

Platform: Famicom

Known as Rockman in Japan, Mega Man is a single-player, multi-scrolling, platform game. The aim of Mega Man is to progress through six stages, defeating the Robot Master boss at the end of each stage, with the ultimate aim of stopping the evil scientist Dr Wily. Set in the year 20XX, you play as the humanoid robot Mega Man, created by Dr Light. At the beginning of the game and after defeating a boss, the player can choose which stage to play. This feature gave the game tremendous replayability. If the player struggled with a particular stage, they had the option to try a different one. This idea would become synonymous with the Mega Man games. As Mega Man, the player can run, jump, and shoot the multitude of different enemies. Mega Man's health bar is displayed on the top left, which can be replenished by picking up energy cells dropped from time to time by destroyed enemies. If Mega Man defeats a Robot Master boss, he will acquire the boss's signature attack weapon. These attacks can be toggled between at any time during gameplay on any other level.

The game became renowned for its perfect blend of arcade-style platforming gameplay and music by Manami Matsumae as well as being a difficult game to complete. Praised by critics and consumers alike Mega Man has spawned a great number of sequels. Some of the most notable are *Mega Man 2* (1988), *Mega Man 3* (1990), *Mega Man 5* (1992), *Mega Man 8* (1996) and *Mega Man 9* (2008). Mega Man himself has become one of Capcom's mascots and most successful franchises.

Phantasy Star

Date of release: December 1987

Region: Japan

Developer: Sega

Publisher: Sega

Platform: Master System

Designed by Kotaro Hayashida, Yuji Naka and Rieko Kodama, Phantasy Star is a single-player JRPG. The aim of Phantasy Star is to defeat the evil tyrannical ruler of the Algol star system, King Lassic. You play as Alis, who swears vengeance upon her brother's death at the hands of Lassic's forces. She gathers a party of three warriors: Noah – a Wizard, Odin – a warrior, and Mayau – a talking cat-like creature. They travel to three of Algol's planets to fulfil her quest. Phantasy Star followed similar game mechanics to other JRPGs of the time. Combat is turn-based with each character having the opportunity to attack, use magic, use an item, talk or run. Characters gain experience by defeating monsters and, in turn, levelling up, increasing their offensive and defensive abilities. Characters can also interact with NPCs and buy and sell items from shops. Like *Dragon Quest* (1986), the player's view in Phantasy Star switches between a top-down perspective during exploration to first-person during combat and interactions between NPCs. The game also featured first-person, fully-scrolling, three-dimensional dungeons, where treasure can be found.

Phantasy Star was one of the first video games to feature first-person, textured 3D environments. The developers were influenced by movies like *Star Wars*. The production team wanted to create an RPG with a science-fiction theme to differentiate it from the usual fantasy-based RPGs of the time. As well as its setting, Phantasy Star was different from other RPGs as it was one of the few video games to feature a female protagonist.

Phantasy Star was well received by critics and consumers and was cited for its accomplished graphics and animation on the Master System. The only thing that held the game back was its high price. The game is considered a milestone in the RPG genre and has seen ports on several platforms over the years, most recently on the Nintendo Switch. Phantasy Star spawned a number of sequels. Most notable of these are *Phantasy Star II* (1989), *Phantasy Star III: Generations of Doom* (1991), *Phantasy Star IV: The End of the Millennium* (1993), *Phantasy Star Online* (2000) and *Phantasy Star Online 2* (2012).

Final Fantasy

Date of release: December 1987

Region: Japan

Developer: Square

Publisher: Square

Platform: Famicom

Designed by Hironobu Sakaguchi, Final Fantasy is a single-player, top-down perspective RPG. The player controls a party of four youths called the Light Warriors. Each carries one of the world's four elemental orbs. The orbs have been darkened by four elemental fiends. The aim of Final Fantasy is to defeat these evil forces and restore light to the orbs, thus saving the world. The further intricacies of the narrative are both detailed and epic which would become a hallmark of the series. Most of the game is played from a top-down perspective. Your party is represented by one character who interacts with NPCs in towns and other areas of the environment. In towns the player can converse with NPCs, thus gathering useful information, buy items in shops, or rest. During the player's time exploring the countryside and dungeons, random battle encounters will often occur. The game switches to turn-based combat mode, displaying your party, the enemy/enemies you face all from a side-view perspective, character statistics and current combat options. Final Fantasy uses standard RPG elements such as magic and the employment of items during combat. Final Fantasy was the first turn-based RPG video game to show combatants facing one another from a side-view perspective, as opposed to a first-person perspective. Once the battle is over the game switches back to a top-down perspective of the surrounding environment. The beautiful music of Final

Fantasy was composed by Nobuo Uematsu. It has become one of the most recognisable and well-loved scores in video game history.

Final Fantasy received high critical praise, even further popularizing the RPG genre in Japan and, in turn, in the West. However, it was criticised by some for its need for the player to grind, necessary to progress through the game.

The original Final Fantasy has been ported to home consoles, handhelds and mobile platforms over the years. The game was ported over to the NES for the USA consumer in 1990. It was many Westerners' first taste of a JRPG, even though it is *Dragon Quest* that was more popular at the time in Japan. Final Fantasy is now considered the more successful of the two, worldwide.

Final Fantasy has spawned many sequels and spin-off titles. It is greatly contested which are the most noteworthy games. That being said, here goes: *Final Fantasy IV* (known as *Final Fantasy II* in the USA) (1991), *Final Fantasy VI (known as Final Fantasy III* in the USA) (1994), *Final Fantasy VII* (1997), *Final Fantasy Tactics* (1997), *Final Fantasy VIII* (1999), *Final Fantasy IX* (2000) and *Final Fantasy XII* (2006). To date, the original Final Fantasy has sold over three million units. Together the Final Fantasy series has sold over 90 million units.

Tecmo Bowl

Date of release: December 1987

Region: Worldwide

Developer: Tecmo

Publisher: Tecmo

Platform: Arcade

Tecmo Bowl is a single-player or multiplayer American Football game. The aim is to score more points than your opponent. Standards rules of American Football apply, albeit over a much shorter period of time. Temco Bowl allowed for four players to participate; two players at a time. The screen is made up of a dual monitor equalling that of a 512 x 256 resolution. The cabinet is twice the size of a standard arcade cabinet to facilitate the two Cathode Ray Tube televisions and player controls.

The teams in the original Temco Bowl are fictional. However, the extremely popular NES port of the game two years later did feature real teams.

Tecmo Bowl spawned the sequels *Tecmo Super Bowl* (1991), *Tecmo Super Bowl II: Special Edition* (1994) and *Tecmo Super Bowl III: Final Edition* (1995).

Project Stealth Fighter

Date of release: December 1987

Region: USA

Developer: MicroProse

Publisher: MicroProse

Platform: Commodore 64 and ZX Spectrum

Project Stealth Fighter is a single-player, first-person, 3D-combat, flight simulator. The player flies a fictional US stealth fighter which they arm with a host of different missiles, laser-guided bombs, cluster weapons, cannons or reconnaissance cameras. The game features more than 100 different missions covering four different locations: Central Europe, Libya, North Cape, and the Persian Gulf.

The game came packaged with a very detailed 113-page operations manual, which went into great detail concerning every aspect of the game.

The game was critically acclaimed for its attention to detail and technical accomplishment on an 8-bit platform. Project Stealth Fighter was MicroProse's precursor to their highly acclaimed *F-19 Stealth Fighter* (1988).

1987 Notable Omissions

1943. Acorn Archimedes. After Burner II. Alex Kidd BMX Trial. Alex Kidd: High-Tech World. Arkanoid: Revenge of Doh. Atari XE. Bivouac. Blasteroids. Blazer. Bureaucracy. California Games. Castlevania II: Simon's Quest. Cybernoid. Dance Aerobics. Dragon Spirit. Earl Weaver Baseball. Faxanadu. Final Lap. Gemini Wing. Karnov. La abadía del crimen. Legacy of the Wizard. Lurking Horror. MIDI Maze. Mike Tyson's Punch-Out. Mr Heli. Nintendo sues Blockbuster. Oids. Penguin Land. Plundered Hearts. Police Quest: In Pursuit of the Death Angel. Pro Wrestler. Quester. Skate or Die. Space Quest II: Vohaul's Revenge. Spay Hunter II. Star Trek: The Rebel Universe. Super Hang-On. The Ancient Art of War at Sea. The Bitmap Brothers is founded. The Fool's Errand. The King of Chicago. The Last Ninja. Trantor: The Last Stormtrooper. Thrust II. Thunder Blade. Tournament

Arkanoid. Wizball. Wizards and Warriors. Wonder Boy in Monsterland. Wonder Momo. Yokai Dochuki. Zarch. Zelda II: The Adventures of Link. Xenophobe.

1988

Wasteland

Date of release: January 1988

Region: USA

Developer: Interplay Productions

Publisher: Electronic Arts

Platform: Apple II, Commodore 64 and IBM compatibles

Wasteland is a single-player, post-apocalyptic RPG. The aim is to investigate a series of disturbances in the nearby areas. You soon discover that a leftover AI is planning to destroy what is left of humanity, your mission is to prevent this from happening. Set in America in the year 2087, after a nuclear holocaust, the player begins the game with a party of four Desert Rangers. This can be expanded to a maximum of seven; however, these extra characters can be unruly at times. The exploration of the game is either done on a world map or in a settlement area. Both are viewed from an above perspective. When the party interacts with shopkeepers or goes into potential combat mode, the screen is split into three. This was fairly traditional at the time. A portrait of the person or creature is illustrated on the top left, together with options buy, sell, run, attack etc, dependent on which kind of character the player encounters. If an attack is initiated, combat is automated. Experience is gained through defeating enemies or carrying out tasks.

Wasteland was one of the first games to feature a persistent game state, saving it for the next play, players could return to previous locations at a later date to find that everything had not reset (as was common at the time) and was, in fact, the way they had left it. The game was known for its vulgar (although mild compared to today's standards) descriptive language and difficult gameplay.

Wasteland was ported to various home computers. *Fallout* (1997) is often cited as the spiritual successor of Wasteland. Wasteland itself has two sequels: *Wasteland 2* (2014) and Wasteland 3 (2020).

Super Contra: The Alien Strikes Back

Date of release: January 1988

Region: Japan

Developer: Konami

Publisher: Konami

Platform: Arcade

Super Contra: The Alien Strikes Back, known as Probotector II: Return of the Evil Forces, in Europe and simply, Super Contra in the USA, was designed by Konami, and is the second game in the Contra series. Super Contra is a single-player or two-player, multi-scrolling, run and gun game. The aim is to infiltrate a former military base and destroy the alien force. You play as either Bill Rizer or Lance Bean. Super Contra contains many of the same elements as the original. New features include power-ups for weapons already in use, making these weapons even more devastating, the 'hyper shell' pick-up item that destroys all on-screen enemies when used, and sections of the game played in a pseudo-3D perspective. The game comprises five stages which take the player through the military base, the jungle and finally the alien lair. At the end of each stage, the player must complete a boss battle.

Super Contra was well received as a good example of the run and gun genre. It was ported to the Famicom/NES, Amiga, MS-DOS and Microsoft Windows.

Electronic Gaming Monthly

Electronic Gaming Monthly (sometimes abbreviated to *EGM*), was a video game magazine, founded in 1988 with its first issue published in the USA in March 1989 by EGM Media LLC. Founded by Steve Harris, *EGM* is a monthly publication offering news and reviews for video games over a variety of console platforms. In 2010 it expanded its mandate to cover PC and mobile games. *EGM*'s original review score was based on 0-10 but it now ranks games on a letter grade system, with C being average and A+ being the highest grade. EGM has a website presence at egmnow.com where games are reviewed on a five-star system.

XZR: Hakai no Gūzō

Date of release: 1988

Region: Japan

Developer: Telenet

Publisher: Telenet

Platform: NEC PC-8801, NEC PC-9801, MSX2 and X1 turbo home computers

XZR is a single-player, action RPG. The game is set in the 12th century in the Middle East. You play as Sadler, a Syrian Assassin on a mission to kill the Caliph. The game is played from a top-down perspective while the player explores their environment and engages with various NPCs, buying, selling and looting chests. Combat happens during side-scrolling areas of the game. As with most RPGs, the player's character gains experience through combat, consequentially increasing their stats. The game also has a strong narrative theme following the anti-hero protagonist as the action takes the player to Baghdad, Babylon, Alexandria and even the Tower of Babel where he encounters the goddess Ishtar. After completing his mission Sadler ends up in the 20th century, where he must assassinate the leaders of Russia and America.

XYR caused a certain amount of controversy concerning its references to religion and politics, not to mention the use of drugs to enhance certain abilities of the player. These included coca (cocaine), marijuana, LSD and opiates.

Despite this controversy, the game was highly praised by critics. XZR is the first game in what is now referred to as the Exile series. The other games in the Exile series are *XZR II: Kanketsuhen* (1988), *Exile* (1991) and *Exile: Wicked Phenomenon* (1992). XZR Hakai no Gūzō was never released outside Japan, though subsequent releases were.

Carrier Command

Date of release: 1988

Region: UK

Developer: Realtime Games

Publisher: Rainbird

Platform: 8-bit and 16-bit home computers

Carrier Command is a single-player, 3D, vehicle simulation and real-time strategy game. The aim is to destroy the enemy's aircraft carrier and island bases. The player controls a futuristic aircraft carrier and its onboard laser cannon. They can also launch any number of its complement of Mantas (Multirole Aircraft for Nautical Tactical Assault) and Walrus (Water and Land Roving Utility Shuttle) vehicles to destroy the enemy. The player controls these aspects with the mouse and the elaborate graphical user interface. The only exception is when the player takes direct control of any Manta or Walrus. A player can switch between any vehicles during gameplay. Vehicles not controlled by the player by default use the autopilot function. Other resource management tools make for a deeper tactical and strategic experience. These can be fully utilised when the player takes control of islands and exploits them for resources, factory or defence.

The game featured filled-in vector graphics to display its 3D landscapes and vehicles. The pace of the game is very similar to *Elite* (1984): if the player is prepared to learn how to play the game and is patient, it can be very rewarding, but it is suited for a particular taste.

Carrier Command was highly praised by critics and consumers who liked these kinds of strategic war games. The game spawned a pseudo-sequel with *Battle Command* (1990). A remake was also released with *Carrier Command: Gaea Mission* (2012). Carrier Command was awarded Best 8-bit Simulation Game of the Year at the 1989/1990 Golden Joystick Awards.

Parodius: The Octopus Saves the Earth

Date of release: April 1988

Region: Japan

Developer: Konami

Publisher: Konami

Platform: MSX

Parodius is a single-player, side-scrolling shooter and is essentially a parody of *Gradius* (1985), with similar gameplay and game mechanics from the Gradius series, such as the power-up system. Characters and themes are derived from various Konami games with cutesy characters. For example, at the start of the game the player can choose to play as an octopus, penguin (from *Antarctic Adventure* 1983), Goemon (from *Mr. Goemon* 1986), the Popolon Knight (from *Knightmare* 1986) or the Viv Viper (from *Gradius* 1985). The game also features references to other video games and Japanese culture. The music changes from typical 1980s video game style to Western classical music, dependent on the stage and which suits the juxtaposition of sprites and environments perfectly. There are six stages in Parodius, each with an end-of-level boss.

Parodius was awarded Best Game that Never Came out in the U.S. by *Electronic Gaming Monthly* in 1992.

Desert Commander/Sensha Senryaku: Sabaku no Kitsune

Date of release: April 1988

Region: Japan

Developer: Kemco

Publisher: Kemco

Platform: Famicom

Desert Commander, known as 'Sensha Senryaku: Sabaku no Kitsune' in Japan, is a single-player or two-player, turn-based strategy game. The aim is to destroy the enemies' HQ first. The game is set in North Africa during World War II. Each player controls several units of either the Allied Forces or the Axis Powers, including tanks, armoured cars, troop transport, infantry, field cannon, anti-aircraft gun, supply truck, bomber and fighter plane. Each unit has a different range on the road, and different fuel and ammunition requirements. Most units are very efficient at destroying one other particular unit, so it is vital to use this and other tactics to win the game.

Desert Commander is a significant milestone in the turn-based strategy genre and can be seen as influencing Nintendo's popular *Advance Wars* series (2001-current date).

F/A-18 Interceptor

Date of release: 1988

Region: USA

Developer: Intellisoft

Publisher: Electronic Arts

Platform: Amiga

F/A-18 Interceptor is a single-player, first-person, 3D combat flight simulator. The aim is to successfully carry out six missions. The player must complete a successful aircraft carrier landing to qualify. All of the missions are set in the San Francisco Bay Area and begin either from the aircraft carrier or a nearby landing field. The six missions are a visual confirmation mission, protection of Air Force One, intercepting and destroying a stolen aircraft, finding a bailed pilot and dropping a rescue pod, intercepting an incoming cruise missile, and destroying a carrier sub and supporting enemy aircraft. Each mission often has an element of immediacy: time is short and, with the use of radar, the player must reach the enemy and take them out with their limited air-to-air heat-seeking AIM-9 Sidewinder missiles, AIM- 120 AMRAAM missiles, or M61 Vulcan Gatling gun. The player can use chaff or flare countermeasures if an enemy locks on and fires with their missiles. Careful attention must be paid to limited fuel: overuse of the plane's afterburner to reach an escaping enemy can leave the player with no fuel, crashing into the ocean. The player could also switch cameras and zoom in/out to get a good view of their surroundings. Some player's favourite manoeuvre would be to do a fly-by underneath the Golden Gate Bridge before getting on with the business at hand.

The game was highly praised by critics of the time and was an alluring way of showing off the Amiga platform's 3D capabilities.

Computer Game Developers' Conference

The first Computer Game Developers' Conference, or GDC, was held in the USA in April 1988. The first conference was organized by Chris Crawford in his living-room with 27 attendees. They now take place in multiple locations around the world with thousands of attendees. A typical conference includes talks and tutorials, awards, workshops and the ever-popular 'Developer's Rant' which began in 2005, allowing developers the opportunity to let off steam about some key problems in the industry and how to solve them.

John Madden Football

Date of release: June 1988

Region: USA

Developers: Trip Hawkins, Robin Antonick and John Madden

Publisher: Electronic Arts

Platform: 8-bit home computers

John Madden Football is a single-player or multiplayer American football game. The game follows traditional American football rules to score the most points in the allotted time. Players could alter the settings at the beginning of each game in areas such as field conditions (hot, cold, windy, rain and snow), time per quarter (8, 10, 12 or 15 minutes), fatigue, injuries, penalties, and announcer. John Madden Football offered two game modes, namely a Quick Mode which provided the player with a traditional arcade experience, and the Standard Game, which gave the player a slower, deeper experience involving them in in-game players' stats.

The game was reviewed favourably, especially for its game mechanics.

John Madden Football is the first in the series, which has seen a game released every year since 1990. The games became known as Madden NFL in 1994 with the release of *Madden NFL '95*. Some of the most notable Madden games over the years are *Madden NFL 2004* (2003), *Madden NFL 2005* (2004), *Madden NFL 2008* (2007), *Madden NFL 2010* (2009) and *Madden NFL 2012* (2011).

Pool of Radiance

Date of release: June 1988

Region: USA

Developer: Strategic Simulations

Publisher: Strategic Simulations

Platform: 8-bit and 16-bit home computers

Designed by Chuck Kroegel and George MacDonald, Pool of Radiance is a single-player, party-based, tactical RPG. It is the first video game adaptation of TSR's (Tactical Studies Rules) immensely popular Advanced Dungeons & Dragons fantasy RPG. As such it derives much of its game mechanics from AD&D as well as other video game RPGs of the time. The aim is to help the city of Phlan defeat the evil creatures and their leader who threaten the surrounding area. The player begins by creating a party of six, choosing a race (dwarf, elf, gnome, half-elf, halfling and human), sex, and class (cleric, fighter, magic-user and thief). The player must also choose character alignments. This will affect how NPCs interact with them. The game screen is split into two or three sections, dependent on the game's mode. During exploration mode, the top left of the screen displays a 3D, first-person perspective, while other parts of the screen display narrative and player status. In combat mode, the display switches to a primitive isometric mode. Players command what each of their character's actions will be per round, and at the end, all the actions are initiated. Combat pauses while the player chooses the actions for the next round. Combat can also be automated if the player so wishes. Included with the game was a 28-page introductory booklet, a 38-page Adventurer's Journal describing the game's background including maps, characters, and a translation decoder wheel, which was the developers' way of combatting piracy. Without the decoder, the player could not enter the correct code and play the game.

The game was fairly well received and sold around 265,000 units.

Pool of Radiance was the first game in a four-part series all developed by SSI's proprietary Gold Box game engine. The other games are *Curse of the Azure Bonds* (1989), *Secret of the Silver Blades* (1990) and *Pools of Darkness* (1991). Since these four games, there have been many AD&D video games, some of the most notable being *Baldur's Gate* (1998), *Planescape Torment* (1999), *Icewind Dale* (2000), *Baldur's Gate II: Shadow of Amn* (2000) and *Neverwinter Nights* (2002).

Forgotten Worlds

Date of release: July 1988

Region: Worldwide

Developer: Capcom

Publisher: Capcom

Platform: Arcade

Known as Lost Worlds in Japan, Forgotten Worlds is a single-player or two-player cooperative, side-scrolling shooter. The aim is to defeat the evil god Bios, the eight gods who serve him and his multitude of minions. You play as one of two super-soldiers. One is armed with a long-range rifle while the other is armed with a short-range wide-spread weapon. The player's character is accompanied by a satellite module that provides extra firepower. A 'megacrush' attack is available to destroy all enemies on screen, except bosses. Some enemies drop coins that can be used in shops to buy power-ups and restore any lost vitality. At the end of each stage, the player must defeat one of the evil gods, defeating the final boss Bios in the ninth and final stage.

The game cabinet featured a rare fire-button mechanic: a dial that could turn 360 degrees to point the character's gun. The player would push this dial down like a normal button to fire. This was Capcom's first use of their new CPS-1 board, which ended up costing around $5 million to produce. Unfortunately, due to the highly saturated shooter genre in the arcades, Forgotten Worlds did not make nearly enough profit.

Forgotten Worlds was released on various 8-bit and 16-bit home computers and consoles.

Battle Chess

Date of release: 1988

Region: USA

Developer: Interplay Productions

Publisher: Interplay Productions

Platform: Amiga

Battle Chess is either a single-player (against the computer) or a two-player chess game. The aim of Battle Chess is the same as normal chess: to put your opponent's king in checkmate. However, in Battle Chess, all the chess pieces are fully animated as they move across the board or take another piece in amusing and delightful ways. For example, a bishop will turn another bishop into a pile of dust, the rook transforms into a rock monster and eats the queen whole, and the queen can vaporise opponents in several different ways. These are just a few of the thirty-five animations in total. A two-player game could be played over a Local Area Network (LAN) or by hot-seat.

With its beautiful graphics and fantastic animations, Battle Chess was popular with retailers for showcasing the Amiga platform. The game ended up selling 250,000 units.

Battle Chess was ported to some 8-bit, most 16-bit home computers, and home consoles. It was later followed by *Battle Chess II: Chinese Chess* (1991) and *Battle Chess 4000* (1992). Battle Chess has also inspired many clones over the years.

Nintendo Power

Nintendo Power was first launched in the USA in July by Nintendo of America. *Nintendo Power* was a monthly publication focusing on Nintendo video games and third-party games released on its platforms. It featured previews, reviews, tips, tricks and strategy guides. Some Nintendo games of this time are infamous for being unbeatable unless certain secrets were revealed within the pages of *Nintendo Power*.

Publication of the magazine switched to Future US in 2007. The final issue of *Nintendo Power* was published in December 2012. It returned as a podcast in December 2017.

Toobin'

Date of release: 1988

Region: USA

Developer: Atari Games

Publisher: Atari Games

Platform: Arcade

Toobin' is a single-player or two-player, recreational sports game. The aim is to reach the finish line before your opponent. You play as Bif or Jet and must travel down the river in your giant inner tube. Players can pass through gates, collect treasures or the letters to spell out Toobin', and pick up cans to increase their score. The cans can be used to throw at your opponent to slow them down. Power-ups can also be collected to allow the players to collect multiple cans. Players must avoid the many hazards along the river. It is possible to take care of these with a can they've collected. There are fifteen rivers in total to navigate, with a wide variety of themes such as Colorado, Nile, Jurassic, Rio Grande, Canals of Mars, and Nightmare.

Toobin' wasn't exactly the most popular arcade at the time, but it was refreshingly different from the usual shooters, fighting and driving games.

Toobin' was ported to various 8-bit and 16-bit platforms of the time.

Altered Beast

Date of release: August 1988

Region: Japan

Developer: Sega

Publisher: Sega

Platform: Arcade

Altered Beast is a single-player or two-player, side-scrolling, beat 'em up with a Greek mythological theme. The aim is to rescue Zeus's daughter, Athena. You play as a centurion who can transform into a beast to help defeat the waves of monsters and the undead which are sent to prevent you from achieving your goal. Specific enemies will drop power-ups which are required to transform your character into a more powerful beast. There are five different beasts, each with different abilities: werewolf, weredragon, werebear, weretiger and a golden weredragon. There are five levels in Altered Beast: the graveyard, the Underworld, a cavern, Neff's Palace and the City of Dis. A boss must be defeated at the end of each level to continue. With the defeat of the final boss, the demon god Neff releases Athena. In the final credits of the game, images are shown of the game characters with wigs off and the beast with his beast costume off, revealing an actor playing him and implying the narrative of the game as a play.

Altered Beast was well received at the arcades. However, some of the ports on the 8-bit and 16-bit home computers and consoles were not so great.

The game never received a true sequel, although *Jūōki: Project Altered Beast*, also known as *Altered Beast*, was released for Playstation 2 in 2005.

The NewZealand Story

Date of release: September 1988

Region: Japan

Developer: Taito

Publisher: Taito

Platform: Arcade

The NewZealand Story is a single-player, multi-scrolling, platform game. You play as a cute little yellow kiwi called Tiki. The aim of The NewZealand Story is to save all the other kiwis, including your girlfriend Phee-Phee, from the leopard seal. The player must traverse through each stage, avoiding or shooting enemies with an assortment of different weapons (Tiki is a weaponised kiwi.). Said enemies turn into fruit that can be collected for more points. The player can also find balloons, blimps and UFOs, or steal them off enemies to help get them through a stage. The game also features underwater areas, the player must be careful not to run out of air during these segments. A very basic on-screen orientation map shows where you are and where the exit is, and therefore your captured kiwi friend. The game also features hidden areas, including a stage called special heaven, which, under specific conditions, allows the player to get back to the main game after losing their final life. There is a time limit applied to each stage, but the only indication the player receives is a jingle followed by a message saying, "Hurry up." When the player's time runs out, an invincible red devil appears and will kill Tikki instantly when touched. At the end of each stage, Tiki releases one of the captured kiwis from a cage. If the player can defeat the leopard seal in the final stage, then Tiki is reunited with his girlfriend.

The NewZealand Story was ported to most 8-bit and 16-bit home computers and consoles.

The NewZealand Story Revolution (a remake) was released in 2007 for the Nintendo DS.

Super Mario Bros. 2/ Super Mario USA

Date of release: October 1988

Region: USA

Developer: Nintendo

Publisher: Nintendo

Platform: Nintendo Entertainment System

Designed by Kensuke Tanabe and Shigeru Miyamoto, Super Mario Bros. 2 is a single-player, side-scrolling platform game. The aim of the game is to defeat Wart, the game's main antagonist. As well as familiar elements from the first Super Mario game, this sequel has a few new features. For example, having the option to choose your character from Mario, Luigi, Toad and Princess Toadstool, each of whom handles differently. Also, instead of jumping on enemies, players can throw objects at them or pick the enemy up and throw them to get them out of the way.

Super Mario 2 was a huge departure from the first Super Mario game, introducing some very different mechanics. The game looks and plays very different from any other Mario game and this became even more apparent with the release *Super Mario Bros. 3* (1988). There is a very good reason for this. The Western release of Super Mario Bros. 2 is, in reality, a game called *Yume Kojo Doki Doki Panic* with changes in graphics and gameplay to make it a Mario sequel for the West. Also, the Japanese version of Super Mario Bros.2 is nothing like the western version. This still causes some confusion to this day. In chronological order here is what happened.

Super Mario Bros. 2 was released in Japan in June 1986. When evaluated by Nintendo of America, it was deemed too hard and so was never released.

Yet the West loved Mario and so a different Super Mario Bros. 2 was developed. A game called *Yume Kojo Doki Doki Panic*, which was never released in the West, was changed to look like and play like a Mario game and was released as Super Mario Bros. 2. In 1988. The West remained, for a time, unaware of both the true origin of the game and the fact that there was an original Super Mario Bros. 2.

The Western version of Super Mario Bros. 2 was released in Japan in 1992 as Super Mario USA.

Japan's version of Super Mario Bros. 2 was released in the West as Super Mario Bros.: The Lost Levels in 1993.

Even though many of the game's mechanics were taken from a different game, it is a testament to Doki Doki Panic's design that many of these features have found their way into the Mario series.

This highly anticipated sequel was highly praised in the west and sold over seven million units.

Ninja Gaiden

Date of release: October 1988

Region: USA

Developer: Tecmo

Publisher: Tecmo

Platform: Arcade

Designed by H. Lijima and Shinobu Iwabayashi of Temco, Ninja Gaiden (Known in Europe as Shadow Warriors) is a single-player or two-player cooperative, side-scrolling, beat 'em up. The aim of Ninja Gaiden is to defeat the evil cult leader Bladedamus, who is a descendant of Nostradamus and seeking to bring about his end-of-the-world prophecy. The player/s must defeat a multitude of enemies using punches, kicks, throws, jump attacks and special attacks performed while hanging from a sign or running up against a wall. The game features destructible environments. Objects such as signposts and telephone booths are destroyed when enemies are thrown into them. This will uncover power-up items, bonus points, health recovery, time extensions and even an extra life. The player/s can also pick up a sword to be used only a limited amount of times. There are seven stages in the game: Los Angeles, Brooklyn, Las Vegas, North Carolina, the Grand Canyon, a transcontinental railroad and finally the enemy's hideout. At the end of the game the player/s defeat Bladedamus and travel back to Tokyo. However, if a player fails at any point a gruesome cut-scene depicts the bound ninja about to killed by a circular saw.

Ninja Gaiden is known for its cut-scenes (especially that one), gameplay, music and high difficulty.

The game was ported to various 8-bit and 16-bit home computers and consoles. The Amiga version was a very close port of the original arcade, and the NES port was very popular. Ninja Gaiden spawned several sequels, some of the most notable being *Ninja Gaiden II: The Dark Sword of Chaos* (1990), *Ninja Gaiden Black* (2005), *Ninja Gaiden: Dragon Sword* (2008) and *Ninja Golden Sigma II* (2009).

Chase H.Q.

Date of release: October 1988

Region: Europe

Developer: Taito

Publisher: Taito

Platform: Arcade

Chase H.Q. is a single-player, vehicular combat and racing game. The aim of the game is to pursue and stop the criminals. At the beginning of each level (of which there are five in total), the player is given a time limit to reach the criminal's car some distance up the highway. An indicator on the right of the screen gives the player an idea of how close they are. Other vehicles must be avoided lest they hinder your progress and the time runs out. The road will fork, and the player must choose the quicker of the two routes or risk running out of time. When the player reaches the criminal's car the timer resets. They must ram the car, maxing out the damage meter on the left before their timer runs out. The player has a red booster button on the gear shift to aid the player but can only use it once per level.

The game was very fast and induced an adrenaline rush thanks to the thrill of the chase. The sound of Nancy talking over the radio and the characters encouraging the player to catch the criminals were integral to the game's appeal. Chase H.Q. was well received in the arcades and was soon ported to most 8-bit and 16-bit home computers and consoles.

The game spawned two sequels: *Special Criminal Investigation* aka *S.C.I.* aka *Chase HQ II*

(1989) and *Super Chase: Criminal Termination* (1992). Chase H.Q. was voted Best Soundtrack of the Year, Best Coin-Op Conversion of the Year (8-bit category) and Arcade Game of the Year at the 1989/1990 Golden Joystick Awards.

Starglider 2

Date of release: 1988

Region: UK

Developer: Argonaut Software

Publisher: Rainbird

Platform: Amiga, Atari ST, MS-DOS, Macintosh and ZX Spectrum

Designed by Jez San and Rick Clucas of Argonaut Software, Starglider 2 is a single-player, 3D, flat-shaded (an evolution of the wireframe rendering of *Starglider* (1986)), first-person, space combat simulator. The aim of Starglider 2 is to destroy an enemy space station using a neutron bomb. To fulfil this aim the player must explore the solar system, destroying any enemies that get in their way, and gather the parts of the neutron bomb. These parts can be found anywhere in space, on or even inside planets.

Starglider 2 was highly praised for not having any loading screens throughout gameplay. A player could fly across an entire planetary system, enter the atmosphere of said planets and explore the surface as well as underground tunnels with no interruption to load up new areas. This was very impressive for the time and a perfect example of what the 16-bit home computers were capable of. The Amiga version was especially lauded.

Super Mario Bros. 3

Date of release: October 1988

Region: Japan

Developer: Nintendo EAD

Publisher: Nintendo

Platform: Famicom and NES

Designed by Shigeru Miyamoto and Takashi Tezuka with music by Koji Kondo, Super Mario. Bros 3 is a single-player or multiplayer, side-scrolling, platform game. The aim of Super Mario Bros. 3 is to save Princess Toadstool from the game's main antagonist, Bowser. You play as either Mario or his brother Luigi. As with other Mario Bros. games, the player can dispose of enemies by jumping on them and can release coins and power-ups by jumping and hitting blocks from below. Many new features were introduced in Super Mario Bros. 3. The super leaf power-up changes Mario into Racoon Mario; he can attack enemies and break blocks with his tail. He could also jump higher and even fly in this state. The frog suit allowed Mario to swim faster and easier. A Hammer Brothers suit lets Mario throw hammers in the air to defeat enemies. With the Tanooki suit, Mario could turn into a statue for a short period of time, rendering him invulnerable. Jugem's Cloud allows the player to pass an action scene without playing it. The Magic Wing item allows Mario unlimited flight until he runs into an enemy. Another feature introduced in Super Mario Bros. 3 was the world map to help players orientate themselves within the game world. In different parts of the world map, there were prize areas, some of which gave the player a power-up straight away, while others required you to play a game of chance. At the end of each stage, Mario could win one of three cards. If the player managed to collect three cards of the same type, they would be awarded extra lives, the amount depending on the card type. There are eight kingdoms in Super Mario Bros. 3, each consisting of several levels. Compared with the previous two games, where each level looked fairly similar throughout the entire game, these kingdoms each have their own distinct environments, such as Ice Land or Desert Land. In the two-player mode, each player takes it in turns to clear a stage. When both Mario and Luigi are in the same area on the world map, they can enter a mini-game. A battle mode version of *Mario Bros.* (1983) is played out, where the two players can work together or against each other, stealing one another's cards if they are able to.

Super Mario Bros. 3 was much loved by critics and consumers alike. The launch of the game in North America in February 1990 turned it from a highly successful video game series into a cultural phenomenon with a lot of coverage from the media and an explosion of merchandise, such as Super Mario Bros. 3 toys, clothes, sweets, stationery, and, of course, *The Adventures of Super Mario Bros. 3* (1990), a Saturday morning cartoon aired by NBC. In short, gamers loved Mario. Even though the game did not reach such reverence in Europe, where it did not arrive until 1991, it was still well known and respected by many.

Super Mario Bros. 3 is regarded as one of the best games for the NES and one of the greatest video games of all time. It marks the pinnacle of the 8-bit platform genre, selling over 17 million units worldwide.

The Sega Mega Drive/Genesis

The Sega Mega Drive, known as the Sega Genesis in North America, was released in Japan in October 1988 by Sega. The Sega Mega Drive is a 16-bit, cartridge-based, fourth-generation video games console capable of 320 x 224 resolution and able to display 61 colours from a 512-colour palette. The controller featured a standard D-pad, three controller buttons and a start button. Unfortunately, the initial release of the console came weeks after the release of *Super Mario Bros. 3* (1988), the popularity of which meant that the initial sales of the Mega Drive in Japan only reached 400,000, rendering it only the third-bestselling console of that generation. However, it was more successful in the West, thanks to a combination of an aggressive marketing campaign (pushing the fact that it was a 16-bit console and the NES was an ageing 8-bit console), some superb arcade ports, sports titles and, finally, the success of *Sonic the Hedgehog* (1991). This was the beginning of what would be known as the console war between Sega and Nintendo. Peripherals which would be launched over the years for the console included light guns, mouse, baseball bat (foam covered) and golf club.

The Sega Mega Drive has sold over 31 million units worldwide. Some of the most notable games for the Sega Mega Drive include *Sonic the Hedgehog* (1991), *Sonic the Hedgehog 2* (1992), *Gunstar Heroes* (1993), *Shining Force* (1993), *Streets of Rage 2* (1993), *Castlevania: Bloodlines* (1994), *Earthworm Jim* (1994), *Ecco: The Tides of Time* (1994), *Super Street Fighter II* (1994), *Comix Zone* (1995) and *Phantasy Star IV* (1995).

NARC

Date of release: 1988

Region: USA

Developer: Williams Electronics

Publisher: WMS Industries

Platform: Arcade

Designed by Nathaniel Davies, Eugene Jarvis and George N. Petro of Williams Electronics, NARC is a single-player or two-player cooperative, side-scrolling, run and gun game. The aim is to kill a multitude of drug offenders using a machine gun with the ultimate aim of stopping Mr Big. You play as one of two narcotics agents, Max Force or Hit Man. The player shoots and kills the drug dealers or can arrest them, awarding them more points at the end of the level. However, it isn't easy to apprehend the criminals when bullets are flying everywhere. Enemies drop cash and drugs which the player can pick up for more points awarded at the end of the level.

NARC was one of the first arcade games to use a 32-bit processor, outputting at a higher resolution than any other arcade of the time. NARC received much controversy due to its ultra-violent nature and the questionable actions of the anti-hero protagonists, such as dealing collected drugs themselves for personal financial benefit. It was believed, by some, that such immoral behaviour might be emulated in real life. NARC has been given a retrospective M rating in the USA (the Entertainment Software Rating Board wasn't established until 1994). The game wasn't even released in Australia where they are particularly strict on video game content.

NARC was ported to various 8-bit and 16-bit home computers and consoles. In 2005 a remake under the original title NARC was released.

Silkworm

Date of release: 1988

Region: Japan

Developer: Tecmo

Publisher: Tecmo

Platform: Arcade

Silkworm is a single-player or two-player, side-scrolling, shoot 'em up. The aim of the game is to destroy the enemy, progress as far as possible and get the highest possible score. One player controls either the jeep, which can change speed, jump and fire in any direction yet is restricted to the ground, or take to the skies with the helicopter which simultaneously fires air-air and air-ground missiles, yet is vulnerable from behind. The allure of Silkworm is for two players to work together for a more enriching shoot 'em up experience. Power-ups are dropped by enemies, such as shields, increased firepower and additional bonus points.

Silkworm is well-renowned for its smooth and cooperative gameplay. It was ported to some of the 8-bit and 16 home computers and consoles. The Amiga port is considered to be the closest to achieving the original arcade experience. The game had no sequel, though *SWIV* (1991) is considered Silkworm's spiritual successor.

Cyberball

Date of release: 1988

Region: USA

Developer: Atari Games

Publisher: Atari Games

Platform: Arcade

Designed by John Salwitz, Cyberball is a single-player or multiplayer sports game. The aim is to score more points than your opponent. Cyberball is played much like American football. The differences are that it is set in the future of 2022 and played with robots. The other major difference is in the mechanics of the ball, which changes state as time passes from 'cool' to 'warm' to 'hot' and, finally, 'critical', at which point it will explode, taking with it any robot player who happens to be holding it. Once the ball explodes, a new ball is introduced, and play continues. Players can upgrade their robots and choose their player formations. The ball will reset if the 50-yard line is crossed.

Cyberball was well received in the arcades. A pseudo-sequel was released which was just an upgraded game called *Tournament Cyberball 2072* (1989).

Exile

Date of release: 1988

Region: UK

Developers: Peter Irvin and Jeremy Smith

Publisher: Superior Software

Platform: Acorn Electron and BBC

Exile (not to be confused with the 1991 game, which is part of the *XZR: Hakai no Gūzō Exile* series) is a single-player, multi-scrolling, action-adventure platform game. The aim of Exile is to help the surviving crew of the spaceship *Pericles* and to stop Triax, a psychotic renegade engineer. The game has some rather fanciful features and game mechanics, considering the limitations of the platforms it was initially made for, such as a complex AI system, realistic gravity, mass and inertia, logical ecosystem, and a teleportation mechanic that has similarities to *Portal* (2007).

Exile was highly praised for these features, many of which were years before their time. Exile was ported to a handful of other 8-bit and 16-bit home computers and consoles.

In 2002 *Edge Magazine* retrospectively awarded Exile 10/10. Only two other games – *Elite* (1984) and *Super Mario Bros.* (1985) – have received such an accolade.

Zak McKracken and the Alien Mindbenders

Date of release: October 1988

Region: USA

Developer: Lucasfilm Games

Publisher: Lucasfilm Games

Platform: Commodore 64

Designed by David Fox, Matthew Alan Kane, David Spangler and Ron Gilbert, Zak McKracken and the Alien Mindbenders is a single-player, graphic adventure. The aim is to assemble all the parts of an alien device, spread all over Earth and Mars. The device is a countermeasure to the Mindbending Machine being used by the aliens, known as the Caponians, which is emitting a strange hum that is reducing the intelligence of everyone on Earth. The player controls four different characters to fulfil this aim.

Zak McKracken and the Alien Mindbenders was only the second game after *Maniac Mansion* to use LucasFilm's proprietary SCUMM engine. It has a similar look and feel, humour and narrative to the aforementioned game.

Zak McKracken and the Alien Mindbenders was ported to several 8-bit and 16-bit home computers.

F-19 Stealth Fighter

Date of release: 1988

Region: USA

Developer: MicroProse

Publisher: MicroProse

Platform: PC DOS

Designed by Sid Meier, Arnold Hendrick, Andy Hollis and Jim Synoski, F-19 Stealth Fighter is a single-player, first-person, 3D, combat flight simulator. The aim of the game is to complete several missions set in the North Cape, the Persian Gulf, Libya and central Europe, with varying conditions such as conventional warfare, limited warfare or cold war. At the beginning of each mission, the player must spend time reviewing and familiarizing themselves with the mission briefing (this is a thinking person's combat simulator), before going on to select an array of armaments and other ordnance, such as a camera or extra fuel, that the player thinks will give them the best chance of success. Upon completion of the mission, the player is shown static cut-scenes and a detailed debrief covering each significant event during the mission. Failure of a mission leads to static cut-scenes, such as a captured or rescued pilot.

The game's designers based the aircraft on what a much-rumoured American stealth aircraft might be like. F-19 Stealth Fighter was released on the same day that the United States Military revealed the existence of such a stealth aircraft: The F-117A Nighthawk stealth fighter. Some revisions of the game renamed the game F-117. Included with the original game was a manual about various US and USSR aircraft, a manual on stealth and aerial fighter tactics, maps and a keyboard overlay. F-19 Stealth Fighter set itself apart from other air combat games by appealing to gamers who were as obsessed with detail and realism as the developers. Players had to take time looking at the manual and paying attention to the briefing, lest they fail. For those who took the time the game could be enormously rewarding.

The game was also ported to the Amiga, Atari ST and PC-98. F-19 Stealth Fighter won Best 8-bit and 16-bit Simulation Game of the Year in the 1990/1991 Golden Joystick Awards.

Speedball

Date of release: November 1988

Region: UK

Developer: The Bitmap Brothers

Publisher: Image Works

Platform: Amiga and Atari ST

Speedball is a single-player or two-player, vertically-scrolling, futuristic sports game. The aim of the game is to score more goals than your opponent, win the match (best out of three games) and ultimately try and win the league, all within the time specified by the player at the beginning of the game. Speedball has similar rules to American football yet is more brutal (knocking over players is necessary and encouraged), and the ball is thrown through a wide hole at either end of the room to score a goal. The game is viewed from an above-perspective and moves with the movement of the ball. Player-control switches dependent on who is closest to the ball. There are five players on each side, including a goalkeeper. There are two warp tunnels, halfway down on either side of the pitch. These can be used by skilled players to pass to teammates on the opposite side of the pitch. There are also bounce domes that deflect the ball. These are placed in different places during different matches. If playing in one-player mode, the opponents will get progressively more difficult to defeat the more matches you win. Coins appear on the pitch. These can be used to increase a player's stats or bribe different officials. Power-ups also appear on the pitch and include getting the ball to teleport to one of your players and electrifying the ball.

Speedball was ported to a handful of other 8-bit and 16-bit platforms. The game spawned one sequel with the even more popular *Speedball 2: Brutal Deluxe* (1990), which has been remade and re-released over the years on multiple platforms. Speedball won Game of the Year (16-bit) at the 1988/1989 Golden Joystick Awards.

Splatterhouse

Date of release: November 1988

Region: Japan

Developer: Namco

Publisher: Namco

Platform: Arcade

Splatterhouse is a single-player, side-scrolling, beat 'em up game. The aim is to save Jennifer from the demonic creatures in the mansion. You play as Rick, a fellow student, who entered the mansion but now finds himself in a dungeon. A mask fused to his face empowers him with superhuman strength. The player must make their way through the dungeon, the forest and finally the mansion, dispatching all manner of foul creatures. The player can perform powerful punches and kicks, either while standing, in a crouch or while jumping. A sliding kick can also take out multiple enemies. The player comes across several weapons, such as the meat-cleaver which slices your enemies clean in half in a bloody mess, or a shotgun that will blow them apart. Each level ends with a boss fight with the player having to defeat the final boss, the Hell Chaos, which has been controlling the mansion and is the embodiment of all its evil.

The developers were influenced by the works of H. P. Lovecraft and American slasher movies of the time. The masked Rick bears an uncanny resemblance to Jason in the *Friday the 13th* movies. The game caused some controversy for its violence and nightmarish graphic imagery. It was possibly the goriest arcade game to date, which made it appealing for some players.

The game was ported to a handful of platforms, some of which admittedly had difficulty reproducing Splatterhouse's high graphical standard. The TurboGrafx-16 port had on the front of the box the following warning: 'The horrifying theme of this game may be inappropriate for young children... and cowards.' Splatterhouse spawned two sequels with *Splatterhouse 2* (1992) and *Splatterhouse 3* (1993) for the Sega Mega Drive/Genesis and was remade in 2010 as a 3D version for PlayStation 3 and Xbox 360.

1987/1988 Golden Joystick Awards

The 1987/1988 Golden Joystick Awards are hosted in London.

Out Run (1986) wins Best Arcade-style Game of the Year and Best Game of the Year.

Nebulus (1987) wins Best Original Game of the Year.

Ghouls 'n Ghosts

Date of release: December 1988

Region: Japan

Developer: Capcom

Publisher: Capcom

Platform: Arcade

Designed by Tokuro Fujiwara, with music composed by Tamyo Kawamoto, Ghouls 'n Ghosts, Known as Daimakaimura (meaning Great Demon World Village) in Japan, is a single-player, side-scrolling, platform game. The aim of Ghouls 'n Ghosts is to restore the souls of Prin Prin and the village people (not the 1970s/80s pop group) by defeating Lucifer. Set three years after *Ghost n' Goblins* (1985), you play as the knight Arthur and, as with the first game in what is known as the Ghost 'n Goblins series (this being the second), you must defeat all manner of Lucifer's demonic creatures. As before, Arthur can pick up different weapons, acquired by destroying chests, to dispatch his enemies. There are other new features in the sequel. The player can now also fire directly up or down, instead of just horizontally. Picking up the gold armour enables you to release a very powerful, charged attack. Each weapon has its own charged attack. There is also an enemy magician who, if you don't have your armour on, will turn you into a duck or an old man for a short amount of time, leaving you especially vulnerable, just in case you were finding the game too easy. There are six levels in Ghouls 'n Ghosts, with the chamber of Lucifer being the final level. After defeating Lucifer, Arthur is reunited with the freed Princess and the village people.

The game was highly praised by critics and consumer alike, and, like its predecessor, was known for its difficulty but not quite to the same insane extent as the original. Ghouls 'n Ghosts was ported to various 8-bit and 16-bit home computers and consoles.

Mega Man 2

Date of release: December 1988

Region: Japan

Developer: Capcom

Publisher: Capcom

Platform: Famicom

Designed by Akira Kitamura and Tokuro Fujiwara, Mega Man 2 is a single-player platformer and the sequel to *Mega Man* (1987). The game is non-linear in that the player can choose any level to play. Mega Man must make his way through eight stages and defeat eight robot masters. Again, Mega Man acquires a special ability from any robot master he defeats. After defeating all the robot masters, the player must defeat Dr Wily. New features in Mega Man 2 include a password system, and energy tanks to refill Mega Man's Health.

Mega Man 2 was far more successful than the original, selling 1.5 million units. The game is often cited as being the best in the Mega Man series and one of the finest games on the NES system.

Winning Run

Date of release: December 1988

Region: Japan

Developer: Namco

Publisher: Namco

Platform: Arcade

Winning Run is a single-player or multiplayer, first-person, 3D, Formula 1 racing game. The aim is to finish first in each race. The player takes control of a Formula 1 car and (after completing a qualifying lap) must not only out-race the other twelve cars but also avoid several hazards on the track.

The player sits down in the arcade cabinet which moves in sync with the player's interaction with the game. Winning Run was the first Arcade racing game to feature fully-3D-shaded polygon environments. The hardware was able to draw a total of 60,000 individual polygons per second, producing the speed necessary for a racing game. The game was lauded for its graphics and realistic racing.

Winning Race had two sequels with *Winning Race Suzuki GP* (1989) and *Winning Run '91* (1991).

1988 Notable Omissions

Arc System Works is formed. Armalyte. Assault. Bad Dudes Vs DragonNinja. Battle Tank. Bionic Commando Rearmed. Blades of Steel. Cabal. Captain Blood. CD-ROM2 System first CD-Tom games console. Conqueror. Dark Chambers. Dark Side. Double Dragon II: The Revenge. Dragon Quest III. Final Fantasy II. Football Manager 2. Gain Ground. Ghostbuster. Golgo 13: Top Secret Episode. Herzog. Hostages: Rescue Mission. Hidden Agenda. Indiana Jones and the Temple of Jones. Insector X. Kenseiden. Laser Squad. Master Blaster. Midway games is formed. Military Madness. Milon's Secret Castle. Mirai Ninja. Nintendo Power Pad. Nintendo Sues Camerica. Operation Thunderbolt. Out Run 3-D. Phelios. Pioneer Plague. Power Drift. R.C. Pro-Am. Robocop. Rocket Ranger. Skate or Die. Super Mario Bros. 2. The Colony. The Guardian Legend. The Manhole. Treasure Island Dizzy. TV Sports: Football. Ultima V: Warriors of Destiny. Vigilante. Walt Disney Computer Software was formed. Will Harvey's Zany Golf. Wonderboy III: Monster Lair. XZR II: Kanketsuhen.

1989

Cadash

Date of release: 1989

Region: Japan

Developer: Taito

Publisher: Taito

Platform: Arcade

Cadash is a single-player or multiplayer, platform RPG. The aim is to rescue Princess Sarasa from the demonic Balrog in the subterranean world. At the beginning of the game, the player/s choose between four characters – fighter, mage, priest or ninja, each with specific strengths and abilities. Players must progress through each stage, dispatching a multitude of monsters, and collect money that can be used to upgrade equipment from various shops. A little health can be replenished by picking up herbs. The rarely encountered elixirs will restore all your health. An antidote will cure you if afflicted by poison. The game comprises of five stages with the final stage set in Castle Cadash. As with most RPGs, players will gain experience through defeating enemies and level-up from time to time, increasing your stats.

The cabinet housed two sets of joysticks and buttons for a two-player game. It was also possible to link two Cadash cabinets and have four players play together.

The game was ported to PC Engine/TurboGrafx-16 and the Mega Drive/Genesis. Cadash is one of the first examples of a side-scrolling, multiplayer platform RPG game, which were to become very popular in Japan.

Midwinter

Date of release: 1989

Region: USA

Developer: Maelstrom Games

Publisher: Microplay Software

Platform: Amiga, Atari ST and IBM-PC

Designed by Mike Singleton, Midwinter is single-player, 3D, first-person, action RPG. The aim is to alert the rest of the islanders of the current invasion and destroy the enemy headquarters. Set in the year 2099, a meteorite strike in the year 2040 has plunged the world into another Ice Age. At the beginning of the game, you play as John Stark, a FVPF (Free Villages Peace Force) soldier and must travel the island, recruiting the civilians of Midwinter Island (formed from massive volcanic activity) and find the other members of the FVPF. The player explores the snow-covered landscape either by skiing, on a snowmobile or by cable car transport system. How likely it is to recruit someone is dependent on which character the player is controlling. Each character has a positive or negative relationship with every other character, determined by the circumstances in the game and the actions taken. Once one of the thirty-two characters is recruited, the player can take control of that character. Each playable character has a certain skill set, some of which are essential to progressing through certain parts of the game. Soldiers can use a rifle, grenades or missiles to defeat the multitude of enemies who possess the same weaponry as the player, as well as a missile-armed snowmobile and mortar fire.

Midwinter received positive reviews at the time. It is also considered a little-known milestone in video game history, despite its primitive, 3D, flat-shaded polygons and the low framerate, it is yet another early example of how some games attempted to stretch across more than just one genre. Like so many games that would come decades later, Midwinter has elements of RPG, simulation, action and strategy.

Midwinter spawned one sequel with *Midwinter II Flames of Freedom* (1991).

Hard Drivin'

Date of release: February 1989

Region: USA

Developer: Atari Games

Publisher: Atari Games

Platform: Arcade

Designed by Rick Moncrief of Atari Games Applied Research Group, Hard Drivin' is a single-player, first-person, 3D, driving simulation game. The aim of the game is simple: complete one or two laps of the current track in the allotted time. Yet it is anything but simple. This is indeed 'hard' driving and the player must use the clutch and gears exactly like in a real car. Compound this with the possibility of stalling and the force feedback steering wheel, which feels like it has a mind of its own, and the game reveals itself to being devilishly challenging. If the player can master staying on the road and avoiding traffic, then they may have the courage to tackle Hard Drivin's other features, such as jumps and stunt loops. Or if the player is able to score in the top ten then they can race against the computer. When (not if) the player crashes, they are treated to a 10-second animated aerial view of the spectacle.

At a time when most racing games used sprite-scaling techniques to give the illusion of moving through a three-dimensional environment, Hard Drivin' with its flat-shaded 3D graphics stood out from the crowd, inviting a lot of attention. The cabinet was very expensive at the time, costing $10,000 per unit. Where most arcades contained an 8-bit or 16-bit processor, Hard Drivin' used two 32-bit graphics-orientated processors, as well as its main CPU. It was no wonder that the 16-bit ports of the game struggled a little, while the 8-bit versions were a far cry from the original.

The game spawned two sequels: *Race Drivin'* (1990) and *Hard Drivin II – Drive Harder* (1991).

SimCity

Date of release: February 1989

Region: USA

Developer: Will Wright

Publisher: Broderbund

Platform: 8-bit and 16-bit home computers

SimCity is a single-player or multiplayer, city-building game. The aim of SimCity is to build and maintain a city. However, beyond this, there are no specific goals or end game, unless specified by choosing to play one of the eight included 'scenarios'. Players view their city from an overhead perspective and can view the map to see where their city sits in the surrounding environment. The land can be broken down into blocks where a player can mark these areas of land as being zoned for commercial, industrial or residential purposes. A power plant must be established (coal or nuclear) and zones must be linked to the power grid and a transport system established so that people can move in and develop these zones. The evolution of each zone is dependent on the surrounding area. Players will need to tax the residents of the city, known as 'Sims' if they want to expand and develop their city and build things, such as airports, churches, fire departments, hospitals, parks, police departments, seaports and stadiums. Players must also deal with crime, pollution and natural disasters (air disaster, earthquake, fire, flood and monsters) which may befall their city.

SimCity initially sold poorly until it was championed by the media of the time. This, coupled with word of mouth from initial buyers, created a snowball effect, turning the game into a commercial success. It sold 300,000 units for the home computer and around 2 million when it was released a couple of years later on the Super Nintendo Entertainment System. SimCity won multiple awards throughout 1989 and 1990. Before SimCity most but not all Video games were about rescuing someone and/or defeating the enemy. SimCity began and popularised a new genre in games, appealing to the innate desire of human beings to create something, as opposed to destroying something.

As well as paving the way for every other city building game and another Will Wright blockbuster game *The Sims* (2000), SimCity has spawned many sequels since its inception. Some of the most notable of these are *SimCity 2000* (1993), *SimCity 3000* (1999) and *SimCity 4: Rush Hour* (2003).

Midnight Resistance

Date of release: 1989

Region: Worldwide

Developer: Data East

Publisher: Data East

Platform: Arcade

Designed by Koji Akibayashi, Midnight Resistance is a single-player or two-player cooperative, multi-scrolling, run and gun game. The aim is to rescue your family from the Crimson King Entity. You play as one of two brothers. The player/s progress through each stage killing a multitude of enemies, some of whom will drop keys. These can be used between stages to unlock a number of special weapons, including 3-way, shotgun, fire (flamethrower), full auto, nitro, and extra ammo for your current special weapon. Players can also collect other power-ups such as the barrier, a super charger for your gun and a 1-up. There is a total of nine stages in the game. During the penultimate stage, you can free members of your family, but how many are dependent on the number of keys you collected in that stage. There are also different endings after defeating the Crimson King, determined by how many family members you've saved.

The arcade cabinet featured a rotatable joystick to allow players to easily move their character whilst shooting in any direction at the same time.

The game was well-received by critics and consumers alike and was soon ported to some of the 8-bit and 16-bit home computers of the time as well as the Sega Mega Drive/Genesis.

Harpoon

Date of release: 1989

Region: USA

Developer: Three-Sixty Pacific

Publisher: Three-Sixty Pacific

Platform: Amiga, MS-DOS and Macintosh

Designed by Larry Bond, Harpoon is a single-player, real-time wargame. There are different aims in the game dependent on the scenario. The player controls either NATO or Soviet forces and focuses on naval combat in the GIUK (Greenland, Iceland & the United Kingdom) Gap, a naval chokepoint in the Atlantic Ocean. The player can control over 100 weapons systems and must make decisions as circumstances consistently change and evolve. Larry Bond was inspired to develop Harpoon after his exposure to NAVTAG (Naval Tactical Analysis Game), a tactical training game developed by the United States Navy. NAVTAG was a computerised version of the 1970 manual training game, SEATAG, which ran on three networked microcomputers: one for the Blue side, the second for the Red side and the third for Game Control. Harpoon came with a user's guide, which included information on superpower politics and maritime strategies in modern warfare, a separate tactical guide for the game itself and a booklet by Tom Clancy about Russian destroyers.

Harpoon received outstanding reviews, frequently achieving the very highest accolades. Praised for its attention to detail and realism to the extent where the military were known to use it at their academies. It has been cited as one of the most significant war games of all time and possibly the most successful naval war game.

There are several games in the Harpoon series, though these do include updates of the original and expansion packs. The two main sequels in the Harpoon series are *Harpoon II* (1994) and *Harpoon III* (2001).

Strider/Strider Hiryu

Date of release: March 1989

Region: USA and Japan

Developer: Capcom

Publisher: Capcom

Platform: Arcade

Designed by Kouichi Yotsui, Tokuro Fujiwara and Shinichi Yoshimoto, Strider is a single-player, side-scrolling, hack and slash, platform game. The aim is to infiltrate the Russian Red Army and return the enemy's secrets to your superiors. Set in the year 2048, you play as Hiryu, one of a secret group of ninjas known as Striders. Strider Hiryu can perform several different moves to help progress through each stage. The game consists of five stages. Hiryu can perform cartwheel jumps (longer cartwheels can be performed if the player gains momentum by running down the many slopes in the game), slide past obstacles or enemies, climb (on walls and ceilings) and use his plasma sword to cut enemies in half. Power-ups in Strider include an extension of Hiryu's blade attack (which is otherwise limited to 100 slashes), extra life, health packs, maximum health increase, and invulnerability coupled with attack-up (limited to 15 seconds). Hiryu can also summon three different types of robotic companions to help defeat his opponents.

Hiryu made his debut in 1988 in the *Strider Hiryu* manga. The Strider arcade game was part of a collaboration between the manga's publisher, Moto Kikaku, and Capcom.

The game was highly praised by critics and consumers alike and was soon ported to some of the 8-bit and 16-bit home computers and consoles of the time. The Mega Drive/Genesis version of the game is often considered the best. Strider spawned two sequels with *Strider II/Journey from Darkness: Strider Returns* (1990) and *Strider 2/Strider Hiryu 2* (1999).

Phantasy Star II

Date of release: March 1989

Region: Japan

Developer: Sega

Publisher: Sega

Platform: Sega Mega Drive/Genesis

Designed by Akinori Nishiyama, Yuji Naka, Rieko Kodama, and with music by Tokuhiko Uwabo, Phantasy Star II is a single-player RPG. The aim is to discover why 'Mother Brain', a giant computer that controls every aspect of life on the planet Mota (called Motovia in *Phantasy Star*), is malfunctioning. Taking place 1000 years after the events of the original game, you play as Rolf, a government agent. The player controls a party of four, meeting more players who can be swapped in and out of the four-player party at any time as the game progresses. Each character has a preferred set of skills and is predetermined to using certain weapons and armour. Phantasy Star II gameplay and game mechanics are very similar to its predecessor, and standard for a JRPG of the time. There are some changes, though. In the first-person combat mode, more than one enemy can be seen at a time, with players able to choose which enemy to attack. The enemies are also fully animated, even when idle, but this was at the expense of having no relevant background, just a generic blue grid on black. The dungeon areas maintained a top-down view used throughout the rest of the gameplay (except for combat) instead of switching to first-person like the first game. Some players missed this first-person part of the game while some have pointed out that it fits in with the rest of the gameplay.

Phantasy Star II was met with very high critical and consumer praise and is regarded as one of the best RPGs of the day. It is noted for its strong narrative, amazing soundtrack and high difficulty. Its science fiction theme set it apart from many of its contemporaries. Phantasy Star II was the first RPG for the Mega Drive. It was also the first game to use the 6 mega-bit cartridge, making it not only the biggest game on the Mega Drive/Genesis but the biggest RPG to date. It was so complex for the time that Sega included a 110-page book of hints in the box. The game's story also had a strong impact on players as it involved a major character's death well into the game.

The game has been ported/remade, with enhanced graphics and music, to the Sega Saturn, Game Boy Advance, Dreamcast, PS2, PSP, Xbox 360 and PS3.

GamePro

GamePro was first launched in the USA in April 1989 by the International Data Group. *GamePro* was a monthly publication focusing on multi-platform games, hardware, news and events. Reviews were rated in five categories on a five-star-based system, with increments of 0.5. The official website GamePro.com was launched in 1998. The magazine published international editions in France, Germany, Spain, Portugal, Italy,

Turkey, Australia, Brazil and Greece. The final issue of the magazine was published at the end of 2011, meaning the publication ran for 32 years and the website for 23 years.

Nintendo Game Boy

The Nintendo Game Boy was released in Japan in April 1989 by Nintendo.

Developed by Satoru Okada and Gunpei Yokoi, the Game Boy is an 8-bit, cartridge-based, fourth-generation handheld game console that uses a 160 x 144 pixel monochrome LCD, measuring 47 x 43 mm. It featured controls in line with the Famicom and NES – a D-Pad, 'A' and 'B' buttons, and the 'SELECT' and 'START' buttons. Over the years several accessories were developed, such as a carrying case, rechargeable battery pack, printer, a camera and a multitude of solutions to help players view the screen in low light as the original Game Boy had no backlight. Players could also connect to other Game Boys using a link cable for use with specific games.

The Nintendo Game Boy was incredibly successful. Multiple variations on the original model were released over the years. It had direct handheld competition from the technically superior Atari Lynx (1989), Sega Game Gear (1990) and the NEC's TurboExpress (1990) but outsold them all. Perhaps this was because it was cheaper and more accessible, or maybe it was the fact that Nintendo's most iconic games could now be played anywhere. Or perhaps it was the deal that Henk Rogers managed to broker which saw a copy of *Tetris* (1984) bundled with every Game Boy. Tetris, being one of the most addictive and the best-selling games of all time, may have contributed to the Game Boy's success.

The original Game Boy has sold around 65 million units worldwide. It was followed by the next generation of Nintendo handhelds with the Game Boy Color (1998) and the Game Boy Advance (2001).

Some of the most notable games for the Gameboy are *Tetris* (1989), *Kirby's Dream Land* (1992), *Super Mario Land 2: 6 Golden Coins* (1993), *The Legend of Zelda: Link's Awakening* (1993), *Donkey Kong* (1994), *Wario Land: Super Mario Land 3* (1994), *Pokémon Red & Blue* (1998) and *Wario Land II* (1998).

Indiana Jones and the Last Crusade: The Graphic Adventure

Date of release: July 1989

Region: USA

Developer: Lucasfilm Games

Publisher: Lucasfilm Games

Platform: Amiga, Atari ST, Macintosh and MS-DOS

Designed by Ron Gilbert, Noah Falstein, David Fox and Steve Purcell, Indiana Jones and the Last Crusade: The Graphic Adventure (released at the same time as the movie) is a single-player, graphic adventure based on the movie of the same name, and the third game to use Lucasfilm Games' proprietary SCUMM engine. The aim of the game is to find your father and, ultimately, the Holy Grail.

What set this game apart from many other graphic adventures was the introduction of a point system called the IQ score or 'Indy Quotient'. This score could be carried over and continued after completion of one game onto a new game, encouraging players to find the many different paths and solutions to confrontations and puzzles. This allowed players to try different styles or play. It also addressed the problem many text and graphical adventures of the time had in that they had no replay value as there was often only one way to solve a problem or finish the game. In Indiana Jones and the Last Crusade: The Graphic Adventure there were multiple ways to play the game and finish it.

Indiana Jones and the Last Crusade: The Graphic Adventure was a critical success selling over 250,000 units. It spawned one sequel with *Indiana Jones and the Fate of Atlantis* (1992).

Kick Off

Date of release: 1989

Region: UK

Developer: Dino Dini and Steve Screech

Publisher: Anco Software

Platform: Atari ST & Amiga

Kick Off is a single-player or multiplayer, multi-scrolling soccer game. The game was viewed from a top-down perspective and featured players with different strategies, fouls with the inclusion of yellow card, red card, penalties, action replays, injuries and injury time. There was also a range of different referees, all with different temperaments.

The Kick Off series of games was very popular for a while. That was until the *Sensible Soccer* series was first released in 1992 and, of course, the *FIFA International Soccer* series that began in 1993.

Kick Off was released on various 8-bit and 16-bit home computers, as well as the NES. The game spawned a whole series of games, some of the most notable of which are *Player Manager* (1990) (the first soccer game to introduce a management system into the game), *Kick Off 2* (1990) and *Kick Off 2 World Cup* (1990).

Golden Axe

Date of release: May 1989

Region: Japan

Developer: Sega

Publisher: Sega

Platform: Arcade

Designed by Makoto Uchida, Golden Axe is a side-scrolling, single-player or multiplayer, fantasy-based beat 'em up. The aim of the game is to rescue the king and the princess from the game's antagonist, Death Adder, who also holds the sacred Golden Axe. The player/s begins the game by choosing one of three characters: Ax Battler the Barbarian, Tyris Flame the Amazon, or Gilius Thunderhead the Dwarf. The player/s must progress through each stage dispatching Death Adder's various minions, some of whom are human and others who aren't. Players can use their standard attack or a jump attack. They can also use a magic attack, raining down such things as fire or lightning, dependent on the character. Players can collect blue potion bottles by intercepting the little sprites who run on screen, catching them before they run off. The potions add to your overall magic power. Characters can also ride and control different creatures using them to attack your enemies to great advantage. For example, the cockatrice can swipe enemies with its tail and the dragons can envelop enemies with its fire breath. After finally defeating Death Adder, the player/s receive a golden axe which grants them immortality.

With Golden Axe, the developers wanted to create a *Double Dragon* type game but with a *Dragon Quest/Conan* backdrop.

The game was ported to most platforms of the time. Golden Axe was well received in the arcades, spawning several sequels that added more players and features. The first two of these, *Golden Axe II* (1991) and *Golden Axe III* (1993) are often considered the best.

Pipe Mania/Pipe Dream

Date of release: June 1989

Region: worldwide

Developer: The Assembly Line

Publisher: Lucasfilm Games

Platform: Amiga

Pipe Mania is a single-player, puzzle game. The aim of Pipe Mania is simple. The player must connect the pieces of pipe, made of different shapes and sizes, from the start position to the end position, ensuring that the 'sewer slime' does not spill out from an open, unconstructed piece of pipe. The slime slowly flows through the pipe and the player must make sure they have laid down the pipe in readiness for it to flow through. If the player is not quick enough and the slime pours out of an open end of the pipe, the game is over. A level is completed when the slime reaches the end position without spillage. Each level becomes more difficult than the last.

Pipe Mania was ported to most 8-bit and 16-bit home computers and consoles and has spawned numerous clones using a similar concept with many variations. It was included also in the Microsoft Windows Entertainment Pack in 1990.

Pipe Mania/Pipe Dream has inspired many mini-games within a game, for example as the means of hacking in *Bioshock* (2007). Its gameplay has also been emulated in many mobile games over the years.

Arthur: The Quest for Excalibur

Date of release: June 1989

Region: USA

Developer: Challenge Inc

Publisher: Infocom

Platform: Amiga, Apple II, MS-DOS and Macintosh

Designed by Bob Bates, Arthur: The Quest for Excalibur is a single-player, text and illustrated adventure game. The aim of the game is to recover the sword in the stone stolen by the evil King Lot. The player takes the role of a young Arthur. You must prove to the wizard Merlin that you have the qualities required to be the future king. The player has three days to fulfil their destiny. Merlin helps by offering advice, and from time to time bestows upon Arthur the power to turn into various animals.

The game included *The Book of Hours*, a Christian prayer book. Used for copy protection, players were referred to this book to input specific lines as passwords.

The game was praised for its graphics, puzzles and parser.

Populous

Date of release: June 1989

Region: worldwide

Developer: Bullfrog Productions

Publisher: Electronic Arts

Platform: Amiga

Designed by Peter Molyneux, Populous is a single-player or multiplayer, isometric, god game. The aim of Populous is to defeat your opponent's followers. You play the part of a divine being with the initial ability to raise or lower the landscape. Flattening the land essentially allows your followers to prosper and multiply. The game works on the concept that the more people who believe in your existence, the more powerful you are, and so it is in your best interests to have them multiply. As your power grows, more divine powers are unlocked, including turning followers into knights, causing earthquakes and floods, and creating swamps and volcanoes. All these can be used to hamper and crush your opponent. Only a small part of the screen is used to view and control the 3D landscape. The top left part of the screen depicts the world map while the top-right displays the level of your divine power and that of your opponent, as well as divine powers available. The bottom left of the screen is used to control your world. There are 500 levels in Populous with a variety of landscapes, such as desert, grassland, ice, lava, rock and snow. There are also several other preferences that can be set before the game begins. Two players could play Populous against one another if they connected their computers together.

Populous received a wealth of critical acclaim and was very popular with PC gamers, selling over four million units which has made it one of the best-selling computer games of all time. It also won multiple awards.

Populous was ported to other 16-bit home computers and consoles, as well as the Game Boy. Bullfrog released a Populous editor in the form of *Populous World Editor*, allowing users to modify the assets of the game. They also released *Populous: The Promised Lands* which added five new landscapes: Silly Land, Wild West, Lego Style Block Land, Revolution Française, and computer-themed Bit Plains. The game had two direct sequels with *Populous II: Trials of the Olympian Gods* (1991) and *Populous: The Beginning* (1998).

Mother

Date of release: July 1989

Region: Japan

Developer: Ape Inc

Publisher: Nintendo

Platform: Famicom

Designed by Shigesato Itoi and Shigeru Miyamoto, Mother is a single-player, turn-based, RPG. The aim of Mother is to find the Eight Melodies and play them to Queen Mary, the ruler of the World of Magicant, and later defeat the alien entity known as Giygas. You play as Ninten, a young boy living in an urban area in late 20th-century America, you must travel with your friends to find the Eight Melodies. The game is viewed from a pseudo-top-down perspective popular at the time, where paths are seen from directly above, trees are depicted in profile and buildings are displayed isometrically. When the player enters combat, it is first-person and turn-based.

Mother is noted for having very similar gameplay and mechanics to the early *Dragon Quest* games: it was inspired by them and often parodies some of its ideas. However, it was quite different from many JRPGs of the time, mainly because it was not exclusively fantasy or sci-fi based, rather set in the late 20th century. It deals with more modern-day objects, such as using the telephone to save your game or cash machines (known as automated teller machines) for banking money. Many NPCs the player interacts with are modern, everyday people. You could also see your whole party while traversing the map as opposed to just the one player representing all, which was also different from most JRPGs.

Mother received a fair to good reception at the time. Some commented that it was a satirical, inferior product to the RPGs it parodied, while others simply disliked the game's high difficulty level. It now lives in the shadow of its sequel *Mother 2/Earthbound* (1994) which refined every aspect of Mother into a better game. The Westernised version of Mother known as *EarthBound Beginnings*, was not officially released until June 2015 for the Wii U Virtual Console.

Gunhed/Blazing Lazers

Date of release: July 1989

Region: Japan

Developer: Compile

Publisher: Hudson Soft

Platform: PC Engine/TurboGrafx-16

Known as Blazing Lazers in the West, Gunhed is a single-player, vertical-scrolling shooter. Based on the 1989 Japanese science fiction action movie *Gunhed*, the aim of the game is to save another galaxy that is under attack by a vast alien space armada called the Dark Squadron. The player controls the Gunhed Advanced Star Fighter. As with many shooters, Gunhed has a system where the player's fire can be changed or upgraded by collecting power-ups. A limited supply of cluster bombs can be used to destroy multiple enemies. The speed of the player's ship is determined by pressing a button that toggles through five different speeds. The game awards extra lives when milestones in the player's scores are reached. There are nine stages in Gunhed, each with a boss which must be destroyed to proceed.

Gunhed was renowned for its graphics and fast, intense, and very smooth gameplay, granting it the status of being one of the best games to be played on the PC Engine/TurboGrafx- 16 Platform.

Batman/Batman: The Movie

Date of release: 1989

Region: UK

Developer: Ocean

Publisher: Ocean

Platform: 8-bit and 16-bit home computers

Batman is a single-player, action adventure game. Based on the huge 1989 hit movie of the same name, the aim of Batman is to stop the Joker. The game is split over five levels. The first level is a multi-scrolling platform game set at the Axis Chemical Plant. Batman can use his Batarangs to take out multiple enemies, and his grapple gun to climb to higher levels or swing across to adjacent levels. Enemies will shoot and throw grenades at him. Toxic gas and acid drops must also be avoided. The second and fourth levels are vehicular games: the Batmobile and then the Batwing. Both are third-person and are extraordinarily difficult, requiring perfect timing and quick reflexes. The third level is a game like the codebreaking game 'Mastermind.' The fifth and final level is another platform section similar to the first level except set in Gotham City Cathedral. When Batman finally reaches the top, he must fire his grappling hook at the perfect time and angle to stop the Joker from climbing up a rope ladder and into a helicopter. If successful, the Joker falls to his death.

The game can be tough to complete. In each level, there is a time limit and the player has only three lives throughout the entire game with no opportunity for extra lives.

In the UK, the game was bundled in what was known as The Batman Pack. This consisted of the Amiga 500 home computer with *Batman* (1989), *F/A-18 Interceptor* (1988), *The NewZealand Story* (1988) and *Deluxe Paint II* (1986) for £399. It was a great offer and helped sell 186,000 Amigas in one year in the UK alone.

Batman was highly commended by many publications of the time and was one of the few very good video games based on a movie – most were terrible. Other versions of a Batman movie licensed game were released over the next couple of years for the NES, Game Boy, Mega Drive/Genesis and Arcade.

Stunt Car Racer/Stunt Track Racer

Date of release: 1989

Region: USA/UK

Developer: MicroStyle

Publisher: MicroPlay /MicroStyle

Platform: Amiga

Designed by Geoff Crammond, Stunt Car Racer is a single-player or two-player, first-person, 3D racing game. The aim of Stunt Car Racer is to complete each track without wrecking your car. The game begins with the player's car being hoisted up and dropped onto an elevated track. Tracks consist of banked turns and an assortment of jumps. The player gets a preview of the track from a bird's eye view to get an idea of what's in store before the race starts. There are eight tracks in Stunt Car Racer, with names like the Big Ramp and the Roller Coaster. Players must hit the jumps at just the right speed, ensuring they are lined up correctly otherwise they will find themselves flying off the track. The crane lifts you back onto the track, however, this takes precious time. The player has limited use of a turbo to make up for lost time. Too many crashes mean you've wrecked your car and the game is over. The tracks get progressively more difficult to complete as you progress. Three laps must be completed to progress to the next track. The game has a league table made up of four divisions, with three drivers in each. Two players can compete by linking two computers together using a null-modem cable and using two separate displays.

The game received favourable reviews, being cited for setting itself apart from other racing games with its unique concept of elevated tracks, 3D graphics (flat-shaded polygons) and gripping gameplay. It was soon ported to some of the other 8-bit and 16-bit home computers.

S.T.U.N. Runner

Date of release: September 1989

Region: USA

Developer: Atari Games

Publisher: Atari Games

Platform: Arcade

S.T.U.N. Runner is a futuristic, single-player, third-person, 3D (flat-shaded polygons), vehicular combat and racing game. S.T.U.N. stands for Spread Tunnel Underground Network. The aim of S.T.U.N. Runner is to complete each track before the timer runs out. There's the added goal of taking on the Ultimate Challenge – a final track that cannot be beaten, only to see how far the player could progress and make it to the highest scores table. The player controls a futuristic vehicle that can reach speeds exceeding 900 mph and can adhere to the walls of the tunnels present in certain parts of the course. A course is made up of different sections: tunnels, construction sites, wide flats, narrow flats, and narrow tunnels. Stars can be collected by racing over them. These can be used to acquire shockwaves. The shockwave can be initialised by the player and travels down the course, destroying everything in its wake. The player can touch boost pads for hyperspeed. During hyperspeed, the player's vehicle turns from flat-shaded polygons to a wireframe model. It's a cool effect to illustrate that the player has entered this mode and to allow players to see what is coming towards them at very high speed. The vehicle also has mounted lasers that the player can use by pressing the trigger buttons on the controller to destroy other vehicles in the way. However, armoured vehicles cannot be destroyed. Smashing into other vehicles breaks off pieces of your vehicle. When the final piece of your vehicle is destroyed then the game is over. Pieces of your vehicle will be replaced if a course is completed. If a course isn't completed in the time allotted, the game is over.

S.T.U.N. Runner's hardware was based on the boards that ran a previous game by Atari Games – *Hard Drivin'* (1989). Player's sat astride the open arcade cabinet, made to look a little bit like the S.T.U.N. Runner vehicle. The control yoke was almost exactly the same as the one used in the very popular *Star Wars* (1983) arcade cabinet. The game is noted for its high speed and 3D graphics, perfect for the arcades as customers were beginning to show great interest in 3D games, and something a bit more fast-paced was needed after the slow-paced *Hard Drivin'* (1989).

S.T.U.N. Runner was ported to several 8-bit and 16-bit home computers and consoles. It is easy to imagine how S.T.U.N Runner might influence a game like *Wipeout (1995).*

Atari Lynx

The Atari Lynx was released in the USA in September 1989 by the Atari Corporation. Developed by Epyx, the Atari Lynx is a 16-bit, cartridge-based, fourth-generation, handheld game console and uses a 3.5-inch screen with a resolution of 160 x 102 and can display 16 colours from a palette of 4,096, with 64 kilobytes of RAM and 4 channels of sound. The Lynx features a D-Pad, two sets of 'A' and 'B' buttons, 'OPTION', 'RESTART' and 'FLIP' buttons.

The initial reception of the Lynx was promising. Its specifications were far superior to those of the Game Boy in every way. Unlike the Game Boy, it had a colour display and this display was back-lit. It could also connect to fifteen other Lynx's, though only a few games used this feature. However, it cost twice as much at $179.99 and its games library was less extensive. The Atari Lynx would go on and sell a total of around three million units, a fraction of the Game Boy's sales. The Atari Lynx was the world's first colour handheld games console and also the first 16-bit handheld. It was also the first-ever device that could be played either way up, with the screen flipping if turned 180 degrees and pressing the flip button. This was a feature that would not become common until well over a decade later with mobile devices. The Atari Lynx was succeeded by the Lynx II (1990).

The most notable games for the Atari Lynx are *California Games* (1989), *Chip's Challenge* (1989), *Klax* (1990), *Todd's Adventure's in Slime World* (1990), *Xenophobe* (1990), *S.T.U.N. Runner* (1991) and *Lemmings* (1993).

Prince of Persia

Date of release: October 1989

Region: USA

Developer: Broderbund

Publisher: Broderbund

Platform: Apple II

Designed by Jordan Mechner, Prince of Persia is a single-player, cinematic platformer. The aim of Prince of Persia is to progress through a series of dungeons, escape and ultimately defeat the Grand Vizier Jaffar and save the princess at the top of the palace tower within the hour. Set in ancient Persia you play as the youth whom the princess loves. The player must find a way out of the dungeon to the palace and finally the palace tower (made up of 12 stages in total), climbing and jumping across pits and defeating any of the Grand Vizier's soldiers they encounter with their sword. Some platforms act as a mechanism to open gates, while others will fall away after a short delay when stood on. The player can lose health by falling too far or touching many of the spike traps and guillotines scattered around the dungeon and palace. Health can be replenished by drinking potions. After defeating the Grand Vizier and saving the princess, the youth is given the title of The Prince of Persia.

The game is similar in style to *Karateka* (1984), which was also designed by Mechner, except the setting is different and there are some new game mechanics. Prince of Persia sold poorly in North America on the Apple II. However, it did very well in Japan and managed to sell two million units once it was ported to the 16-bit home computers and consoles. Prince of Persia is noted for the smooth animation of its characters, which was achieved using rotoscoping. Mechner used video of his brother as reference material.

Prince of Persia spawned a whole series of Prince of Persia games. Some of the most notable are *Prince of Persia: Sands of Time* (2003), *Prince of Persia: Warrior Within* (2004), *Prince of Persia: The Two Thrones* (2005) and *Prince of Persia* (2008).

Pomping World/Pang/Buster Bros.

Date of release: November 1989

Region: Japan

Developer: Mitchell Corporation

Publisher: Mitchell

Platform: Arcade

Designed by Yoshiki Okamoto and Toshihiko Uda, Pomping World, also known as Pang or Buster Bros. outside of Japan, is a single-player or co-operative two-player, action game. The aim of Pomping World is to destroy all the bouncing balloons and progress to the next stage within the allotted time. You play as one of two brothers armed with a harpoon weapon that fires a wire upwards. If it hits one of the balloons it will break into smaller ones (similar to *Asteroids but with* balloons) until they are destroyed completely. When hit the balloons may drop temporary power-ups/weapons (similar to *Arkanoid*), such as double wire – firing two wires at the same time; power wire – a static wire that can destroy multiple balloons and stay intact; Vulcan missile – a machine gun; force field; the hourglass – slows the balloons down; the clock – stops the balloons, and the dynamite – pops all the balloons down to their smallest size, which sounds good but can be disastrous as it can fill the screen with a multitude of balloons to dodge. If you are hit by the balloons or one of the creatures that move onto the screen from time to time, then you will lose a life. The player begins the game with three lives. There are 50 stages in Pomping World, moving across 17 different locations all over the world, illustrated as beautiful 16-bit backgrounds. For example, Mount Fuji, Paris, London, New York, Egypt, Easter Island, Athens and the Taj Mahal.

Pomping World was ported to most 8-bit and 16-bit home computer and consoles where it received high praise from critics and consumers alike.

Pomping World spawned a number of sequels. These were *Super Buster Bros./Super Pang* (1990), *Pang 3* (1995), *Mighty! Pang* (2000), *Pang: Magical Michael* (2010) and *Pang Adventures* (2016).

Teenage Mutant Ninja Turtles

Date of release: November 1989

Region: USA

Developer: Konami

Publisher: Konami

Platform: Arcade

Teenage Mutant Ninja Turtles is a single-player or multiplayer, side-scrolling beat 'em up, based on the hit animated television series of the same name. The aim is to save the turtles' mentor Splinter and friend reporter April O'Neil from the evil Shredder and his henchman. Up to four players can play together, each choosing one of the four turtles: Donatello, Leonardo, Michelangelo and Raphael. Every turtle uses a different weapon with advantages and disadvantages. Different attacks can be performed by the player/s. Objects and other parts of the environment can be utilised to enable players to dispatch the multitude of enemies sent your way. At the end of each stage, the turtles must defeat a boss to continue, ultimately defeating Shredder at the end to complete the game.

Even though four-player cooperative arcade games had been around for some time now with games like *Gauntlet* (1985), Teenage Mutant Ninja Turtles would begin a new wave of side-scrolling, multiplayer co-ops, with *Captain America and The Avengers* (1991), *The Simpsons* (1991) and *X-Men* (1992).

Teenage Mutant Ninja Turtles was also released for 8-bit and 16-bit home computers and consoles. The NES version was titled *Teenage Mutant Ninja Turtles II: The Arcade Game* (1990), so as not to confuse it with their Teenage Mutant Ninja Turtles game released in June 1989.

Shadow of the Beast

Date of release: 1989

Region: UK

Developer: Reflections Interactive

Publisher: Psygnosis

Platform: Amiga

Designed by Martin Edmondson, Paul Howarth, Richard Swinfen and Steven Hammond, with music by David Whittaker, Shadow of the Beast is a single-player platform game. The aim of the game is to defeat the evil beast lord, Maletoth. You play as a creature who was kidnapped as a child and corrupted into a beast by Maletoth. If you can defeat the final boss at the end of the game, you are freed from the Shadow of the Beast curse and regain your human form. The player can run, jump, crouch, and climb ladders. Throughout each level, you must dispatch a multitude of Maetoth's minions. You do this by simply punching them, later in the game the player acquires a weapon to deal with these foes.

What the game lacked in gameplay it made up for in sound and graphics. Shadow of the Beast was designed to push the Amiga platform to its limits and show gamers something they had never seen before: displays of up to 128 colours on screen, and 12 levels of parallax scrolling, in the foreground, the background and the sky. The game was known for its clunky controls yet it was visually stunning. The style and the technique it used would influence games for years to come.

Shadow of the Beast received two sequels: Shadow of the Beast II (1990) and Shadow of the Beast III (1992). A remake was released in the form of *Shadow of the Beast* (2016).

Final Fight

Date of release: December 1989

Region: Worldwide

Developer: Capcom

Publisher: Capcom

Platform: Arcade

Designed by the team who would work on the legendary *Street Fighter II* (1991), Final Fight is a single-player or two-player, cooperative beat 'em up. The aim of Final Fight is to rescue Mike Haggar's daughter, Jessica, from the Mad Gear Gang. The player/s can play as pro-wrestler and Mayor of Metro City, Mike Haggar, Jessica's boyfriend Cody, or Cody's best friend, Guy. The player can execute several different attacks while standing or jumping. Combos can be performed by pressing buttons and moving the joystick in various directions. The enemies encountered can be thrown or a grab attack can be implemented by the player. Weapons can be discovered and used by smashing crates and barrels. Weapons have limited use before they disappear. There are six stages in Final Fight. The player must defeat a boss at the end of each stage to continue.

The game was originally promoted in trade shows as a Street Fighter sequel entitled *Street Fighter '89* starring Ryu and Ken. However, since the game was nothing like the original, the game's title and protagonists were changed. Final Fight was well-received in 1989, distinguished for its graphics, characters (most notably Mike Hagger) and soundtrack. The game was ported to most 8-bit and 16-bit home computers and home consoles.

Final Fight spawned five direct sequels: *Final Fight Guy* (1992), *Final Fight 2* (1993), *Final Fight 3* (1995), *Final Fight Revenge* (1999) and *Final Fight: Streetwise* (2006).

PC Genjin/Bonk's Adventure

Date of release: December 1989

Region: Japan

Developer: Red Company/Atlus

Publisher: Hudson Soft

Platform: PC Engine

PC Genjin is a single-player, side-scrolling platformer. The aim of PC Genjin is to rescue Princess Za from the evil tyrannosaurus-rex King Drool. You play as PC Genjin (or Bonk on the TurboGrafx-16 Western version), a caveboy, who dispatches his enemies by hitting them with his head. If PC Genjin eats different kinds of meat, he will power-up and change state and name too. If he eats a small amount of meat, he will become PC Enjin (Monkey Man), giving him the ability to stun enemies by pounding the ground. Eating a second small amount of meat changes him again, this time into PC Henjin (a weird person) and making him invincible. These states are temporary. The player has three lives. Each life depletes when damage is taken but can be restored by collecting fruit and vegetables. A red heart will fill an entire life up. The rare blue heart adds an extra heart to PC Genjin's maximum health.

PC Genjin was ported to the Amiga, Arcade, NES and Game Boy.

PC Genjin/Bonk's Adventure was followed by *PC Genjin 2/Bonk's Revenge* (1991), *PC Genjin 3/Bonk 3: Bonk's Big Adventure* (1993), *Chō Genjin, Super B.C. Kid/Super Bonk* (1994) and *Super Genjin 2* (1995).

Dragon Slayer: The Legend of Heroes

Date of release: December 1989

Region: Japan

Developer: Nihon Falcom

Publisher: Nihon Falcom

Platform: NEC PC-8801

Designed by Nihon Falcom, Dragon Slayer: The Legend of Heroes is a single-player, turn-based, RPG. The aim of the game is to defeat Baron Drax, the usurper of the throne, and rid the land of monsters. You play as you King Logan, and with your companions, you must travel the land to fulfil your destiny.

The game was ported to various Japanese home computers and consoles.

Dragon Slayer: The Legend of Heroes is the sixth in the *Dragon Slayer* series and the first in *The Legend of Heroes* series of games. Other notable games in this latter series include *The Legend of Heroes: Trails in the Sky the 3rd* (2007), *The Legend of Heroes: Trails of Cold Steel II* (2014), *The Legend of Heroes: Trails of Cold Steel III* (2017) and *The Legend of Heroes: Trails of Cold Steel IV* (2018).

Castlevania III: Dracula's Curse

Date of release: December 1989

Region: Japan

Developer: Konami

Publisher: Konami

Platform: Famicom

Castlevania III: Dracula's Curse is a single-player, action, horror-themed platformer. The aim of Castlevania III: Dracula's Curse is to slay Dracula and his army of undead creatures who threaten to sweep the Earth clean of life and bring everlasting darkness. It has similar game mechanics to the first two games. Taking place more than 100 years before the events of the first two Castlevania games, you play as Trevor Belmont. However, in this third instalment, the player is accompanied by a choice of three playable characters, to whom the player can switch in order to use their unique skills to progress through the game. These characters are Sypha Belnades who can use powerful magic, Grant Danasty who can change direction in mid-air while jumping and climb walls, and Alucard (Dracula's son) who can shoot fireballs and transform into a bat. The game comprises sixteen stages but branches into two different routes, making the game non-linear. One route takes the player across the lake over the bridge and through the front gate of Dracula's Castle. This is generally regarded as the easier of the two routes. The second involves taking the player through tunnels and caverns before entering the castle by the cliffside. This is regarded as the more difficult route.

The game was praised for returning to the form of the original after the disappointment of the second game in the series. Castlevania III: Dracula's Curse is renowned for its difficulty and soundtrack.

1988/1989 Golden Joystick Awards

The 1988/1989 Golden Joystick Awards is hosted in London.

Armalyte (1988) wins Best Graphics of the Year.

Bionic Commando (1988) wins Best Soundtrack of the Year.

Operation Wolf (1987) wins Best Game of the Year.

Herzog Zwei

Date of release: December 1989

Region: Japan

Developer: Technosoft

Publisher: Sega

Platform: Mega Drive/Genesis

Designed by Takashi Iwanaga, Herzog Zwei (meaning Duke Two in German) is a single-player or two-player, multi-scrolling, futuristic, real-time strategy game. The aim of Herzog Zwei is to defeat your opponent by destroying their base. Viewed from a top-down perspective, the player/s initially control a jet fighter that can transform into a giant mech. At the top of the screen are four energy bars:

- B is your base's 'health' and if it reaches zero you lose the game.
- D is the durability of your jet/mech. If it reaches zero your jet/mech explodes and you are taken back to your base with a new jet/mech.
- G is the gun energy of your jet/mech.
- E is the energy of your jet/mech which depletes as you move. When it reaches zero it has the same effect as losing durability.

Other units can be produced at your base and given orders, but both these things cost money. The units the player/s can produce, and use are the ARM-51D (armoured car), TAX-52 (tank), SAM-42 (surface to air missile unit), supply (supply vehicle), GRM-34a (ground turret), infantry, and FWA (motorbikes). Units can be airlifted by the jet/mech and deployed to either patrol, garrison or capture an enemy base. A maximum of 50 units can be produced. There are also nine outposts spread out across the map that is initially chosen by the player/s. These outposts produce additional revenue, acting as waypoints towards destroying your opponents and are critical to winning a game.

Herzog Zwei was met with a lukewarm reception, possibly due to the Mega Drive/Genesis being aimed more at teenagers who played arcade-type games. Retrospectively it has received more merit than at the time of its release. Herzog Zwei is often cited as the first real-time strategy (RTS) game in that it closely represents such modern-day games. It has had a heavy influence on games such as *Dune II* (1992), *Warcraft: Orcs & Humans* (1994), *Total Annihilation* (1997) and *StarCraft* (1998). Because the player controls a single character as well as their armies, Herzog Zwei is sometimes considered a precursor to the Multiplayer Online Battle Arena (MOBA) subgenre of RTS games.

Wonder Boy III: The Dragon's Trap

Date of release: December 1989

Region: Japan

Developer: Westone

Publisher: Sega

Platform: Sega Master System

Wonder Boy III: The Dragon's Trap is a single-player, side-scrolling, action-adventure platform game, and despite its name is the fourth game in the Wonder Boy series. The aim of the game is to defeat the Vampire Dragon and obtain the Salamander Cross, which can lift the curse placed on Wonder Boy by the Mecha Dragon.

The game begins where *Wonder Boy in Monster Land* (1987) finished off. Wonder Boy defeated the Mecha Dragon but was transformed into a green dragon. To find the Salamander Cross and lift the curse, Wonder Boy must explore the game world and find clues. A multitude of different enemies that hinder Wonder Boy's progress must be defeated, including bosses at the end of specific areas. The game is non-linear so areas can be explored in any order. However, access may be limited in Wonder Boy's current form. As the player progresses through the game. Wonder Boy will assume other forms such as Hawk-Man, Lion-Man, Mouse-Man and Piranha-Man. These forms allow the player to access new areas by flying, climbing and swimming.

Weapons, such as sword, fireball, tornado, arrows, boomerang and thunder, as well as armour, shields and keys, can be purchased at shops using gold acquired by killing enemies. Health, depicted as a row of hearts on the top left of the screen, can be replenished in hospitals as well as by the possibility of purchasing a life potion that will automatically refill your health should you die in combat. If the player doesn't possess a life potion and your hearts are reduced to nothing, then it's game over.

Sweet Home

Date of release: December 1989

Region: Japan

Developer: Capcom

Publisher: Capcom

Platform: Famicom

Designed by Tokuro Fujiwara (*Ghost 'n Goblins* (1985)) and Juzo Itami and based on a Japanese horror film of the same name, Sweet Home is a single-player, survival horror RPG. The aim of Sweet Home is to find the precious paintings inside a huge haunted mansion. The player controls a party of five, seen from a top-down view, and can control them in groups or as individuals. This is necessary to complete certain puzzles and for the management of carrying items. Certain characters have certain abilities therefore the player must choose wisely whom to choose for each escapade. Combat takes place in the first person and is like other RPGs of the time. However, Sweet Home was rather unique at the time for its emphasis on horror and survival, something that would become the cornerstone of the survival horror genre.

Sweet Home was never released in the West partially due to its horror elements which were not usually a staple of Nintendo's marketing in places like North America.

Sweet Home is considered by some to be the first true survival horror game, becoming a cult classic and inspiring the *Resident Evil* games also by Capcom. Sweet home was also released as a South Korean television series in 2020.

1989 Notable Omissions

A Boy and his Blob. Adventures of LoLo. Alex Kidd in the Enchanted Castle. Amagon. Arch Rivals. *Armalyte*. Avalon: The Legend Lives. Baseball Stars. Beast Busters. Blood Money. Bonk's Revenge. Budokan. Chip's Challenge. Columns. Crack Down. Darius II. Duck Tails. Dungeon Explorer. Dungeon Master: Chaos Strikes Back. Escape from the planet of the Robot Monsters. Exterminator. Fantasy World Dizzy. FM Towns. Galaxy Force. Ikari III: The Rescue. Indianapolis 500: The Simulation. It Came from the Desert. Leisure Suit Larry III: Passionate Patti in Pursuit of the Pulsating Pectorals. Mappy Kids. Mercs. Minesweeper. Myth. North & South. Off Road. Power Glove. Prehistoric Island in 1930. Project Firestart. Quest for Glory. Rastan Saga II. River City Ransom/Street Gangs. R-Type II. Shadow Dancer. Shadowgate. Skull & Crossbones. Sly Spy. Special Criminal Investigation aka S.C.I.. Super Mario Land. The Guardian Legend. The Adventures of Bayou Billy. The Revenge of Shinobi. U-Force. Tiger Electronic LCD Handheld games. The Legendary Axe. The Untouchables. The Revenge of Shinobi. Toki. Tommy Lasorda Baseball. Tournament Cyberball 2072. Turbo Out Run. Vette!. Winning Race Suzuki GP. Wonder Boy III: The Dragon's Trap. WWF Wrestle Mania. Xenon 2 Megablast. Zero Wing.

Notes

Dear reader. I love video games and I love lists. Here are some retrospective notes on the history of video games between 1947-1989. It can be interesting and useful to collate information into categories such as game genres and console generations. Enjoy.

Significant milestones in the Text-Based Video Game genre

1971. Star Trek. Mike Mayfield. SDS Sigma 7 mainframe computer and HP 2000C Minicomputer.

1971. Oregon Trail. Don Rawitsch and Bill Heinemann. Teleprinter

1976. The Colossal Cave Adventure game. William Crowther. PDP-10 computer

1977. Zork (AKA Zork: The Great Underground Empire – Part 1 or Zork 1). Infocom. Tim Anderson. Marc Blank. Dave Lebling and Bruce Daniels. PDP-10.

1980. Eamon (The Wonderful World of Eamon). Donald Brown. Apple II.

1980. Essex MUD (Essex Multi-User Dungeon. MUD or MUD 1). Roy Trubshaw and Richard Bartie. DEC PDP-10.

1982 The Hobbit. Beam Software. Various 8-bit platforms.

1982. Time Zone. Sierra On-Line. Roberta Williams. Apple II.

1983. Planetfall. Infocom. Steve Meretzky. Multiple 8-bit home computer platforms.

1984. The Hitchhiker's Guide to the Galaxy. Infocom. Various 8-bit platforms.

1984. King's Quest I. Sierra On-Line. Roberta Williams. PCjr.

1986. Space Quest I. Sierra On-Line. Mark Crowe, Scott Murphy and Sol Ackerman. DOS and Apple.

1987. The Guild of Thieves. Magnetic Scrolls. Rob Steggles. 8-bit and 16-bit home computers.

Significant milestones in the Graphic Adventure Game genre

1980. Mystery House. On-Line Systems. Ken and Roberta Williams. Apple II.

1985. Where in the World Is Carmen Sandiego? Broderbund. Apple II.

1985. Déjà Vu. Mindscape. ICOM Simulations Inc. Macintosh.

1987. Leisure Suit Larry in the Land of the Lounge Lizards. Sierra On-Line. Apple II and PC DOS.

1987. Maniac Mansion. Lucasfilm Games. Apple II & Commodore 64.

1988. Zak McKracken and the Alien Mindbenders. Lucasfilm Games. David Fox, Matthew Alan Kane, David Spangler and Ron Gilbert. Commodore 64.

1989. Indiana Jones and the Last Crusade: The Graphic Adventure. Lucasfilm Games. Ron Gilbert, Noah Falstein, David Fox and Steve Purcell. Amiga, Atari ST, Macintosh and MS-DOS.

Significant precursors to the First-Person Shooter (FPS) genre

1973. Maze War. NASA Ames Research Centre. Steve Colley, Greg Thompson and Howard Palmer.

1974. Spasim. Developed by Jim Bowery for the PLATO computer network.

1975. Panther. John Edo Haefeli. PLATO System.

1979. Tail Gunner. Cinematronics. Arcade.

1979. Star Raiders. Atari 400 and Atari 800. Written by Doug Nebauer.

1980. Battlezone. Atari. Edward Rotberg, Owen Rubin and Roger Hector. Arcade.

1983. Star Wars. Atari. Mike Hally. Arcade.

1984. Elite. Acornsoft. David Braben. Ian Bell. BBC Micro.

1985. Tau Ceti. CRL Group PLC. Peter Cooke. ZX Spectrum.

1987. Driller/Space Station Oblivion. Incentive Software. 8-bit and 16-bit home computers.

1988. Starglider 2. Argonaut Software. 8-bit and 16-bit home computers.

Significant milestones in the Multi-Directional Shooter genre

1977. Combat. Atari. Atari 2600.

1979. Asteroids. Atari. Lyle Rains, Ed Logg and Dominic Walsh. Arcade.

1980. Berzerk. Stern Electronics. Alan McNeil. Arcade.

1981. Space Dungeon. Taito. Rex Battenberg. Arcade.

1981. Bosconian. Namco. Arcade.

1982. Gravitar. Atari. Mike Hally and Rich Adam. Arcade.

1982. Robotron:2084. Williams Electronics. Eugene Jarvis and Larry DeMar. Arcade.

1983. Sinistar. Williams Electronics. Arcade.

1987. Alien Syndrome. Arcade.

Significant milestones in the Shooter/Shoot 'em up genre

1962. Spacewar. Steve Russel. DEC PDP-1

1971. Galaxy Game. Bill Pitts and Hugh Tuck. Arcade.

1971. Computer Space. Nolan Bushnell and Ted Dabney. Arcade.

1977. Space Wars. Cinematronics. Larry Rosenthal. Arcade.

1978. Space Invaders. Taito. Tomohiro Nishikado. Arcade.

1979. Galaxian. Namco. Arcade.

1979. Radar Scope. Nintendo. Shigeru Miyamoto. Arcade.

1980. Missile Command. Atari. David Theurer. Arcade.

1980. Phoenix. Centuri. Arcade.

1980. Star Castle. Cinematronics. Tim Skelly and Scott Boden. Arcade.

1981. Gorf. Midway. Dave Nutting. Arcade.

1981. Centipede. Atari. Donna Bailey and Ed Logg. Arcade.

1981. Galaga. Namco. Arcade.

1981. Defender. Williams Electronics. Eugine Jarvis. Arcade.

1981. Scramble. Konami. Arcade.

1981. Vanguard. SNK. Dave Payne. Arcade.

1981. Stargate. Electronica. Eugene Jarvis and Larry DeMar. Arcade.

1982. Zaxxon. Sega. Arcade.

1982. Moon Patrol. Irem. Arcade.

1982. Choplifter. Broderbund. Apple II.

1982. Xevious. Namco. Masanobu Endo. Arcade.

1984. 1942. Capcom. Yoshiki Okamoto. Arcade.

1985. Gradius/Nemesis. Konami. Hiroyaso Machiguchi. Arcade.

1986. Salamander. Konami. Arcade.

1987. Darius. Taito. Toshio Kohno. Arcade.

1987. Galaga '88. Namco. Arcade.

1987. R-Type. Irem. Arcade.

1987. Wizball. Ocean Software. John Hare, Chris Yates and Peter Johnson. Commodore 64.

1988. Silkworm. Tecmo. Arcade.

1988. Forgotten Worlds. Capcom. Arcade.

1988. Parodius: The Octopus Saves the Earth. Konami. MSX.

Significant milestones in the Dungeon Crawl Role-Playing video game

1975. PEdity5 also known as The Dungeon. Rusty Rutherford. PLATO System.

1975. Dnd. Gary Whisenhunt and Ray Wood. PLATO system.

1975. Moria. Kevet Duncombe. PLATO system.

1979. Temple Of Apshai. Automated Simulations. TRS-80 and Commodore PET.

1979. Akalabeth: World of Doom. Richard Garriot. Apple II

1979. Adventure. Atari. Warren Robinett. Arcade.

1980. Rogue. Michael Toy and Glenn Wichman. Unix-based mainframe systems.

1980. Ultima 1 (AKA Ultima 1: The First Age of Darkness). Richard Garriot. Apple II

1981. Wizardry: Proving Grounds of the Mad Overlord. Sir-Tech. Apple II

1982. Hack. Jay Fenlason. Unix.

1982. Dragonstomper. Starpath. Stephen Landrum. Atari 2600.

1982. Swordquest: Earthworld. Atari. Atari 2600.

1983. Dandy. Atari. John Howard Palevich. 8-bit.

1985. Gauntlet. Atari Games. Ed Logg. Arcade.

1986. The Legend of Zelda. Nintendo. Shigeru Miyamoto, Takashi Tezuka and music by Koji Knondo. Nintendo.

1987. Ys 1: Ancient Ys Vanished. Nihon Falcom Masaya Hashimoto, Tomoyoshi Miyazaki. PC-8801.

1987. NetHack. The NetHack DevTeam. MS-DOS.

1987. Dungeon Master. FTL Games. Doug Bell. Atari ST.

Significant milestones in the modern-day Role-Playing video game

1975. Dnd. Gary Whisenhunt and Ray Wood. PLATO system.

1975. Moria. Kevet Duncombe. PLATO system.

1979. Temple Of Apshai. Automated Simulations. TRS-80 and Commodore PET.

1979. Akalabeth: World of Doom. Richard Garriot. Apple II

1979. Adventure. Atari. Warren Robinett. Arcade.

1980. Ultima 1 (AKA Ultima 1: The First Age of Darkness). Richard Garriot. Apple II.

1980. Eamon/The Wonderful World of Eamon. Donald Brown. Apple II.

1981. Wizardry: Proving Grounds of the Mad Overlord. Sir-Tech. Apple II

1982. Dragonstomper. Starpath. Stephen Landrum. Atari 2600.

1982. Swordquest: Earthworld. Atari. Atari 2600.

1984. The Black Onyx. Bullet-Proof Software. Henk Rogers. NEC-8801.

1984. Dragon Slayer. Nihon Falcom. Yoshio Kiya. NEC-8801.

1985. Tales of the Unknown: Volume 1. The Bard's Tale. Electronic Arts. Michael Cranford. Apple II.

1985. Ultima IV: Quest of the Avatar. Origin Systems. Richard Garriot. Apple II.

1985. Dragon Slayer II: Xanadu. Nihon Falcom. Yoshio Kiya. PC-8801.

1986. Dragon Quest/Dragon Warrior. Chunsoft. Famicom.

1987. Phantasy Star. Sega. Kotaro Hayashida, Yuji Naka and Rieko Kodama. Sega Master System.

1987. Final Fantasy. Square. Hironobu Sakaguchi. Famicom.

1988. Wasteland. Electronic Arts. Interplay Productions. Apple II, Commodore 64 and IBM compatibles.

1988. Pool of Radiance. Strategic Simulations, Inc (SSI). Chuck Kroegel and George MacDonald. 8-bit and 16-bit home computers.

1989. Phantasy Star II. Sega. Akinori Nishiyama, Yuji Naka, Rieko Kodama, with music by Tokuhiko Uwabo. Sega Mega Drive/Genesis.

1989. Dragon Slayer: The Legend of Heroes. Nihon Falcom. NEC PC-8801.

Evolution of the Sports Game genre

1954. Pool/Billiards. William Brown and Ted Lewis. MIDSAC computer.

1956. Tennis for Two. William Higinbotham.

1967. The Brown Box ping pong game. Ralph Baer. The Brown Box.

1972. Pong. Nolan Bushnell and Allan Alcorn. Arcade.

1973. Soccer. Taito. Arcade.

1976. Heavyweight Champ. Sega. Arcade.

1978. Atari Football. Atari. Dave Theurer. Arcade.

1980. Olympic Decathlon. Microsoft Consumer Products. Timothy W. Smith. TRS-80.

1982. Football Manager. Addictive Games. ZX80. ZX81. ZX Spectrum.

1983. Punch Out!!. Nintendo. Genyo Takeda and Shigeru Miyamoto. Arcade.

1983. Track & Field. Konami. Arcade.

1984. Hyper Sports. Konami. Arcade.

1984. Summer Games. U.S. Gold. Epyx. Commodore 64.

1985. Hang-On. Sega. Yu Suzuki. Arcade.

1986. Leader Board. Bruce Carver and Roger Carver. Commodore 64.

1986. 720°. Atari. John Salwitz and Dave Ralston. Arcade.

1987. Tecmo Bowl. Tecmo. Arcade.

1988. John Madden Football. Electronic Arts. Trip Hawkins, Robin Antonick and John

Madden. 8-bit home computers.

1989. Kick Off. Anco Software. Dino Dini and Steve Screech. Atari ST.

Evolution of the Racing Game genre/Vehicular Combat genre

1974. Gran Trak 10. Atari. Arcade.

1975. Wheels. Midway. Arcade.

1975. Indy 800. Atari. Arcade.

1976. Death Race. Exidy. Arcade.

1976. Night Driver. Atari. Arcade.

1979. Speed Freak. Vectorbeam. Arcade.

1979. Head On. Sega. Arcade.

1979. Monaco GP. Sega. Arcade.

1980. Rally-X. Namco. Arcade.

1981. Turbo. Sega. Steve Hanawa. Arcade.

1982. Pole Position. Namco. Toru Iwatani. Arcade.

1983. Spy Hunter. Bally Midway. George Gomez. Arcade.

1984. Excitebike. Nintendo. Shigeru Miyamoto. Famicom.

1985. Buggy Boy/Speed Buggy. Tatsumi. Arcade.

1985. Hang-On. Sega. Yu Suzuki. Arcade.

1986. Super Sprint. Atari. Robert Weatherby and Kelly Turner. Arcade.

1986. Out Run. Sega. Yu Suzuki. Arcade.

1988, Chase-H.Q. Taito. Arcade.

1988. Winning Run. Namco. Arcade.

1989. Stunt Car Racer. MicroStyle. Microplay. Geoff Crammond. Amiga.

1989. S.T.U.N. Runner. Atari Games. Arcade.

Evolution of the Maze genre

1959. Mouse in the Maze. Alan Kotok and Peter Samson. TR-0 computer.

1976. Blockade. Gremlin. Arcade.

1979. Head On. Sega. Arcade.

1980. Pac-Man. Namco. Toru Iwatani. Arcade.

1980. Rally-X. Namco. Arcade.

1980. Wizard of Wor. Midway. Dave Nutting. Arcade.

1981. Ms. Pac-Man. Midway. Arcade.

1981. Amidar. Stern. Konami. Arcade.

1981. Lady Bug. Universal. Kazutoshi Ueda. Arcade.

1982. Dig Dug. Namco. Arcade.

1982. Mr. Do! Taito. Universal. Arcade.

1982. Pengo. Sega. Coreland. Arcade.

1983. Bomberman. Hudson Soft. NEC PC-8801.

1983. Crystals Castles. Atari. Scott Fuller, Franz X. Lanzinger and Sam Lee. Arcade.

1984. Sabre Wulf. Ultimate Play the Game. ZX Spectrum

1984. Tower of Druaga. Namco. Massanobu Endo. Arcade.

1984. Boulder Dash. First Star Software. Atari 8-bit.

1985. Eggerland Mystery. HAL Laboratory. MSX.

1987. Pac-Mania. Namco. Toru Iwatani, Akira Usikura and music by Yuriko Keino and Yoshito Tomuro. Arcade.

Evolution of the Flight Simulator/ Flight Combat Simulator

1979. Flight Simulator. SubLogic. Bruce Artwick. Apple II.

1980. Red Baron. Atari. Arcade

1982. Microsoft Flight Simulator 1.0. Microsoft. IBM PC.

1984. Skyfox. Ray Tobey. Electronic Arts. Apple II.

1987. Project Stealth Fighter. MicroProse. Commodore 64 and ZX Spectrum.

1988. F/A-18 Interceptor. Electronic Arts. Intellisoft. Amiga.

1988. F-19 Stealth Fighter. MicroProse. Sid Meier, Arnold Hendrick, Andy Hollis and Jim Synoski. Various 8-bit and 16-bit home computers.

Evolution of the Fighting or Beat 'em Up genre

1979. Warrior. Vectorbeam. Arcade.

1984. Karate Champ & Karate Champ Player vs Player. Data East. Arcade.

1984. Karateka. Broderbund. Jordan Mechner. Apple II.

1984. Kung-Fu Master. Irem. Takashi Nishiyama. Arcade.

1985. Yie Ar Kung-Fi. Konami. Arcade.

1985. The Way of the Exploding Fist. Melbourne House. Gregg Barnett. Commodore 64.

1987. Double Dragon. Taito. Yoshihisa Kishimoto, Shinichi Saito and Koji Kai. Arcade.

1987. Street Fighter. Capcom. Takashi Nishiyama and Hiroshi Matsumoto. Arcade.

1987. International Karate+/Chop N' Drop. System 3. 8-bit and 16-bit home computers.

1988. Vigilante. Irem. Arcade.

1988. Altered Beast. Sega. Arcade.

1988. Ninja Gaiden/Shadow Warriors. Temco. H. Lijima and Shinobu Iwabayashi. Arcade.

1988. Splatterhouse. Namco, Namco Splatter Team. Arcade.

1989. Golden Axe. Sega. Makoto Uchida. Arcade.

1989. Teenage Mutant Ninja Turtles. Konami. Arcade.

1989. Final Fight. Capcom. Arcade.

Significant milestones in the Platform genre

1980. Crazy Climber. Nichibutsu. Arcade. Atari 2600. Famicon. Sharp X68000.

1980. Space Panic. Universal. Chris Crawford. Arcade.

1981. Donkey Kong. Nintendo. Shigeru Miyamoto. Arcade.

1981. Jump Bug. Hoei Corporation. Coreland. Sega. Arcade.

1982. Pitfall. Activision. David Crane. Arcade.

1982. Donkey Kong jr. Nintendo. Arcade.

1982. BurgerTime. Data East. Arcade.

1982. Joust. Williams Electronics. Arcade.

1982. Miner 2049er. Big Five Software. Bill Hogue. Atari 8-bit.

1982. Q*bert. Gottlieb. Warren Davis and Jeff Lee. Arcade.

1983. Mappy Namco. Arcade.

1983. JetPac. Ultimate Play the Game. Developed by Tim and Chris Stamper. Various 8-bit home computers.

1983. Mario Bros.. Nintendo. Shigeru Miyamoto and Gunpei Yokoi. Arcade.

1983. Chuckie Egg. A&F Software. Nigel Alderton. Various 8-bit home computers.

1983. Lode Runner. Broderbund. Douglas E. Smith. Various 8-bit home computers.

1983. Major Havoc. Atari. Owen Rubin and Mark Cerny. Arcade.

1983. Manic Miner. Bug-Byte. Mathew Smith. Various 8-bit home computers.

1984. H.E.R.O. Activision. John Van Ryzin. Atari 2600.

1984. Bomb Jack. Tehkan. Michitaka Tsuruta and Kazotoshi Ueda. Arcade and Various 8-bit home computers.

1984. Boulder Dash. First Star Software. Peter Liepa and Chris Gray. Various 8-bit home computers.

1984. Skool Daze. Microsphere. David and Helen Reidy, and Keith Warrington. Various 8-bit home computers.

1984. Impossible Mission. Epyx. Dennis Caswell. Various 8-bit home computers.

1984. Jet Set Willy. Software Projects. Matthew Smith. Various 8-bit home computers.

1984. Pac-Land. Namco. Arcade.

1984. Bounty Bob Strikes Back!. Big Five Software. Bill Hogue. Atari 8-bit.

1985. Ghost 'n Goblins. Capcom. Tokuro Fujiwara. Arcade.

1985. Super Mario Bros. Nintendo. Shigeru Miyamoto. Famicom/NES

1986. Wonder Boy. Sega. Ryuichi Nishizawa. Arcade.

1986. Imogen. Micro Power. Michael St Aubyn. BBC Micro.

1986. Metroid. Nintendo. Satoru Okada, Gunpei Yokoi, Hiroji Kiyotake and Yoshio Sakamoto. Nintendo.

1986. Solomon's Key. Michitaka Tsuruta. Temco. Arcade.

1986. Bubble Bobble. Taito. Fukio Mitsuji. Arcade.

1986. Castlevania. Konami. Famicom.

1986. Alex Kidd in Miracle World. Sega. Sega Master System.

1986. Rolling Thunder. Namco. Arcade.

1986. Kid Icarus AKA Light Mythology: Palutena's Mirror. Nintendo. Gunpei Yokoi. Famicom.

1987. Head Over Heels. Ocean Software. Jon Ritman, Bernie Drummond, Guy Stevens.

Various 8-bit home computers.

1987. Spindizzy. Codemasters. Andrew Oliver and Philip Oliver. Various 8-bit home computers.

1987. Nebulus. Hewson Consultants. John M. Philips. 8-bit and 16-bit home computers.

1987. Rainbow Islands: The Story of Bubble Bobble 2. Taito. Fukio Mitsuji. Arcade.

1987. Mega Man. Capcom. Famicom.

1988. The New Zealand Story. Taito. Arcade.

1988. Super Mario Bros. 3. Nintendo. Shigeru Miyamoto and Takashi Tezuka with music by Koji Kondo. Famicom and NES.

1988. Exile. Superior Software. Peter Irvin and Jeremy Smith. Acorn Electron and BBC Micro.

1988. Ghouls 'N Ghosts. Capcom. Tokuro Fujiwara, with music composed by Tamyo Kawamoto Arcade.

1988. Mega Man 2. Capcom. Famicom.

1989. Prince of Persia. Broderbund. Jordan Mechner. Apple II.

1989. PC Genjin/Bonk's Adventure. Hudson Soft. Red Company and Atlus. PC Engine.

1989. Castlevania III: Dracula's Curse. Konami. Famicom/NES.

1989. Wonder Boy III: The Dragon's Trap. Sega. Westone. Sega Master System.

Significant milestones in the Run and Gun genre

1982. Front Line. Taito. Tetsuya Sasaki. Arcade.

1985. Ninja Princess. Sega. Arcade.

1985. Commando. Capcom. Tokuro Fujiwara. Arcade.

1985. Green Beret/Rush 'n Attack. Konami. Arcade.

1986. Ikari Warriors. Tradewest. Arcade.

1986. Rolling Thunder. Namco. Arcade.

1987. Contra/Gryzor/Probotector. Konami. Koji Hiroshita. Arcade.

1987. Bionic Commando. Tokuro Fujiwara. Arcade.

1987. Alien Syndrome. Sega. Arcade.

1988. Super Contra: The Alien Strikes Back. Konami. Arcade.

1988. Narc. WMS Industries. Nathaniel Davies, Eugene Jarvis. Arcade.

1989. Midnight Resistance. Data East. Koji Akibayashi. Arcade.

Significant milestones in the Turn-Based Strategy genre

1973. Empire 1. John Daleske. Plato System.

1981. Eastern Front. Atari. Chris Crawford. Atari 8-bit.

1981. Utopia. Mattel. Don Daglow. Intellivision.

1983. Archon: The Light and the Dark. Electronic Arts. Atari 8-Bit.

1983. M.U.L.E. Ozark Softscape. Danielle Bunten Berry. Atari 8-bit.

1986. Defender of the Crown. Cinemaware. Kelly Beck and James D. Sachs. Amiga.

1987. Desert Commander/Sensha Senryaku: Sabaku no Kitsune. Kemco. NES.

Evolution of the Stealth game

1981. Castle Wolfenstein. Muse Software. Silas Warner. Apple II.

1987. Metal Gear. Konami. Hideo Kojima. MSX2.

Evolution of the Action-Adventure game

1979. Superman. Atari. John Dunn. Atari 2600.

1979. Adventure. Atari. Warren Robinett.

1982. Swordquest: Earthworld. Atari. Dan Hitchens and Tod Frye. Atari 2600.

1984. Knight Lore. Ultimate Play the Game. Stamper Brothers. ZX Spectrum.

1986. The Legend of Zelda. Nintendo. Shigeru Miyamoto, Takashi Tezuka and music by Koji Knondo. Nintendo.

Evolution of the Real-Time Strategy genre

1984. The Ancient Art of War. Broderbund. Dave and Barry Murry of Evryware Inc. Apple II.

1988. Carrier Command. Rainbird. 8-bit and 16-bit home computers.

1989. Harpoon. Three-Sixty Pacific. Larry Bond. Amiga, MS-DOS and Macintosh.

1989. Herzog Zwei. Sega. Takashi Iwanaga of Technosoft. Mega Drive/Genesis.

Significant precursors to the modern-day Survival Horror genre

1982. Haunted House. James Andreasen. Atari. Atari 2600.

1982. 3D Monster Maze. Malcolm Evans. Sinclair ZX81.

1983. Ant Attack. Quicksilva. ZX Spectrum.

1989. Sweet Home. Capcom. Famicom.

Significant milestones of the Puzzle genre

1982. Sokoban. Thinking Rabbit. NEC PC-8801.

1984. Tetris. Alexey. Pajitnov. Electronika 60.

1985. Paradroid. Graftgold. Andrew Braybrook. Commodore 64.

1989. Pipe Mania/Pipe Dream. Lucasfilm Games. Assembly Line. Amiga.

Significant milestones in the Game creation genre

1982. The Arcade Machine. Broderbund. Doug Carlston and Chris Jochumson. Apple II.

1983. Pinball Construction Set. Electronic Arts. Bill Budge. Apple II

1984. Adventure Construction Set. Electronic Arts. Stuart Smith. Commodore 64.

Significant milestones in the Simulation genre

1985. Little Computer People. Activision. David Crane & Rich Gold. Commodore 64.

1989. SimCity. Broderbund. 8-bit and 16-bit home computers.

Significant milestones in the Rail Shooter genre

1983. Star Wars. Atari. Mike Hally. Arcade.

1987. Operation Wolf. Taito. Arcade.

Significant Open World Games

1984. Elite. Acornsoft. David Braben. Ian Bell. BBC Micro.

1987. Sid Meier's Pirates!. Microprose. Commodore 64.

Early milestones in the 3D graphics

1973. Maze War is written at the NASA Ames Research Centre in California by Steve Colley. Greg Thompson and Howard Palmer. First Hidden Line Wireframe game.

1974. Spasim. is released in March. Developed by Jim Bowery for the PLATO computer network. Hidden Line Wireframe.

1975. Panther. John Edo Haefeli. PLATO System.

1975. Moria. Kevet Duncombe. PLATO system. Hidden Line Wireframe.

1978. Star Hawk. . Cinematronics. Tim Skelly. Arcade & Vectrex. Hidden Line Wireframe.

1979. Speed Freak. Vectorbeam. Larry Rosenthal. Arcade. Hidden Line Wireframe.

1979. Flight Simulator. SubLogic. Apple II. Hidden Line Wireframe.

1979. Akalabeth: World of Doom. Richard Garriot. Apple II. Seen Line Wireframe.

1979. Tail Gunner. Cinematronics. Arcade. Hidden Line Wireframe.

1980. Red Baron. Atari. Arcade. Seen Line Wireframe.

1980. Battlezone. Atari. Ed Rotberg, Owen Rubin, Roger Hector. Arcade. Seen Line Wireframe.

1981. Wizardry: Proving Grounds of the Mad Overlord. Sir-Tech. Andrew C. Greenberg. Robert Woodhead. Apple II. Hidden Line Wireframe.

1982. Microsoft Flight Simulator 1.0. Microsoft. IBM PC. Flat-Shaded Polygons.

1982. Wayout. Sirius Software. Paul Allen Edelstein. Flat-Shaded Polygons.

1983. Star Wars. Atari. Mike Hally. Arcade. Hidden Line Wireframe.

1984. Elite. Acornsoft. David Braben. Ian Bell. BBC Micro. Hidden Line Wireframe.

1984. Rescue on Fractalus! Lucasfilm Games. David Fox. Flat-Shaded Polygons.

1984. I Robot. Atari. Dave Theurer. Arcade. Flat-Shaded Polygons.

1984. Plasma Line. Various 8-bit and 16-bit home computers.

1985. Mercenary. Novagen. Paul Woakes, Bruce Jordan, Mo Warden. Various 8-bit and 16-bit home computers. Hidden Line Wireframe & Flat-Shaded Polygons.

1985. The Eidolon. Lucasfilm Games. Charlie Kellner, Lance Saleme. Various 8-bit home computers. Flat-Shaded Polygons.

1986. The Sentinel/The Sentry. Firebird. Geoff Crammond. Various 8-bit and 16-bit home computers. Flat-Shaded Polygons.

1987. Driller/Space Station Oblivion. Incentive Software. Major Developments. 8-bit and 16-bit home computers. Flat-Shaded Polygons.

1987. Phantasy Star. Sega. Sega Master System. Textured Flat-Shaded Polygons.

1987. Zarch/Virus. Superior/Acornsoft. David Braben. Various 8-bit and 16-bit home computers. Acorn Archimedes. Flat-Shaded Polygons.

1987. Falcon. Spectrum HoloByte. Sphere Inc. Various 8-bit and 16-bit home computers.

1988. The Colony. Mindscape. David Alan Smith. Amiga, Macintosh & MS-DOS. Flat-Shaded Polygons.

1988. Carrier Command. Rainbird. 8-bit and 16-bit home computers. Flat-Shaded Polygons.

1988. Starglider 2. Rainbird. Various 8-bit and 16-bit home computers. Flat-Shaded Polygons.

1989 Hard Drivin'. Atari Games. Rick Moncrief. Flat-Shaded Polygons.

1989. Midwinter. Microplay Software. Mike Singleton. Amiga, Atari ST and IBM-PC. Flat-Shaded Polygons.

Notable Early Video Game Music

1975. Gun Fight (First example of music in a video game).

1978. Space Invaders (Continuous basic beat music).

1980. Rally-X (Continuous melodic music). Toshio Kai

1981. Vanguard (Music from the movies 'Star Trek: The Motion Picture', and 'Flash Gordon' were used in-game).

1982. Tron (music from the movie).

1983. Journey (music from a rock band).

1983. Star Wars (music from the movie).

1983. Gyruss (extra processor used for music and played in stereo). Masahiro Inoue.

1983. Spy Hunter. Bob Libbe, Michael Bartlow and Neil Falconer.

1983. Mr Do's Castle (one of the author's personal favourites).

1984. Deus Ex Machina (the first video game to be played with an accompanying soundtrack and narration, Synchronised with the game on a tape recorder).

1984. Marble Madness (Different music per level). Brad Fuller and Hal Canon.

1985. Paperboy. Hal Canon and Earl Vickers.

1985. Ghost 'N Goblins. Ayako Mori.

1985. Super Mario Bros. Koji Kondo.

1985. Space Harrier. Hiroshi Kawaguchi.

1986. The Legend of Zelda. Koji Kondo.

1986. Out Run. Hiroshi Kawaguchi.

1988. King's Quest IV: The Perils of Rosella. First Hollywood composer William Goldstein to produce a score.

Early Significant Multiplayer, PvP (player Vs player) games

1958. Tennis for Two. William Higinbotham. Oscilloscope.

1962. SpaceWar! Steve Russell. DEC PDP-1.

1967. The Brown Box. Ralph Baer.

1971. Galaxy Game. Bill Pitts and Hugh Tuck. Arcade.

1971. Computer Space. Nolan Bushnell and Ted Dabney. Arcade.

1972. Table Tennis. Ralph Baer. Magnavox Odyssey.

1972. Pong. Atari. Nolan Bushnell and Allan Alcorn. Arcade.

1973. Empire 1. John Daleske. Plato System.

1973. Soccer. Taito. Arcade.

1974. Spasim. Jim Bowery. PLATO System.

1974. Tank. Kee games. Steve Bistow and Lyle Rains. Arcade.

1975. Indy 800. Atari. Arcade.

1975. Home Pong. Atari.

1977. Combat. Atari. Atari 2600.

1978. Atari Football. Atari. Steve Bristow. Arcade.

1979. Warrior. Vectorbeam. Tim Skelly. Arcade.

1980. Fishing Derby. Activision. David Crane. Atari 2600.

1980. Warlords. Atari. Steve Fawkner. Arcades.

1980. Wizard of Wor. Midway. David Nutting. Arcade.

1985. Yie Ar Kung-Fu. Konami. Arcade.

1985. The Way of the Exploding Fist. Melbourne House. Gregg Barnett. Various 8-bit and 16-bit home computers.

1987. Street Fighter. Capcom. Takashi Nishiyama and Hiroshi Matsumoto. Various 8-bit and 16-bit home computers and consoles.

1987. International Karate+/Chop N' Drop. System 3. Archer MacLean and music by Rob Hubbard. Various 8-bit and 16-bit home computers and consoles.

Early Significant Cooperative games

1973. Empire 1. John Daleske. Plato System.

1974. Spasim. Jim Bowery. PLATO System.

1980. Armour Attack. Cinematronics. Tim Kelly. Arcade.

1980. Essex MUD. Roy Trubshaw and Richard Bartle. DEC PDP-10.

1980. Wizard of Wor. Midway. David Nutting. Arcade.

1983. Mario Bros. Nintendo. Shigeru Miyamoto and Gunpei Yokoi. Arcade.

1983. Dandy. Atari. John Howard Palevich. Atari 8-bit.

1985. Gauntlet. Atari. Ed Logg. Arcade.

1986. Bubble Bobble. Taito. Fukio Mitsuji. Arcade.

1986. Ikari Warriors. SNK. Tradewest. Arcade.

1986. Salamander. Konami. Arcade.

Most Successful First-Generation Gaming Platforms

1977. Nintendo Color TV-Game series. Nintendo. 3 million units.

1976. Coleco Telstar series. Coleco. 1976. 1 million units.

1975. TV Tennis Electrotennis. Epoch Co., Magnavox. 1975. 440,000 units.

1972. Magnavox Odyssey. Magnavox. 350,000 units.

1975. Atari Home Pong. Atari, Sears Tele-Games. 150,000 units.

Most Successful Second-Generation Gaming Platforms

1977. Atari VCS/2600. Atari. 30 million units.

1982. Colecovision. Coleco. 6 million units.

1980. Intellivision. Mattel. 3 million+ units.

1978. Magnavox Odyssey^2. Magnavox. 2 million units.

1982. Atari 5200. Atari. 1 million.

1982. Vectrex. General Consumer Electric & Milton Bradley. Est 600,000 units.

1976. Fairchild Channel F. Fairchild Semiconductor. 250, 000 units.

Most Successful Third-Generation Gaming Platforms

1983. Nintendo Famicom/NES. Nintendo. 62 million units.

1982. NEC PC-98. Nippon Electric. 18 million units.

1985. Sega Master System/Sega Mark III. Sega. 17.8 million units.

1983. Commodore 64. Commodore. 12.5 million units.

1983. MSX. ASCII Corporation & Microsoft. 9.2 million units.

1982. ZX Spectrum. Sinclair Research. 5 million.

1985. Amiga 1000. Commodore. 4.9 million units.

1986. Atari 7800.Atari. 3.7 million units

1983. Sega SG-1000. Sega. 2 million units.

Most Successful Fourth-Generation Gaming Platforms

1990. Nintendo Super Famicom/SNES. Nintendo. 49 million units.

1988. Mega Drive/Genesis. Sega. 32 million+ units.

1987. PC Engine/TurboGrafx-16. NEC. 11 million units.

1985. Amiga 500. Commodore. 4.9 million.

1991. Philips CD-i. Philips. 1 million.

Glossary

1-up. An extra life.

8-Bit. Referring to computer hardware that processes 8 bits (see Bit) of information at a time.

16-Bit. Referring to computer hardware that processes 16 bits (see Bit) of information at a time.

3D Wireframe. A graphical representation of a 3D object which only displays the edges of said object. For example, a cube is displayed with 12 lines. This technique requires the least amount of computational resources to display a 3D object.

3D Wireframe with Hidden Line Removal. A 3D wireframe of a 3D object, except the internal lines, are removed giving the impression that the object is more solid. To remove the internal lines of an object requires more computational resources.

Action Adventure Game. A video game in which the emphasis is on high action, exploration and puzzle-solving with an intriguing narrative.

ASCII. Abbreviation for American Standard Code for Information: a way of storing numbers, letters, or symbols for exchanging information between computer systems. In games has been a way to represent dungeons on-screen using little memory. For example, dots and lines make up the structure of the rooms, the player's character is displayed as an @ symbol, a snake is represented by an S, and so on and so forth.

Axonometric Projection. An efficient way for the hardware of the time to display 3D isometric-looking graphics.

BASIC. A Common computer programming language that uses instructions that are similar to English. Basic is an acronym for Beginner's All-purpose Symbolic Instruction Code.

Beat 'em up. Refers to a genre of game where the player/s must frequently use hand to hand combat to defeat numerous waves of enemies.

Bedroom Coder/s. A term used to describe either a very small team, often just one person, writing code for a game in their bedroom.

Bit. A unit of information in a computer that must be either 1 or 0.

Bitmap. A computer image formed from pixels.

Boss. An enemy often found at the end of a level or game that is significantly stronger and more difficult to beat than other enemies.

Bullet Hell. A sub-genre of the shoot 'em up where the screen is almost filled with enemy bullets.

Byte. A unit of information consisting of eight bits e.g. 10101110. A byte of information can represent one character e.g. the letter 'a'

CAD. Abbreviation for Computer-Aided Design. The use of computers to design objects.

CD-ROM. Abbreviation for Compact Disc Read-Only Memory. This is a compact disc that holds large amounts of information that can be read by a computer but cannot be changed.

City Building Game. A game where the player acts as the city planner managing resources, keeping citizens happy and expanding/evolving the city.

Clone. An unlicensed copy of a video game.

Colour Overlay. A primitive way of creating colour graphics by placing a coloured acetate overlay onto a monochromatic screen.

Copy Protection. A technique used to prevent the use of copied games. In the early days of video games, this might mean having the player refer to a code or specific location in a guide book included with a genuine copy of the game.

CRT. A monitor, television or projector that displays an image using a Cathode-Ray-Tube

Cut-Scene. An in-game movie where the player has little to no control over the characters. The cut-scene is often a way to inform the player and progress story.

Demo Scene. Referring to audio-visual demonstrations emphasising and pushing the boundaries of what specific computer hardware can do

Dogfighting. Close-range aerial or space battle.

D-Pad. Short for directional pad, the D-pad is a four-way (although there are models which operate in more than four directions) directional button, usually operated by the player's left thumb.

Dungeon Crawl. A genre of game that involves the player navigating through a labyrinthian game world.

Eighth Generation. Refers to the eighth generation of home video game consoles (Sony Playstation 4, Nintendo Wii U & Switch and Microsoft Xbox One) and their games, between 1998-2015.

Eroge. A Japanese genre of erotic games.

Esports. An organised video game competition where players or teams of players compete against one another.

Experience Points. Also known as XP. A number that conveys a character's experience. A player's character gains experience points through battle and other encounters, or by fulfilling a quest. More XP results in higher stats such as attack strength, speed, defence etc.

Fantasy Text-Based RPG. An RPG that exclusively or mainly uses text for input and output, set against a fantasy-themed backdrop.

Feelies. Objects such as a map, coins, models, badges etc included with a video game.

Fifth Generation. Also known as the 32-bit era, refers to the fifth generation of home video game consoles - Sony Playstation, Sega Saturn & Nintendo 64 and their games, between 1993-2006.

Final Boss. An enemy, often at the end of the game and the game's main antagonist, which is stronger and more difficult to beat than any other enemy in a game.

First Generation. Refers to the first generation of home video game consoles (Magnavox Odyssey, Atari Home Pong & Nintendo Color TV-Game series) and their games, between 1972-1983.

First-Person. Refers to a video game where you play/see as though you are the character in the game.

Fixed Shooter. A sub-genre of the shooter, where the player's movement is restricted to only two directions of movement, often left and right.

Flat-Shaded. A graphical representation of a 3D object which displays each side, known as a polygon, as a uniform colour. For example, a cube is displayed with 6 polygons, though often only between one- three sides are displayed at one time. This requires more computational resources to display than a wireframe 3D object.

Flight Simulator. A game or simulation, the purpose of which is to emulate as many characteristics between the pilot, plane and the environment.

Flip-Screen. A game world larger than the screen, so that the next part of the environment 'flips' to reveal the next screen, when the player reaches the edge of the screen.

FOCAL. A computer programming language that uses instruction that is similar to English. FOCAL is an acronym for Formulating On-Line Calculation in Algebraic Language.

Fourth Generation. Also known as the 16-bit era, refers to the fourth generation of home video game consoles (Super Famicom/SNES, Sega Mega Drive/Genesis, PC Engine/TurboGrafx- 16 & SNK Neo Geo) and their games, between 1987-2004.

FPS. Abbreviation for Frames Per Second: the rate at how many frames are displayed per second. It is also an abbreviation for First Person Shooter, popularised in the Nineties.

Free-Roaming. Allowing the player to move freely through the game world and/or choose the game narrative and objectives at will.

Game Engine. Software specifically built for game development, often includes its own scripting, 3D editor, physics engine, lighting editor, sound editor, cutscene editor and a level editor.

Game Mechanic. The underlying rules of a game.

Gameplay. How the game feels through its interface and the character/s they play, to interact with the game.

GG. Abbreviation for Good Game/Great Game. Often used (in the in-game chat facility) by players at the end of a multiplayer game.

God Game. A game where the player takes the role of a powerful deity who manipulates NPCs and the environment to achieve their aims.

Graphical Adventure Game. An adventure game that relies heavily or exclusively on graphics with a graphical user interface (GUI) for issuing commands.

Grind/Grinding. A term used when a player resorts to a repetitive task for long periods of time, whether that be combat or acquiring loot, to gain abilities, XP or level-up.

GUI. Abbreviation for Graphical User Interface. It is an interface that allows users to interact with electronic devices through graphical icons and audio indicators instead of text-based user interfaces, typed command labels or text navigation.

Hack and Slash. Refers to a genre of game where the emphasis is put on the player violently dispatching a massive number of enemies. It distinguishes itself from the 'beat 'em up' as being more violent and often involves more elaborate weapons and magic.

Homebrew. Referring to a game written by a hobbyist.

Hot Seat. Refers to a mode of multiplayer gaming, often found in turn-based games, where players use the same machine to play the game and so must take turns, sitting down and then getting up.

IP. Abbreviation for Intellectual Property. An idea, invention or creation protected by law.

Isometric. A method of drawing three-dimensional shapes using two dimensions.

Isometric Shooter. A shooter game taking place on an isometric grid.

JRPG. Acronym for a Japanese Role-Playing Game.

Killer App. In this case, a video game that will cause a consumer to buy a console or computer to play that game, often exclusive to that or only a select few platforms.

Kilobyte (K or KB). A unit of computer information consisting of 1,024 Bytes or 8,192 Bits of data.

LaserDisc. An optical disc storage for video and audio, that can be read using a laser, first released in 1978.

LCD. Abbreviation for Liquid Crystal Display. Refers to an electronic display.

Level Editor. A development tool to more easily facilitate the building of levels, maps or environments for a specific game.

Levelling Up. An in-game event which means that the player's character has reached a new level e.g. risen from level 8 to level 9. It results in higher stats or access to new, usable items and quests only available for characters above a certain level.

Light Gun. A device resembling a gun that allows players to shoot at and thus interact with pixels on a screen.

Local Area Network (LAN). A term to describe several computers which are linked together in relatively close proximity.

Mainframe. A very large, powerful computer with a lot of memory that many people can use at the same time.

Maze Game. A genre of game where the player is placed within a maze.

Memory. The part of a computer in which information or programs are stored either permanently or temporarily, or the amount of space available on it for storing information.

Menu-Driven Adventure. An adventure game which has the player utilise a set menu of commands (as opposed to inputting text) to control characters, solve puzzles and progress the narrative.

Microcomputer. A small computer containing a microprocessor, often used in homes.

Microprocessor. A part of a computer that controls its main operations.

Minicomputer. A computer that is smaller than a mainframe computer, yet larger than a microcomputer.

MMORPG. (Massively Multiplayer Online Role-Playing Game.) A role-playing game that involves hundreds or thousands of players, playing at the same time in the same world.

MOBA. (Multiplayer Online Battle Arena.) A genre of video game in which you play as a specific class of character working with a small team to destroy the enemy base, against another group of human players with the same aim.

MUD. Abbreviation for Multi-User Dungeon.

Multiplayer (Game). A game in which more than one person can play within the same gaming environment, whether working in teams or on your own against the other players.

Multi-Scrolling. A game that scrolls in any four directions, rather than being restricted to only two.

NPC (Non-Player Character). Any character in a video game not controlled by a player.

Open Architecture. Hardware or software architecture that easily facilitates changes by other users.

Oscilloscope. A device that represents oscillations by displaying them on a Cathode Ray Tube

Parallax Scrolling. An animation technique often used in 2D side-scrolling games where different layers, e.g. foreground, midground and background, move at different speeds to give the illusion of depth.

Parser. A program or part of a program that interprets input to a computer by recognising keywords or analysing sentence structure.

Party-Based System. A system in a game where the player controls one character (in which case the AI controls the other players), or more than one character, in a group, working together for a common goal.

PC. Personal Computer.

Pixel. The smallest area of illumination on a display from which graphics are composed.

Platform. The type of system you are using. Examples are PC, Playstation, IOS and Arcade.

Platformer. A platformer or platform game is a game with an emphasis on jumping, climbing and sometimes combat, in an environment of platforms of varying height.

Polygon. A polygon is a 2D geometric shape. These can be used to make a 3D object. For example, six quadrilaterals can form a cube. Though most shapes are broken down into triangles. Very complex 3D objects made of thousands or millions of polygons, called meshes, can be used in the development of video games.

Port. Adapting a game to run on a different platform.

Power-Up. An item that adds benefits for the player. Examples are extra firepower or temporary invulnerability.

Pre-Rendered Graphics. Computer graphics that are not rendered in real-time. Video footage, where each frame is rendered beforehand and played back later.

Procedurally Generated. Graphics or assets which are generated using algorithms rather than created by human input.

PvE. Short for player versus environment, the environment is controlled by the computer hardware.

PvP. Short for player versus player. Can refer to just two players competing head to head or multiple players.

RAM. Abbreviation for Random Access Memory. A type of computer memory that can be searched in any order and changed, as necessary. Also, known as active memory.

Raster. A type of computer image made of pixels.

Real-Time Strategy (RTS). RTS games usually involve gathering resources, building armies and then defeating your opponent's army in real-time, as opposed to turn-based strategy games where the player can take their time to make a move.

Roguelike. A genre of game characterized by level randomisation, turn-based movement and permanent death.

ROM. Abbreviation for Read-Only Memory. A type of memory that holds information that can be accessed but not changed or added to.

Rotoscoping. The tracing of a series of still images from footage of people or animals in motion (for example) to present more natural-looking animation.

RPG. Acronym for a Role-Playing Game.

Run & Gun. A sub-genre of the shoot 'em up or shooters, where the player is on foot running and shooting a multitude of various enemies.

Sandbox Game. A game with an emphasis on freedom and creativity and allowing the player to go anywhere and do anything, as opposed to a game that is linear or requires something from the player to progress to another level or area.

Scaling Sprites. The technique of scaling graphics in quick succession over a series of frames to give the illusion of three-dimensional movement.

Screen Resolution. The ability of a display to show things clearly and with a lot of detail. The higher the resolution, the clearer the image.

Scrolling. The continuous movement of text or images on a display screen in either a horizontal or vertical direction.

Second Generation. Refers to the second generation of home video game consoles (Fairchild Channel F, Atari 2600 & Intellivision) and their games, between 1976-1992.

Seventh Generation. Refers to the seventh generation of home video game consoles (Sony Playstation 3, Nintendo Wii & Microsoft Xbox 360) and their games, between 2005-2021.

Shooter. A genre of video game where the main conceit is that of shooting the enemy.

Side-Scrolling. In reference to a game that is viewed from the side and the camera scrolls left or right with the player's character.

Single-Player. A game that involves only one player's input.

Sixth Generation. Refers to the sixth generation of home video game consoles (Sega Dreamcast, Sony Playstation 2, Nintendo Gamecube & Microsoft Xbox) and their games, between 1998-2015.

Speech Synthesis. The artificial electronic reproduction of human speech.

Sprite. A two-dimensional image or animation that is integrated into a larger scene.

Strategy Video Game. A game with an emphasis on planning and strategy to win the game.

Survival Horror. A game that contains strong horror elements with action adventure. The emphasis is often on lack of resources thus heightening the survival aspect of the game.

Tape/Cassette. Thin plastic in a long, narrow strip with a magnetic covering that allows sounds and data to be recorded/stored and played/loaded.

Tape Recorder. A machine that is used for playing/loading and recording/storing sound/information onto a tape.

Third Generation. Also known as the 8-bit era, refers to the third generation of home video game consoles (Famicom/NES, SG-1000, Sega Master System & Atari 7800) and their games, between 1983-2003.

Third Person. Refers to a video game where you view the character or object that you control in the game.

Tile-Based. Often referring to games where movement and attack range is restricted to tile-based blocks.

Tube Shooter. Refers to a sub-genre of the shoot 'em up games where the player can move around the entirety of the screen shooting towards the middle at enemies as if they were flying down a giant tube.

Turn-Based Strategy. A game where players take turns playing.

Twin-Stick Shooter. Also referred to as multi-directional shooters, the twin-stick shooter features two joysticks, one for movement and one for firing, allowing the player to fire in any direction independent of their movement.

Vector Graphics. The use of mathematical equations to draw computer graphics.

Virtual Reality. (VR). Virtual Reality involves using hardware and software to immerse a player in a simulated world.

Wireframe. A method of displaying a 3D digital model of something in which only lines are displayed.

Sources Used

To cite every source that has had bearing on this book would be an exercise in futility, however, here are some examples of some of the most valuable resources.

Books

Martin Amis. Invasion of the Space Invaders. (1982). Published by Johnathan Cape Vintage Publishing.

Steven L. Kent. The Ultimate History of Video Games. (2001). Three Rivers Press.

Dave Morris & Leo Haratas. The Art of Game Worlds. (2004). ILEX Press Limited.

Triston Donovan. Replay: The History of Video Games. (2010). UK. Yellow Ant.

Frans Mayra. An Introduction to Game Studies, Games in Culture. (2010). SAGE Publications Ltd.

Larissa Hjorth. (2011). Games and Gaming, An Introduction to new media. Berg.

Jane McGonical. Reality is Broken: Why Games Make Us Better and How They Can Change the World. (2011). Vintage Digital.

Harold Goldberg. All Your Base Are Belong To Us: How Fifty Years of Videogames Conquered Pop Culture. (2011). USA. Three Rivers Press.

Tony Mott. 1001 Video Games You Must Play Before You Die. (2013).UK. Cassell.

Steven Howlett. Diary of An 80s Computer Geek: A Decade of Micro Computers, Video Games and Cassette Tape. (2014). CreateSpace.

Scott Rogers. Level Up! The Guide to Great Video Game Design. (2014). Wiley.

Kurt Kalata. Hardcore Gaming 101 Presents: The 200 Best Games of All Time. (2015). CreateSpace.

Chris Kohler. power-up how Japanese video games gave the world an extra life. (2016). Dover Publications Inc.

Katherine Isbister. How Games Move Us: Emotion by Design (Playful Thinking). (2016).

The MIT Press.

Kurt Kalata. Hardcore Gaming 101 Presents: The Guide to Retro Indie Games Vol 1. (2017). CreateSpace.

Simon Parkin. An illustrated History of 151 Video Games. (2017). USA. Annes Publishing Ltd.

Nicholas Sinard. A short History of Video Games. (2017). Independently Published.

Kurt Kalata. Hardcore Gaming 101 Digest Vol. 3: The Guide to Retro Horror. (2018). CreateSpace.

Iain Simons & James Newman. A History of Videogames. (2018). Carlton Books Ltd.

Marty Allen. Retro Games. (2018). Dog 'n' Bone.

Dustin Hansen. Game On!: Video Game History from Pong and Pac-Man to Mario, Minecraft, and More. (2019). Square Fish.

Richard Stanton. (2019). A Brief History of Video Games: From Atari to Virtual Reality. (2019). UK. Robinson.

Mike Diver. Retro Gaming: A Byte-sized History of Video Games. (2019). Michael O'Mara Books Limited.

Magazines

Edge Magazine. (1993-present.) Future Publishing.

Games TM. (2002-2018). Highbury Entertainment and then Future Publishing.

PC Gamer Magazine. (2016-present). Future Publishing.

Retro Gamer Magazine. (2004-present). Live Publishing (2004-2005). Future Publishing (2005-2016). Future Publishing (2016-present).

Online

www.computerhistory.org/timeline/

listverse.com/2010/05/11/15-firsts-in-video-game-history/

en.wikipedia.org/wiki/History_of_video_games

bigboxcollection.com/#CollectionOverview

vgsales.fandom.com/wiki/Video_Game_Sales_Wiki

www.giantbomb.com/

virtualspeech.com/blog/history-of-vr

www.arcade-museum.com/

videogamehistorian.wordpress.com/2014/01/22/the-priesthood-at-play-computer-games-in-the-1950s/

self.gutenberg.org/articles/video_game_crash_of_1977#Early_arcade_video_games_.281971.E2.80.931977.29

retroconsole.xyz/history-of-video-games/video-games-1988/

docs.google.com/file/d/0BxluaTgKKEs4MGFsZ2NpSHctVVE/edit

mobygames.com

The Angry Video Game Nerd

Kim Justice

Metal Jesus Rocks

John's Arcade Game Reviews & Tech

Ashens

LGR

TNT Amusements Inc

Retro Game On

Retroware

Index

B

C

D

E

F

G

H

I

J

K

L

M

N

O

P

Q

R

S

T

U

V

W

X

Y

Z